American Dreams

OTHER TITLES IN THE LONGMAN TOPICS READER SERIES

College Culture, Student Success
Debra J. Anderson

Translating Tradition
Karen E. Beardslee

Reading City Life
Patrick Bruch and Richard Marback

Diversity: Strength and Struggle
Joseph Calabrese and Susan Tchudi

Legends, Lore, and Lies: A Skeptic's Stance
Joseph Calabrese

The People and Promise of California
Mona Field and Brian Kennedy

Citizenship Now
Jon Ford and Marjorie Ford

The Changing World of Work
Marjorie Ford

Issues of Gender
Ellen G. Friedman and Jennifer D. Marshall

Youth Subcultures: Exploring Underground America
Arielle Greenberg

Education Matters: Exploring Issues in Education
Morgan Gresham and Crystal McCage

Science and Society
Richard W. Grinnell

International Views: America and the Rest of the World
Keith Gumery

Listening to Earth: A Reader
Christopher Hallowell and Walter Levy

Body and Culture
Greg Lyons

Writing Places
Paula Mathieu, George Grattan, Tim Lindgren, and Staci Shultz

Peace, War, and Terrorism
Dennis Okerstrom

The World of the Image
Trudy Smoke and Alan Robbins

Hip Hop Reader
Tim Strode and Tim Wood

The Counterculture Reader
E. A. Swingrover

Discovering Popular Culture
Anna Tomasino

Music and Culture
Anna Tomasino

Ethics in the 21st Century
Mary Alice Trent

Considering Culture Difference
Pauline Uchmanowicz

Language and Prejudice
Tamara M. Valentine

CyberReader, Abridged Edition
Victor J. Vitanza

A LONGMAN TOPICS READER

American Dreams

LARRY R. JUCHARTZ
Mott College

ELIZABETH A. STOLAREK
Ferris State University

CHRISTY RISHOI
Mott College

PEARSON
Longman

New York San Francisco Boston
London Toronto Sydney Tokyo Singapore Madrid
Mexico City Munich Paris Cape Town Hong Kong Montreal

Senior Vice President and Publisher: Joseph Opiela
Senior Acquisitions Editor: Katherine Meisenheimer
Senior Marketing Manager: Sandra McGuire
Production Manager: Savoula Amanatidis
Project Coordination, Text Design, and Electronic Page Makeup:
GGS Book Services, Inc.
Cover Design Manager: John Callahan
Cover Photo: Courtesy of Getty Images
Senior Manufacturing Buyer: Alfred C. Dorsey

For permission to use copyrighted material, grateful acknowledgment is made to the copyright holders on pp. 241–242, which are hereby made part of this copyright page.

Library of Congress Cataloging-in-Publication Data

American dreams / [edited by] Larry R. Juchartz, Elizabeth A. Stolarek, Christy Rishoi.
p. cm.— (A Longman topics reader)
ISBN-13: 978-0-205-52079-4
ISBN-10: 0-205-52079-0
1. College readers. 2. English language—Rhetoric—Problems, exercises, etc. I. Juchartz, Larry R. II. Stolarek, Elizabeth A. III. Rishoi, Christy
PE1417.A395 2008
808'.0427—dc22

2007039013

Please visit us at www.ablongman.com

ISBN-13: 978-0-205-52079-4
ISBN-10: 0-205-52079-0

In memory of Olive Dougherty and Rosa Wicklein

—L. J.

In memory of Evelyn and Mitchell Zdunek

—E. S.

For Niel and Jan

—C. R.

CONTENTS

PREFACE

The concept of an "American Dream" is everywhere: in investment brochures, in essays and articles, in TV ads for the latest electronics. This book tracks the evolution of a related idea: what makes a person an American? Does an American live within particular geographical boundaries? Is an American someone who pledges allegiance to a particular form of government, and who agrees to support that form of government by paying taxes and obeying laws? Does an American simply share a particular set of beliefs and values with a community of others called Americans?

In looking at "America" as a geographical area, many have argued compellingly that the term *America* more correctly refers to the entire mass of the North and South American continents, not just to the area of the United States. But the concept of *America* as visualized in this book begins with the hopes and aspirations of the people who first colonized areas of North America for England, and of their descendants who established the first democracy in this part of the world. It continues with the sorrows and frustrations of those who believed that dream was beyond their grasp, and with the dreams of millions of immigrants who left their homes to take their chances with this new system of government in a new land. It concludes with comments from later generations who have modified the concept of the American Dream to fit the demands and structures of their rapidly evolving society.

The evolution of the American Dream can be seen in the works of the writers included in this text. The writers speak of their individual interpretations with passion and conviction, and they use the art of *rhetoric* to persuade readers of the validity and importance of their ideas. To better understand the concept of the American Dream and the way it has been developed and advanced through time, it is necessary to understand the principles of rhetoric itself. Many people today hear the term mostly through negative phrases such as "campaign rhetoric," "advertising rhetoric," and "rhetorical question," all of which suggest that rhetoric deals with unethical or meaningless communication.

But rhetoric is more properly defined as "the art of effective communication," with the word *effective* meaning successful; communication that is effective succeeds in doing the job it was intended to do. One of the earliest definitions of rhetoric comes from the philosopher Aristotle, who described it as "the art of determining, in all situations, the best possible means of persuasion." Aristotle recognized that the key element in persuading an audience is an understanding of their thoughts and feelings about a topic, as well as the most effective methods of persuading them. This book invites you, not only to read about and understand the dreams that led to the foundation and development of the United States, but also to understand the national rhetoric that caused the dreams of a few to be shared by millions.

We would like to thank the following reviewers for their helpful comments: Meredith Love, Francis Marion University; Debbie Mael, Newbury College; Amanda Miller Plaizier, Utah State University; David Schmid, University at Buffalo; and Richard Zumkhawala-Cook, Shippensburg University.

LARRY R. JUCHARTZ
Mott College

ELIZABETH A. STOLAREK
Ferris State University

CHRISTY RISHOI
Mott College

CHAPTER 1

Founders' Dream/ Dreamers Found

The selections that follow initiate discussion of the American Dream by looking at its inception—at the voices of those who first entertained the possibility of forming a new type of society in what was then called the New Land. Spanning the period from the establishment of the first permanent settlement in New England to just before the Civil War, they detail early Americans' hopes, dreams, aspirations, and disappointments.

As you read these selections, think about the image or images of the American Dream they express. What qualities of life are envisioned by these early Americans? Do all authors seem to share the same dream about the possibilities open to them? If not, how do their dreams differ? How do their dreams differ from your own concept of the American Dream?

Also, concentrate on the various techniques and strategies the authors use to present themselves. Who are their audiences for these selections? What assumptions do the authors seem to be making about their audiences? What is the message of each selection, and how is it presented in order to be persuasive?

The Origin of the Longhouse—Seneca Legend

ARTHUR PARKER

Many Americans believe that the first settlers from Europe found a lawless, savage land, but contemporary historians dispute that belief. Many Native American tribes had formed complex, long-lasting governments and alliances well before European colonization. "The Origin of the Longhouse" tells the story of the founding of the Confederacy of the Five Nations, also called the Iroquois Confederacy, a union of five tribes (Mohawk, Onondaga, Oneida, Seneca, and Cayuga) believed to date back to around 1450. (Excerpts from the Iroquois Constitution appear later in this chapter.)

Arthur Parker (1881–1955), an anthropologist and archeologist who was part Seneca himself, collected Iroquois legends and compiled them into his 1923 book Seneca Myths and Folk Tales.

✦

Where the Mohawk river empties into the Hudson in ancient times there was a Mohawk village. The people there were fierce and warlike and were continually sending out war parties against other settlements and returning would bring back long strings of scalps to number the lives they had destroyed. But sometimes they left their own scalps behind and never returned. They loved warfare better than all other things and were happy when their hands were slimy with blood. They boasted that they would eat up all other nations, and so they continued to go against other tribes and fight with them.

Now among the Mohawks was a chief named Deganawida, a very wise man, and he was very sad of heart because his people loved war too well. So he spoke in council and implored them to desist lest they perish altogether, but the young warriors would not hear him and laughed at his words; but he did not cease to warn them until at last despairing of moving them by ordinary means, he turned his face to the west and wept as he journeyed onward and away from his people. At length he reached a lake whose shores were fringed with bushes, and being tired he lay down to rest. Presently, as he lay meditating, he heard the soft spattering of water sliding from a skillful paddle and peering out from his hiding place, he saw in the red light of sunset a man leaning over his canoe and dipping into the shallow water with a basket. When he raised it up it was full of shells, the shells of the periwinkles that live in shallow pools. The man pushed his canoe toward the shore and sat down on the beach, where he kindled a fire. Then he began to string his shells and, finishing a string, would touch the shells and talk. Then, as if satisfied, he would lay it down and make another until he had a large number. Deganawida watched the strange proceeding with wonder. The sun had long since set, but Deganawida still watched the man with the shell strings sitting in the flickering light of the fire that shadowed the bushes and shimmered over the lake.

After some deliberation he called out, "*Kwē*, I am a friend!" and stepping out upon the sand stood before the man with the shells. "I am Deganawida," he said, "and come from the Mohawk."

"I am Hiawatha of the Onondaga," came the reply.

Then Deganawida inquired about the shell strings for he was 5
very curious to know their import and Hiawatha answered, "They are the rules of life and laws of good government. This all white string is a sign of truth, peace and good will; this black string is a sign of hatred, of war and of a bad heart; the string with the alternate beads, black and white, is a sign that peace should exist between the nations. This string with white on either end and black in the middle is a sign that wars must end and peace be declared." And so Hiawatha lifted his strings and read the laws.

Then said Deganawida, "You are my friend indeed, and the friend of all nations. Our people are weak from warring and weak from being warred upon. We who speak one tongue should combine against the Hadiondas instead of helping them by killing one another, but my people are weary of my advising and would not hear me."

"I, too, am of the same mind," said Hiawatha, "but Tatodaho slew all my brothers and drove me away. So I came to the lakes and have made the laws that should govern men and nations. I believe that we should be as brothers in a family instead of enemies."

"Then come with me," said Deganawida, "and together let us go back to my people and explain the rules and laws."

So when they had returned, Deganawida called a council of all the chiefs and warriors and the women, and Hiawatha set forth the plan he had devised. The words had a marvelous effect. The people were astonished at the wisdom of the strange chief from the Onondaga, and when he had finished his exposition the chiefs promised obedience to his laws. They delegated Deganawida to go with him to the Oneida and council with them, then to go onward to Onondaga and win over the arrogant erratic Tatodaho, the tyrannical chief of the Onondaga. Thus it was that together they went to the Oneida country and won over their great chief and made the people promise to support the proposed league. Then the Oneida chief went with Hiawatha to the Cayugas and told them how by supporting the league they might preserve themselves against the fury of Tatodaho. So when the Cayuga had promised allegiance, Deganawida turned his face toward Onondaga and with his comrades went before Tatodaho. Now when Tatodaho learned how three nations had combined against him he became very angry and ran into the forest where he gnawed at his fingers and ate grass and leaves. His evil thoughts became serpents and sprouted from his skull and waving in a tangled mass hissed out venom. But Deganawida did not fear him and once more asked him to give his consent to a league of peace and friendship; but he was still wild until Hiawatha combed the snakes from his head and told him that he should be the head chief of the confederacy and govern it according to the laws that Hiawatha had made. Then he recovered from his madness and asked why the Seneca had not been visited, for the Seneca outnumbered all the other nations and were fearless warriors. "If their jealousy is aroused," he said, "they will eat us."

Then the delegations visited the Seneca and the other nations to the west but only the Seneca would consider the proposal. The other nations were exceedingly jealous.

Thus a peace pact was made and the Long House built, and Deganawida was the builder, but Hiawatha was its designer.

Now moreover, the first council of Hiawatha and Deganawida was in a place now called Albany at the mouth of a small stream that empties into the Hudson.

1450

For Discussion and Writing

1. "The Origin of the Longhouse" was an oral narrative, passed from generation to generation. How does the language of the legend facilitate oral, as opposed to written, transmission between speakers and audiences? Some of Western literature's most important works also began as oral narratives, the Greek myths and the Bible being prime examples. Do you see any similarities in the writing styles of these three narrative traditions?
2. What do you believe was the significance of the shell strings?
3. While much of the legend is told in a straightforward manner, occasional mythical elements appear (e.g., "His evil thoughts became serpents and sprouted from his skull and waving in a tangled mass hissed out venom"). What do mythical elements add to the story?
4. Following the style of "The Origin of the Longhouse," write a short narrative explaining the origin of some phenomenon, institution or product.

The Mayflower Compact

The Mayflower Compact is the first constitution written by European colonists to America. It expresses the dreams and aspirations of some of the earliest immigrants to the New Land, 101 Pilgrims who left Plymouth, England, on September 16, 1620, intent on establishing a settlement in Virginia. After many setbacks, they finally landed off the coast of Cape Cod on November 21, 1620, in what is now Massachusetts. They wrote and signed The Mayflower Compact to establish rules for governing Plymouth, the first permanent settlement in New England.

In the Name of God, Amen. We whose names are underwritten, the loyal subjects of our dread Sovereign Lord King James, by the Grace of God of Great Britain, France and Ireland, King, Defender of the Faith, etc.

Having undertaken, for the Glory of God and advancement of the Christian Faith and Honour of our King and Country, a Voyage to plant the First Colony in the Northern Parts of Virginia, do by these presents solemnly and mutually in the presence of God and one another, Covenant and Combine ourselves together into a Civil Body Politic, for our better ordering and preservation and furtherance of the ends aforesaid; and by virtue hereof to enact, constitute and frame such just and equal Laws, Ordinances, Acts, Constitutions and Offices, from time to time, as shall be thought most meet and convenient for the general good of the Colony, unto which we promise all due submission and obedience. In witness whereof we have hereunder subscribed our names at Cape Cod, the 11th of November, in the year of the reign of our Sovereign Lord King James, of England, France and Ireland the eighteenth, and of Scotland the fifty-fourth. Anno Domini 1620.

1620

For Discussion and Writing

1. What goals and ideals are evident in "The Mayflower Compact"? What type of life did its authors envision in their new settlement?
2. Who is the audience for "The Mayflower Compact"? Can you define more than one audience for this document?

3. What methods did the authors use to establish their credibility? Think of both the content and the style of the document.
4. Have you ever, perhaps when you were a child, written some type of charter or constitution for an organization of your friends or classmates (perhaps for an interest-based club or secret society)? Did the language in that document resemble the language in "The Mayflower Compact"? What is the purpose of using "official-sounding" language in such documents? Where do our ideas about "proper" language for specific kinds of documents come from?

From "A Model of Christian Charity"

John Winthrop

John Winthrop (1587–1649) left England to lead a band of Puritans to America. As the first governor of the Massachusetts Bay Colony, he was both the colonists' legal and religious leader, believing that he was destined by God to create a holy community. "A Model of Christian Charity," often called the "City Upon a Hill" sermon, was delivered as the colonists were about to disembark. In this sermon, Winthrop set out rules for creating a community based on justice and mercy.

✦

Thus stands the cause between God and us. We are entered into covenant with Him for this work, we have taken out a commission, the Lord hath given us leave to draw our own articles we have professed to enterprise these actions upon these and these ends, we have hereupon besought Him of favor and blessing. Now if the Lord shall please to hear us, and bring us in peace to the place we desire, then hath He ratified this covenant and sealed our commission, [and] will expect a strict performance of the articles contained in it, but if we shall neglect the observations of these articles which are the ends we have propounded, and dissembling with our God, shall fall to embrace this present world and prosecute our carnal intentions seeking great things for ourselves and our posterity, the Lord will surely break out in wrath against us, be revenged of such a perjured people, and make us know the price of the breach of such a covenant.

Now the only way to avoid this shipwreck and to provide for our posterity is to follow the counsel of Micah, to do justly, to love mercy, to walk humbly with our God. For this end we must be knit together in this work as one man, we must entertain each other in brotherly affection, we must be willing to abridge ourselves of our superfluities for the supply of others' necessities, we must uphold a familiar commerce together in all meekness, gentleness, patience, and liberality, we must delight in each other, make others' conditions our own, rejoice together, mourn together, labor and suffer together, always having before our eyes our commission and community in the work, our community as members of the same body. So shall we keep the unity of the spirit in the bond of peace. The Lord will be our God and delight in all our ways, so that we shall see much more of His wisdom, power, goodness, and truth than formerly we have been acquainted with. We shall find that the God of Israel is among us, when ten of us shall be able to resist a thousand of our enemies, when He shall make us a praise and glory, that men shall say of succeeding plantations, the Lord make it like that of New England. For we must consider that we shall be as a city upon a hill, the eyes of all people are upon us. So that if we shall deal falsely with our God in this work we have undertaken and so cause Him to withdraw His present help from us, we shall be made a story and byword throughout the world, we shall open the mouths of enemies to speak evil of the ways of God and all professors for God's sake, we shall shame the faces of many of God's worthy servants, and cause their prayers to be turned into curses upon us till we be consumed out of the good land whither we are going. And to shut up this discourse with that exhortation of Moses, that faithful servant of the Lord in His last farewell to Israel, Deut. 30., Beloved there is now set before us life and good, death and evil, in that we are commanded this day to love the Lord our God, and to love one another, to walk in His ways and to keep His commandments and His ordinance, and His laws, and the articles of our covenant with Him that we may live and be multiplied, and that the Lord our God may bless us in the land whither we go to possess it. But if our hearts shall turn away so that we will not obey, but shall be seduced and worship other Gods, our pleasures, our profits, and serve them, it is propounded unto us this day we shall surely perish out of the good land whither we pass over this vast sea to possess it. Therefore let us choose life, that we, and our seed, may live, and by obeying His voice, and cleaving to Him, for He is our life and our prosperity.

1630

For Discussion and Writing

1. The place of religion in government is one of the most hotly debated topics of discussion and argument in contemporary American life. John Winthrop believed that the arrival of the Puritans at Massachusetts Bay was a clear sign of God's acceptance of the colonists' covenant. What was that covenant? What did the colonists have to do to maintain the covenant? What were the dangers they faced it they did not follow it?
2. Winthrop set out to build a self-sustaining community. What rules of behavior did he set out for the colonists' relationships with each other? What is your opinion of his rules? Are they idealistic? Practical? Likely to succeed?
3. Winthrop uses the image of the city upon a hill to promote good behavior among the colonists, because their actions would be viewed and judged by all. How does a visual image, such as a city on a hill, help an audience to understand what the speaker or writer is saying? What other visual images do you see in Winthrop's sermon?
4. For many, the American Dream includes material prosperity, while others maintain that the Dream has been defiled through greed and excessive materialism. What passages in Winthrop foreshadow an emphasis on prosperity as an element of the American Dream?

Give Me Liberty or Give Me Death

PATRICK HENRY

Patrick Henry, shopkeeper, lawyer, orator and patriot, delivered this speech in support of an armed militia to the second Virginia Convention in St. John's Church, Richmond, VA, on March 23, 1775.

No man thinks more highly than I do of the patriotism, as well as abilities, of the very worthy gentlemen who have just addressed the House. But different men often see the same subject in different lights; and, therefore, I hope it will not be thought disrespectful to those gentlemen if, entertaining as I do opinions of a character very opposite to theirs, I shall speak forth my sentiments freely and without reserve. This is no time for ceremony. The questing before the House is one of awful moment to this country. For my own part, I consider it as nothing less than a question of freedom or slavery; and in proportion to the magnitude of the subject ought to be the freedom of the debate. It is only in this way that we can hope to arrive at truth, and fulfill the great responsibility which we hold to God and our country. Should I keep back my opinions at such a time, through fear of giving offense, I should consider myself as guilty of treason towards my country, and of an act of disloyalty toward the Majesty of Heaven, which I revere above all earthly kings.

Mr. President, it is natural to man to indulge in the illusions of hope. We are apt to shut our eyes against a painful truth, and listen to the song of that siren till she transforms us into beasts. Is this the part of wise men, engaged in a great and arduous struggle for liberty? Are we disposed to be of the number of those who, having eyes, see not, and, having ears, hear not, the things which so nearly concern their temporal salvation? For my part, whatever anguish of spirit it may cost, I am willing to know the whole truth; to know the worst, and to provide for it.

I have but one lamp by which my feet are guided, and that is the lamp of experience. I know of no way of judging of the future but by the past. And judging by the past, I wish to know what there has been in the conduct of the British ministry for the last ten years to justify those hopes with which gentlemen have been pleased to solace themselves and the House. Is it that insidious smile with which our petition has been lately received? Trust it not, sir; it will prove a snare to your feet. Suffer not yourselves to be betrayed with a kiss. Ask yourselves how this gracious reception of our petition comports with those warlike preparations which cover our waters and darken our land. Are fleets and armies necessary to a work of love and reconciliation? Have we shown ourselves so unwilling to be reconciled that force must be called in to win back our love? Let us not deceive ourselves, sir. These are the implements of war and subjugation; the last arguments to which kings resort. I ask gentlemen, sir, what means this martial array, if its purpose be not to force us to submission? Can gentlemen assign any other possible motive for it? Has Great Britain any enemy, in this quarter of the world, to call for all this accumulation of navies and armies? No, sir, she has none. They are meant for us: they can be meant for no other. They are sent over to bind and rivet upon us those chains which the British ministry have been so long forging. And what have we to oppose to them? Shall we try argument? Sir, we have been trying that for the last ten years. Have we anything new to offer upon the subject? Nothing. We have held the subject up in every light of which it is capable; but it has been all in vain. Shall we resort to entreaty and humble supplication? What terms shall we find which have not been already exhausted? Let us not, I beseech you, sir, deceive ourselves. Sir, we have done everything that could be done to avert the storm which is now coming on. We have petitioned; we have remonstrated; we have supplicated; we have prostrated ourselves before the throne, and have implored its interposition to arrest the tyrannical hands of the ministry and Parliament. Our petitions have been slighted; our remonstrances have produced additional violence and insult; our supplications have been disregarded; and we have been spurned, with contempt, from the foot of the throne! In vain, after these things, may we indulge the fond hope of peace and reconciliation. There is no longer any room for hope. If we wish to be free—if we mean to preserve inviolate those inestimable privileges for which we have been so long contending—if we mean not basely to abandon the noble struggle in which we have been so long engaged, and which we have pledged ourselves never to abandon until the glorious object of our contest shall be obtained—we must fight! I repeat it, sir, we must fight! An appeal to arms and to the God of hosts is all that is left us!

They tell us, sir, that we are weak; unable to cope with so formidable an adversary. But when shall we be stronger? Will it be the next week, or the next year? Will it be when we are totally disarmed, and when a British guard shall be stationed in every house? Shall we gather strength by irresolution and inaction? Shall we acquire the means of effectual resistance by lying supinely on our backs and hugging the delusive phantom of hope, until our enemies shall have bound us hand and foot? Sir, we are not weak if we make a proper use of those means which the God of nature hath placed in our power. The millions of people, armed in the holy cause of liberty, and in such a country as that which we possess, are invincible by any force which our enemy can send against us. Besides, sir, we shall not fight our battles alone. There is a just God who presides over the destinies of nations, and who will raise up friends to fight our battles for us. The battle, sir, is not to the strong alone; it is to the vigilant, the active, the brave. Besides, sir, we have no election. If we were base enough to desire it, it is now too late to retire from the contest. There is no retreat but in submission and slavery! Our chains are forged! Their clanking may be heard on the plains of Boston! The war is inevitable—and let it come! I repeat it, sir, let it come.

5 It is in vain, sir, to extenuate the matter. Gentlemen may cry, Peace, Peace—but there is no peace. The war is actually begun! The next gale that sweeps from the north will bring to our ears the

clash of resounding arms! Our brethren are already in the field! Why stand we here idle? What is it that gentlemen wish? What would they have? Is life so dear, or peace so sweet, as to be purchased at the price of chains and slavery? Forbid it, Almighty God! I know not what course others may take; but as for me, give me liberty or give me death!

1775

For Discussion and Writing

1. Patrick Henry's introductory paragraph is very complimentary and conciliatory toward the preceding speakers, who had advocated accommodating the British and avoiding war. What was Henry's purpose in beginning his speech this way?
2. Contemporary Americans often debate the propriety of criticizing the government, especially during a time of war, but Henry states that withholding his opinions to avoid giving offence would be treason to his country and disloyalty to God. In a short essay, state your opinion on the propriety of criticizing the government during a crisis and the major reasons that support your opinion.
3. Henry advances his case through a series of questions designed to illustrate that appeasing the British would not work. How effective is his questioning? In supporting an unpopular position, what would be the advantage of using questions instead of statements?
4. Henry references sources that would have been familiar to his classically educated audience. To what is he referring when he alludes to "the song of the siren"? "Betrayed by a kiss"?
5. Henry's stirring conclusion, "Give me liberty or give me death!," became a rallying call for the American revolutionaries and one of the best-known and most quoted American statements. What other passages from the speech are familiar to you? What, in your opinion, makes a statement memorable?

Declaration of Independence

THOMAS JEFFERSON

The Declaration of Independence proclaims the independence of the thirteen British colonies of America and establishes a new country, the United States of America. It documents the grievances the colonists held against their ruler, King George III of England, and establishes a political philosophy for the new country. The language and statement of principles in The Declaration of Independence are so powerful that they have been adopted by many other countries.

Thomas Jefferson (1743–1826) drafted the document while a delegate to the Second Continental Congress. The Congress made some revisions, of which the most disappointing to Jefferson was the deletion of language against slavery, and adopted the Declaration on July 4, 1776. Jefferson, although achieving much as the governor of Virginia, George Washington's Secretary of State, and the third president of the United States, considered writing the Declaration of Independence one of his most noteworthy accomplishments.

When in the Course of human events it becomes necessary for one people to dissolve the political bands which have connected them with another and to assume among the powers of the earth, the separate and equal station to which the Laws of Nature and of Nature's God entitle them, a decent respect to the opinions of mankind requires that they should declare the causes which impel them to the separation.

We hold these truths to be self-evident, that all men are created equal, that they are endowed by their Creator with certain unalienable Rights, that among these are Life, Liberty and the pursuit of Happiness.—That to secure these rights, Governments are instituted among Men, deriving their just powers from the consent of the governed,—That whenever any Form of Government becomes destructive of these ends, it is the Right of the People to alter or to abolish it, and to institute new Government, laying its foundation on such principles and organizing its powers in such form, as to them shall seem most likely to effect their Safety and Happiness. Prudence, indeed, will dictate that Governments long established should not be changed for light and transient causes; and accordingly all experience hath shewn that mankind are more disposed to suffer, while evils are sufferable than to right themselves by abolishing the forms to which they are accustomed. But when a long train of abuses and usurpations, pursuing invariably the same Object evinces a design to reduce them under absolute Despotism, it is their right, it is their duty, to throw off such Government, and to provide new Guards for their future security.—Such has been the patient sufferance of these Colonies; and such is now the necessity which constrains them to alter their former Systems of Government. The history of the present King of Great Britain is a history of repeated injuries and usurpations, all having in direct object the establishment of an absolute Tyranny over these States. To prove this, let Facts be submitted to a candid world.

He has refused his Assent to Laws, the most wholesome and necessary for the public good.

He has forbidden his Governors to pass Laws of immediate and pressing importance, unless suspended in their operation till his Assent should be obtained and when so suspended, he has utterly neglected to attend to them.

He has refused to pass other Laws for the accommodation of 5
large districts of people, unless those people would relinquish the right of Representation in the Legislature, a right inestimable to them and formidable to tyrants only.

He has called together legislative bodies at places unusual, uncomfortable, and distant from the depository of their Public Records, for the sole purpose of fatiguing them into compliance with his measures.

He has dissolved Representative Houses repeatedly, for opposing with manly firmness his invasions on the rights of the people.

He has refused for a long time, after such dissolutions, to cause others to be elected, whereby the Legislative Powers, incapable of Annihilation, have returned to the People at large for their exercise; the State remaining in the mean time exposed to all the dangers of invasion from without, and convulsions within.

He has endeavoured to prevent the population of these States; for that purpose obstructing the Laws for Naturalization of Foreigners; refusing to pass others to encourage their migrations hither, and raising the conditions of new Appropriations of Lands.

He has obstructed the Administration of Justice by refusing 10
his Assent to Laws for establishing Judiciary Powers.

He has made Judges dependent on his Will alone for the tenure of their offices, and the amount and payment of their salaries.

He has erected a multitude of New Offices, and sent hither swarms of Officers to harass our people and eat out their substance.

He has kept among us, in times of peace, Standing Armies without the Consent of our legislatures.

He has affected to render the Military independent of and superior to the Civil Power.

15 He has combined with others to subject us to a jurisdiction foreign to our constitution, and unacknowledged by our laws; giving his Assent to their Acts of pretended Legislation:

For quartering large bodies of armed troops among us:

For protecting them, by a mock Trial from punishment for any Murders which they should commit on the Inhabitants of these States:

For cutting off our Trade with all parts of the world:

For imposing Taxes on us without our Consent:

20 For depriving us in many cases, of the benefit of Trial by Jury:

For transporting us beyond Seas to be tried for pretended offences:

For abolishing the free System of English Laws in a neighbouring Province, establishing therein an Arbitrary government, and enlarging its Boundaries so as to render it at once an example and fit instrument for introducing the same absolute rule into these Colonies:

For taking away our Charters, abolishing our most valuable Laws and altering fundamentally the Forms of our Governments:

For suspending our own Legislatures, and declaring themselves invested with power to legislate for us in all cases whatsoever.

25 He has abdicated Government here, by declaring us out of his Protection and waging War against us.

He has plundered our seas, ravaged our coasts, burnt our towns, and destroyed the lives of our people.

He is at this time transporting large Armies of foreign Mercenaries to compleat the works of death, desolation, and tyranny, already begun with circumstances of Cruelty & Perfidy scarcely paralleled in the most barbarous ages, and totally unworthy the Head of a civilized nation.

He has constrained our fellow Citizens taken Captive on the high Seas to bear Arms against their Country, to become the executioners of their friends and Brethren, or to fall themselves by their Hands.

He has excited domestic insurrections amongst us, and has endeavoured to bring on the inhabitants of our frontiers, the merciless Indian Savages whose known rule of warfare, is an undistinguished destruction of all ages, sexes and conditions.

30 In every stage of these Oppressions We have Petitioned for Redress in the most humble terms: Our repeated Petitions have been answered only by repeated injury. A Prince, whose character is thus marked by every act which may define a Tyrant is unfit to be the ruler of a free people.

Nor have we been wanting in attentions to our British brethren. We have warned them from time to time of attempts by their legislature to extend an unwarrantable jurisdiction over us. We have reminded them of the circumstances of our emigration and settlement here. We have appealed to their native justice and magnanimity, and we have conjured them by the ties of our common kindred, to disavow these usurpations, which would inevitably interrupt our connections and correspondence. They too have been deaf to the voice of justice and of consanguinity. We must, therefore, acquiesce in the necessity, which denounces our Separation, and hold them, as we hold the rest of mankind, Enemies in War, in Peace Friends.

We, therefore, the Representatives of the United States of America, in General Congress, Assembled, appealing to the Supreme Judge of the world for the rectitude of our intentions, do, in the Name, and by Authority of the good People of these Colonies, solemnly publish and declare, That these United Colonies are, and of Right ought to be Free and Independent States, that they are Absolved from all Allegiance to the British Crown, and that all political connection between them and the State of Great Britain, is and ought to be totally dissolved; and that as Free and Independent States, they have full Power to levy War, conclude Peace, contract Alliances, establish Commerce, and to do all other Acts and Things which Independent States may of right do.—And for the support of this Declaration, with a firm reliance on the protection of Divine Providence, we mutually pledge to each other our Lives, our Fortunes and our sacred Honor.

1776

For Discussion and Writing

1. Who is the audience for The Declaration of Independence? Look particularly at the first and last paragraphs.
2. Jefferson states that "all men are created equal, that they are endowed by their Creator with certain unalienable Rights, that among these are Life, Liberty and the pursuit of Happiness." "Life" and "liberty" seem pretty straightforward; what might the "pursuit of happiness" mean? What does that phrase mean to you?
3. According to the Declaration, what is the purpose of government? What is the responsibility of the people if their government does not meet their needs? Discuss the ways in which this argument continues today.
4. The delegates to the Continental Congress had been governed by a constitutional monarchy. Although those governed held certain rights, the king's

power was transferred through inheritance. How would you expect King George III and his loyal subjects to respond to this document?
5. In the final sentence, the delegates "pledge to each other our lives, our Fortunes and our sacred Honor." How does this pledge establish their credibility? In what other ways does Jefferson establish the credibility of the signers of the document?

From "Common Sense"

THOMAS PAINE

During his lifetime Thomas Paine (1737–1809) was a minister, an inventor, and a writer, but the job description "revolutionary" probably best describes him. Born in England, he immigrated to the colonies in 1774, just in time to lend his support to the American Revolution. Common Sense, *which advocated independence from England, was an immediate success. Later Paine traveled to France to support the French Revolution, which cost him a year in prison and very nearly his life. He was a lifelong opponent of monarchs and a supporter of what he called "natural rights."*

INTRODUCTION

Perhaps the sentiments contained in the following pages, are not yet sufficiently fashionable to procure them general favor; a long habit of not thinking a thing wrong, gives it a superficial appearance of being right, and raises at first a formidable outcry in defence of custom. But tumult soon subsides. Time makes more converts than reason.

As a long and violent abuse of power is generally the means of calling the right of it in question, (and in matters too which might never have been thought of, had not the sufferers been aggravated into the inquiry,) and as the king of England hath undertaken in his own right, to support the parliament in what he calls theirs, and as the good people of this country are grievously oppressed by the combination, they have an undoubted privilege to inquire into the pretensions of both, and equally to reject the usurpations of either. . . .

The cause of America is, in a great measure, the cause of all mankind. Many circumstances have, and will arise, which are not local, but universal, and through which the principles of all lovers of mankind are affected, and in the event of which, their affections are interested. The laying a country desolate with fire and sword, declaring war against the natural rights of all mankind, and extirpating the defenders thereof from the face of the earth, is the concern of every man to whom nature hath given the power of feeling; of which class, regardless of party censure, is

The author. . . .

THOUGHTS ON THE PRESENT STATE OF AMERICAN AFFAIRS

In the following pages I offer nothing more than simple facts, plain arguments, and common sense; and have no other preliminaries to settle with the reader, than that he will divest himself of prejudice and prepossession, and suffer his reason and his feelings to determine for themselves; that he will put *on,* or rather that he will not put *off,* the true character of a man, and generously enlarge his views beyond the present day.

Volumes have been written on the subject of the struggle 5
between England and America. Men of all ranks have embarked in the controversy, from different motives, and with various designs; but all have been ineffectual, and the period of debate is closed. Arms, as the last resource, decide the contest; the appeal was the choice of the king, and the continent hath accepted the challenge.

It hath been reported of the late Mr Pelham (who tho' an able minister was not without his faults) that on his being attacked in the house of commons, on the score, that his measures were only of a temporary kind, replied, *"they will last my time."* Should a thought so fatal and unmanly possess the colonies in the present contest, the name of ancestors will be remembered by future generations with detestation.

The sun never shined on a cause of greater worth. 'Tis not the affair of a city, a country, a province, or a kingdom, but of a continent—of at least one eighth part of the habitable globe. 'Tis not the concern of a day, a year, or an age; posterity are virtually involved in the contest, and will be more or less affected, even to the end of time, by the proceedings now. Now is the seed time of continental union, faith and honor. The least fracture now will be like a name engraved with the point of a pin on the tender rind of a young oak; The wound will enlarge with the tree, and posterity read it in full grown characters.

By referring the matter from argument to arms, a new æra for politics is struck; a new method of thinking hath arisen. All plans, proposals, &c. prior to the nineteenth of April, *i.e.* to the commencement of hostilities, are like the almanacks of the last year; which, though proper then, are superceded and useless now. Whatever was advanced by the advocates on either side of the question then, terminated in one and the same point, viz. a union with Great-Britain; the only difference between the parties was the method of effecting it; the one proposing force, the other friendship; but it hath so far happened that the first hath failed, and the second hath withdrawn her influence.

As much hath been said of the advantages of reconciliation, which, like an agreeable dream, hath passed away and left us as we were, it is but right, that we should examine the contrary side of the argument, and inquire into some of the many material injuries which these colonies sustain, and always will sustain, by being connected with, and dependant on Great-Britain. To examine that connexion and dependance, on the principles of nature and common sense, to see what we have to trust to, if separated, and what we are to expect, if dependant.

10 I have heard it asserted by some, that as America hath flourished under her former connexion with Great-Britain, that the same connexion is necessary towards her future happiness, and will always have the same effect. Nothing can be more fallacious than this kind of argument. We may as well assert that because a child has thrived upon milk, that it is never to have meat, or that the first twenty years of our lives is to become a precedent for the next twenty. But even this is admitting more than is true, for I answer roundly, that America would have flourished as much, and probably much more, had no European power had any thing to do with her. The commerce, by which she hath enriched herself are the necessaries of life, and will always have a market while eating is the custom of Europe.

But she has protected us, say some. That she hath engrossed us is true, and defended the continent at our expence as well as her own is admitted, and she would have defended Turkey from the same motive, viz. the sake of trade and dominion.

Alas, we have been long led away by ancient prejudices, and made large sacrifices to superstition. We have boasted the protection of Great-Britain, without considering, that her motive was *interest* not *attachment*; that she did not protect us from *our enemies* on *our account,* but from *her enemies* on *her own account,* from those who had no quarrel with us on any *other account,* and who will always be our enemies on the *same account.* Let Britain wave her pretensions to the continent, or the continent throw off the dependance, and we should be at peace with France and Spain were they at war with Britain. The miseries of Hanover last war ought to warn us against connexions.

It hath lately been asserted in parliament, that the colonies have no relation to each other but through the parent country, *i.e.* that Pennsylvania and the Jerseys, and so on for the rest, are sister colonies by the way of England; this is certainly a very roundabout way of proving relationship, but it is the nearest and only true way of proving enemyship, if I may so call it. France and Spain never were, nor perhaps ever will be our enemies as *Americans,* but as our being the *subjects of Great-Britain.*

But Britain is the parent country, say some. Then the more shame upon her conduct. Even brutes do not devour their young, nor savages make war upon their families; wherefore the assertion, if true, turns to her reproach; but it happens not to be true, or only partly so, and the phrase *parent* or *mother country* hath been jesuitically adopted by the king and his parasites, with a low papistical design of gaining an unfair bias on the credulous weakness of our minds. Europe, and not England, is the parent country of America. This new world hath been the asylum for the persecuted lovers of civil and religious liberty from *every part* of Europe. Hither have they fled, not from the tender embraces of the mother, but from the cruelty of the monster; and it is so far true of England, that the same tyranny which drove the first emigrants from home, pursues their descendants still.

In this extensive quarter of the globe, we forget the narrow 15
limits of three hundred and sixty miles (the extent of England) and carry our friendship on a larger scale; we claim brotherhood with every European christian, and triumph in the generosity of the sentiment. . . .

But admitting, that we were all of English descent, what does it amount to? Nothing. Britain, being now an open enemy, extinguishes every other name and title: And to say that reconciliation is our duty, is truly farcical. The first king of England, of the present line (William the Conqueror) was a Frenchman, and half the Peers of England are descendants from the same country; wherefore, by the same method of reasoning, England ought to be governed by France.

Much hath been said of the united strength of Britain and the colonies, that in conjunction they might bid defiance to the world. But this is mere presumption; the fate of war is uncertain, neither do the expressions mean any thing; for this continent would never suffer itself to be drained of inhabitants, to support the British arms in either Asia, Africa, or Europe.

Besides, what have we to do with setting the world at defiance? Our plan is commerce, and that, well attended to, will secure us the peace and friendship of all Europe; because, it is the interest of all Europe to have America a *free port*. Her trade will always be a protection, and her barrenness of gold and silver secure her from invaders.

I challenge the warmest advocate for reconciliation, to shew, a single advantage that this continent can reap, by being connected with Great Britain. . . .

It is repugnant to reason, to the universal order of things to all examples from former ages, to suppose, that this continent can longer remain subject to any external power. The most sanguine in Britain does not think so. The utmost stretch of human wisdom cannot, at this time, compass a plan short of separation, which can promise the continent even a year's security. Reconciliation is *now* a falacious dream. Nature hath deserted the connexion, and Art cannot supply her place. For, as Milton wisely expresses, "never can true reconcilement grow where wounds of deadly hate have pierced so deep." . . .

Small islands not capable of protecting themselves, are the proper objects for kingdoms to take under their care; but there is something very absurd, in supposing a continent to be perpetually governed by an island. In no instance hath nature made the satellite larger than its primary planet, and as England and America, with respect to each other, reverses the common order of nature, it is evident they belong to different systems: England to Europe, America to itself.

I am not induced by motives of pride, party, or resentment to espouse the doctrine of separation and independance; I am clearly, positively, and conscientiously persuaded that it is the true interest of this continent to be so; that every thing short of *that* is mere patchwork, that it can afford no lasting felicity,—that it is leaving the sword to our children, and shrinking back at a time, when, a little more, a little farther, would have rendered this continent the glory of the earth. . . .

A government of our own is our natural right: And when a man seriously reflects on the precariousness of human affairs, he will become convinced, that it is infinitely wiser and safer, to form a constitution of our own in a cool deliberate manner, while we have it in our power, than to trust such an interesting event to time and chance. . . .

Ye that tell us of harmony and reconciliation, can ye restore to us the time that is past? Can ye give to prostitution its former innocence? Neither can ye reconcile Britain and America. The last cord now is broken, the people of England are presenting addresses against us. There are injuries which nature cannot forgive; she would cease to be nature if she did. As well can the lover forgive the ravisher of his mistress, as the continent forgive the murders of Britain. The Almighty hath implanted in us these unextinguishable feelings for good and wise purposes. They are the guardians of his image in our hearts. They distinguish us from the herd of common animals. The social compact would dissolve, and justice be extirpated from the earth, or have only a casual existence were we callous to the touches of affection. The robber, and the murderer, would often escape unpunished, did not the injuries which our tempers sustain, provoke us into justice.

O ye that love mankind! Ye that dare oppose, not only the 25
tyranny, but the tyrant, stand forth! Every spot of the old world is overrun with oppression. Freedom hath been hunted round the globe. Asia, and Africa, have long expelled her.—Europe regards her like a stranger, and England hath given her warning to depart. O! receive the fugitive, and prepare in time an asylum for mankind. . . .

1776

For Discussion and Writing

1. What do you believe Paine meant by the statement, "The cause of America is, in a great measure, the cause of all mankind"? To what extent do you think it is true in today's world?
2. Beginning in paragraph 10, Paine delineates objections colonists had expressed to separating from England, then counter-argues each objection. This is an ancient rhetorical technique, called *anticipation of objection* (anticipating what your opponents would say) and rebuttal (arguing against them). What is the value of including anticipation of opposition and rebuttal in an argument?
3. Many Americans are concerned about immigration and a global economy, seeing these as relevantly recent phenomena, but Paine addresses both these issues in *Common Sense*. What are his opinions on immigration? On free trade?

4. In paragraph 21, Paine uses analogy to support his argument, saying "In no instance hath nature made the satellite larger than its primary planet," to argue that England is too small to govern a large entity like America. What other analogies does Paine use? How useful do you believe analogy is in furthering an argument?
5. Reread paragraph 7, concentrating particularly on the language. What is the effect of such series of phrases as, "'Tis not the affair of a city, a country, a province, or a kingdom" or, "'Tis not the concern of a day, a year, or an age." The emotive language (language used to stir the emotions) seen in paragraph 7 gives Paine's essay power beyond his statements of fact and logic. Find other examples of emotive language in *Common Sense*. How do they affect you?

Letter to John Adams: Remember the Ladies (1776)

ABIGAIL ADAMS

Both the wife (John Adams) and mother (John Quincy Adams) of presidents, Abigail Adams (1744–1818) was a force for change in her own right. Self-educated and a lifelong writer, her letters to her husband during the Continental Congress and the Revolutionary War reveal her to be his trusted and outspoken confidant, and give us many insights into colonial life. "Remember the Ladies," which was written in stages between March 31 and April 5, 1776, showcases her interest in women's rights.

✦

Braintree, March 31, 1776

I wish you would ever write me a Letter half as long as I write you; and tell me if you may where your Fleet are gone? What sort of Defence Virginia can make against our common Enemy? Whether it is so situated as to make an able Defence? Are not the Gentery Lords and the common people vassals, are they not like the uncivilized Natives Brittain represents us to be? I hope their Riffel Men who have shewen themselves very savage and even Blood thirsty; are not a specimen of the Generality of the people.

I am willing to allow the Colony great merrit for having produced a Washington but they have been shamefully duped by a Dunmore.

I have sometimes been ready to think that the passion for Liberty cannot be Eaquelly Strong in the Breasts of those who have been accustomed to deprive their fellow Creatures of theirs. Of this I am certain that it is not founded upon that generous and christian principal of doing to others as we would that others should do unto us.

Do not you want to see Boston; I am fearfull of the small pox, or I should have been in before this time. I got Mr. Crane to go to our House and see what state it was in. I find it has been occupied by one of the Doctors of a Regiment, very dirty, but no other damage has been done to it. The few things which were left in it are all gone. Cranch [Crane?] has the key which he never deliverd up. I have wrote to him for it and am determined to get it cleand as soon as possible and shut it up. I look upon it a new acquisition of property, a property which one month ago I did not value at a single Shilling, and could with pleasure have seen it in flames.

The Town in General is left in a better state than we expected, 5
more oweing to a percipitate flight than any Regard to the inhabitants, tho some individuals discoverd a sense of honour and justice and have left the rent of the Houses in which they were, for the owners and the furniture unhurt, or if damaged sufficent to make it good.

Others have committed abominable Ravages. The Mansion House of your President [John Hancock] is safe and the furniture unhurt whilst both the House and Furniture of the Solisiter General [Samuel Quincy] have fallen a prey to their own merciless party. Surely the very Fiends feel a Reverential awe for Virtue and patriotism, whilst they Detest the paricide and traitor.

I feel very differently at the approach of spring to what I did a month ago. We knew not then whether we could plant or sow with safety, whether when we had toild we could reap the fruits of our own industery, whether we could rest in our own Cottages, or whether we should not be driven from the sea coasts to seek shelter in the wilderness, but now we feel as if we might sit under our own vine and eat the good of the land.

I feel a gaieti de Coar to which before I was a stranger. I think the Sun looks brighter, the Birds sing more melodiously, and Nature puts on a more chearfull countanance. We feel a temporary peace, and the poor fugitives are returning to their deserted habitations.

Tho we felicitate ourselves, we sympathize with those who are trembling least the Lot of Boston should be theirs. But they cannot be in similar circumstances unless pusilanimity and cowardise should take possession of them. They have time and warning given them to see the Evil and shun it. I long to hear that you have declared an independancy and by the way in the new Code of Laws which I suppose it will be necessary for you to make I desire you would Remember the Ladies, and be more generous and favourable to them than your ancestors. Do not put such unlimited power into the hands of the Husbands. Remember all Men would be tyrants if they could. If perticuliar care and attention is not paid to the Laidies we are determined to foment a Rebelion, and will not hold ourselves bound by any Laws in which we have no voice, or Representation.

That your Sex are Naturally Tyrannical is a Truth so thoroughly established as to admit of no dispute, but such of you as wish to be happy willingly give up the harsh title of Master for the more tender and endearing one of Friend. Why then, not put it out of the power of the vicious and the Lawless to use us with cruelty and indignity with impunity. Men of Sense in all Ages abhor those customs which treat us only as the vassals of your Sex. Regard us then as Beings placed by providence under your protection and in immitation of the Supreem Being make use of that power only for our happiness.

1776

John Adams' Response to "Remember the Ladies" (1776)

On April 14, 1776, John Adams responded to Abigail's letter in the following manner.

As to your extraordinary Code of Laws, I cannot but laugh. We have been told that our Struggle has loosened the bands of Government every where. That Children and Apprentices were disobedient—that schools and Colledges were grown turbulent—that Indians slighted their Guardians and Negroes grew insolent to their Masters.

But your Letter was the first Intimation that another Tribe more numerous and powerfull than all the rest were grown discontented.—This is rather too coarse a Compliment but you are so saucy, I wont blot it out.

Depend upon it, We know better than to repeal our Masculine systems. Altho they are in full Force, you know they are little more than Theory. We dare not exert our Power in its full Latitude. We are obliged to go fair, and softly, and in Practice you know We are the subjects. We have only the Name of Masters, and rather than give up this, which would compleatly subject Us to the Despotism of the Peticoat, I hope General Washington, and all our brave Heroes would fight. I am sure every good Politician would plot, as long as he would against Despotism, Empire, Monarchy, Aristocracy, Oligarchy, or Ochlocracy.

1776

For Discussion and Writing

1. Abigail Adams' many letters to her husband provide a good look at colonial life during a time beset by the ravages of war and disease. What household concerns does Adams express? What were her concerns about the outcome of the revolution?
2. During colonial times and long after the revolution, only adult males who owned property could vote; women were not granted suffrage until the passage of the 19th Amendment in 1920. Men had the right to punish their wives, including through beatings, and to confiscate their wages and any property they inherited. In addition, men were regularly granted custody of all children after divorce. With these policies in mind, why was it so important to Abigail Adams that her husband and his colleagues "remember the ladies"?
3. Based on his response to his wife, would you expect John Adams to have become known in history as a supporter of women's rights? What rights did he believe women possessed through their "Despotism of the Petticoat"?

Constitution of the Iroquois Nations—The Great Binding Law (*Gayanashagowa*)

Dekanawidah

"The Origin of the Longhouse," printed earlier in this chapter, tells the story of the beginning of the Confederacy of the Five Nations, an alliance of tribes that inhabited parts of New York, Pennsylvania, Ontario, and Quebec. Gayanashagowa, or the Great Binding Law, is the constitution of that alliance. While the text has generally been

dated at mid-fifteenth century, recent archeological studies suggest it may have been written three hundred years earlier, in the mid-twelfth century. Many historians believe that some elements of the United States Constitution were based on The Great Binding Law.

---

1. I am Dekanawidah and with the Five Nations' Confederate Lords I plant the Tree of Great Peace. I plant it in your territory, Adodarhoh, and the Onondaga Nation, in the territory of you who are Firekeepers.

I name the tree the Tree of the Great Long Leaves. Under the shade of this Tree of the Great Peace we spread the soft white feathery down of the globe thistle as seats for you, Adodarhoh, and your cousin Lords.

We place you upon those seats, spread soft with the feathery down of the globe thistle, there beneath the shade of the spreading branches of the Tree of Peace. There shall you sit and watch the Council Fire of the Confederacy of the Five Nations, and all the affairs of the Five Nations shall be transacted at this place before you, Adodarhoh, and your cousin Lords, by the Confederate Lords of the Five Nations.

2. Roots have spread out from the Tree of the Great Peace, one to the north, one to the east, one to the south and one to the west. The name of these roots is The Great White Roots and their nature is Peace and Strength.

If any man or any nation outside the Five Nations shall obey the laws of the Great Peace and make known their disposition to the Lords of the Confederacy, they may trace the Roots to the Tree and if their minds are clean and they are obedient and promise to obey the wishes of the Confederate Council, they shall be welcomed to take shelter beneath the Tree of the Long Leaves.

We place at the top of the Tree of the Long Leaves an Eagle who is able to see afar. If he sees in the distance any evil approaching or any danger threatening he will at once warn the people of the Confederacy.

3. To you Adodarhoh, the Onondaga cousin Lords, I and the other Confederate Lords have entrusted the caretaking and the watching of the Five Nations Council Fire.

When there is any business to be transacted and the Confederate Council is not in session, a messenger shall be dispatched either to Adodarhoh, Hononwirehtonh or Skanawatih, Fire Keepers, or to their War Chiefs with a full statement of the case desired to be considered. Then shall Adodarhoh call his cousin Lords together and consider whether or not the case is of sufficient importance to demand the attention of the Confederate Council. If so, Adodarhoh shall dispatch messengers to summon all the Confederate Lords to assemble beneath the Tree of the Long Leaves. . . .

RIGHTS, DUTIES AND QUALIFICATIONS OF LORDS

17. A bunch of a certain number of shell (*wampum*) strings each two spans in length shall be given to each of the female families in which the Lordship titles are vested. The right of bestowing the title shall be hereditary in the family of the females legally possessing the bunch of shell strings and the strings shall be the token that the females of the family have the proprietary right to the Lordship title for all time to come, subject to certain restrictions hereinafter mentioned.

18. If any Confederate Lord neglects or refuses to attend the Confederate Council, the other Lords of the Nation of which he is a member shall require their War Chief to request the female sponsors of the Lord so guilty of defection to demand his attendance of the Council. If he refuses, the women holding the title shall immediately select another candidate for the title.

No Lord shall be asked more than once to attend the Confederate Council.

19. If at any time it shall be manifest that a Confederate Lord has not in mind the welfare of the people or disobeys the rules of this Great Law, the men or women of the Confederacy, or both jointly, shall come to the Council and upbraid the erring Lord through his War Chief. If the complaint of the people through the War Chief is not heeded the first time it shall be uttered again and then if no attention is given a third complaint and warning shall be given. If the Lord is contumacious the matter shall go to the council of War Chiefs. The War Chiefs shall then divest the erring Lord of his title by order of the women in whom the titleship is vested. When the Lord is deposed the women shall notify the Confederate Lords through their War Chief, and the Confederate Lords shall sanction the act. The women will then select another of their sons as a candidate and the Lords shall elect him. Then shall the chosen one be installed by the Installation Ceremony. . . .

NAMES, DUTIES AND RIGHTS OF WAR CHIEFS....

37. There shall be one War Chief for each Nation and their duties shall be to carry messages for their Lords and to take up the arms of war in case of emergency. They shall not participate in the proceedings of the Confederate Council but shall watch its progress and in case of an erroneous action by a Lord they shall receive the complaints of the people and convey the warnings of the women to him. The people who wish to convey messages to the Lords in the Confederate Council shall do so through the War Chief of their Nation. It shall ever be his duty to lay the cases, questions and propositions of the people before the Confederate Council.

38. When a War Chief dies another shall be installed by the same rite as that by which a Lord is installed.

39. If a War Chief acts contrary to instructions or against the provisions of the Laws of the Great Peace, doing so in the capacity of his office, he shall be deposed by his women relatives and by his men relatives. Either the women or the men alone or jointly may act in such a case. The women title holders shall then choose another candidate.

40. When the Lords of the Confederacy take occasion to dispatch a messenger in behalf of the Confederate Council, they shall wrap up any matter they may send and instruct the messenger to remember his errand, to turn not aside but to proceed faithfully to his destination and deliver his message according to every instruction.

41. If a message borne by a runner is the warning of an invasion he shall whoop, "Kwa-ah, Kwa-ah," twice and repeat at short intervals; then again at a longer interval.

If a human being is found dead, the finder shall not touch the body but return home immediately shouting at short intervals, "Koo-weh!"

CLANS AND CONSANGUINITY

42. Among the Five Nations and their posterity there shall be the following original clans: Great Name Bearer, Ancient Name Bearer, Great Bear, Ancient Bear, Turtle, Painted Turtle, Standing Rock, Large Plover, Deer, Pigeon Hawk, Eel, Ball, Opposite-Side-of-the-Hand, and Wild Potatoes. These clans distributed through their respective Nations, shall be the sole owners and holders of the soil of the country and in them is it vested as a birthright.

43. People of the Five Nations members of a certain clan shall recognize every other member of that clan, irrespective of the Nation, as relatives. Men and women, therefore, members of the same clan are forbidden to marry. 20

44. The lineal descent of the people of the Five Nations shall run in the female line. Women shall be considered the progenitors of the Nation. They shall own the land and the soil. Men and women shall follow the status of the mother.

45. The women heirs of the Confederated Lordship titles shall be called *Royaneh* (Noble) for all time to come.

46. The women of the Forty Eight (now fifty) *Royaneh* families shall be the heirs of the Authorized Names for all time to come.

When an infant of the Five Nations is given an Authorized Name at the Midwinter Festival or at the Ripe Corn Festival, one in the cousinhood of which the infant is a member shall be appointed a speaker. He shall then announce to the opposite cousinhood the names of the father and the mother of the child together with the clan of the mother. Then the speaker shall announce the child's name twice. The uncle of the child shall then take the child in his arms and walking up and down the room shall sing: "My head is firm, I am of the Confederacy." As he sings the opposite cousinhood shall respond by chanting, "Hyenh, Hyenh, Hyenh, Hyenh," until the song is ended. . . . .

It is not good nor honorable for a Confederate Lord to allow his people whom he has called to go hungry. 25

51. When a Lord holds a conference in his home, his wife, if she wishes, may prepare the food for the Union Lords who assemble with him. This is an honorable right which she may exercise and an expression of her esteem.

52. The *Royaneh* women, heirs of the Lordship titles, shall, should it be necessary, correct and admonish the holders of their titles. Those only who attend the Council may do this and those who do not shall not object to what has been said nor strive to undo the action.

53. When the *Royaneh* women, holders of a Lordship title, select one of their sons as a candidate, they shall select one who is trustworthy, of good character, of honest disposition, one who manages his own affairs, supports his own family, if any, and who has proven a faithful man to his Nation.

54. When a Lordship title becomes vacant through death or other cause, the *Royaneh* women of the clan in which the title is hereditary shall hold a council and shall choose one from among their sons to fill the office made vacant. Such a candidate shall not be the father of any Confederate Lord. If the choice is unanimous the name is referred to the men relatives of the clan. If they should disapprove it shall be their duty to select a candidate from among their own number. If then the men and women are unable to decide which of the two candidates shall be named, then the matter shall be referred to the Confederate Lords in the Clan. They shall decide which candidate shall be named. If the men and the women agree to a candidate his name shall be referred to the sister clans for confirmation. If the sister clans confirm the choice, they shall refer their action to their Confederate Lords who shall ratify the choice and present it to their cousin Lords, and if the cousin Lords confirm the name then the candidate shall be installed by the proper ceremony for the conferring of Lordship titles. . . .

RIGHTS AND POWERS OF WAR

79. Skanawatih shall be vested with a double office, duty and with double authority. One-half of his being shall hold the Lordship title and the other half shall hold the title of War Chief. In the event of war he shall notify the five War Chiefs of the Confederacy and command them to prepare for war and have their men ready at the appointed time and place for engagement with the enemy of the Great Peace.

80. When the Confederate Council of the Five Nations has for its object the establishment of the Great Peace among the people of an outside nation and that nation refuses to accept the Great Peace, then by such refusal they bring a declaration of war upon themselves from the Five Nations. Then shall the Five Nations seek to establish the Great Peace by a conquest of the rebellious nation.

81. When the men of the Five Nations, now called forth to become warriors, are ready for battle with an obstinate opposing nation that has refused to accept the Great Peace, then one of the five War Chiefs shall be chosen by the warriors of the Five Nations to lead the army into battle. It shall be the duty of the War Chief so chosen to come before his warriors and address them. His aim shall be to impress upon them the necessity of good behavior and strict obedience to all the commands of the War Chiefs. He shall deliver an oration exhorting them with great zeal to be brave and courageous and

never to be guilty of cowardice. At the conclusion of his oration he shall march forward and commence the War Song and he shall sing:

> Now I am greatly surprised
> And, therefore I shall use it—
> The power of my War Song.
> I am of the Five Nations
> And I shall make supplication
> To the Almighty Creator.
> He has furnished this army.
> My warriors shall be mighty
> In the strength of the Creator.
> Between him and my song they are
> For it was he who gave the song
> This war song that I sing!

RIGHTS OF THE PEOPLE OF THE FIVE NATIONS

93. Whenever a specially important matter or a great emergency is presented before the Confederate Council and the nature of the matter affects the entire body of the Five Nations, threatening their utter ruin, then the Lords of the Confederacy must submit the matter to the decision of their people and the decision of the people shall affect the decision of the Confederate Council. This decision shall be a confirmation of the voice of the people.

94. The men of every clan of the Five Nations shall have a Council Fire ever burning in readiness for a council of the clan. When it seems necessary for a council to be held to discuss the welfare of the clans, then the men may gather about the fire. This council shall have the same rights as the council of the women.

95. The women of every clan of the Five Nations shall have a Council Fire ever burning in readiness for a council of the clan. When in their opinion it seems necessary for the interest of the people they shall hold a council and their decisions and recommendations shall be introduced before the Council of the Lords by the War Chief for its consideration.

96. All the Clan council fires of a nation or of the Five Nations may unite into one general council fire, or delegates from all the council fires may be appointeed to unite in a general council for discussing the interests of the people. The people shall have the right to make appointments and to delegate their power to others of their number.

When their council shall have come to a conclusion on any matter, their decision shall be reported to the Council of the Nation or to the Confederate Council (as the case may require) by the War Chief or the War Chiefs.

97. Before the real people united their nations, each nation had its council fires. Before the Great Peace their councils were held. The five Council Fires shall continue to burn as before and they are not quenched. The Lords of each nation in future shall settle their nation's affairs at this council fire governed always by the laws and rules of the council of the Confederacy and by the Great Peace.

98. If either a nephew or a niece see an irregularity in the performance of the functions of the Great Peace and its laws, in the Confederate Council or in the conferring of Lordship titles in an improper way, through their War Chief they may demand that such actions become subject to correction and that the matter conform to the ways prescribed by the laws of the Great Peace.

RELIGIOUS CEREMONIES PROTECTED

99. The rites and festivals of each nation shall remain undisturbed and shall continue as before because they were given by the people of old times as useful and necessary for the good of men. . . .

PROTECTION OF THE HOUSE

107. A certain sign shall be known to all the people of the Five Nations which shall denote that the owner or occupant of a house is absent. A stick or pole in a slanting or leaning position shall indicate this and be the sign. Every person not entitled to enter the house by right of living within it upon seeing such a sign shall not approach the house either by day or by night but shall keep as far away as his business will permit. . . .

1450

For Discussion and Writing

1. What is the tone of The Great Binding Law? If you were a member of one of the five founding tribes of the alliance, what would your response be on hearing the Law? What particular sections of the Law seem designed to promote acceptance and conciliation?

2. What were the rights and responsibilities of women under the Law?
3. The Law requires that War Chiefs not be part of the Confederate Council, a situation very different from the United States Constitution, which gives the president the powers of Commander in Chief of the military. Why do you think the framers of the Law felt it important that war commanders not have anything to do with civil government?
4. The Law sets out various rituals (hospitality, naming, war, etc.) to be followed by all alliance members, while giving those members leeway to continue with their own rituals as well. What is the role of ritual in forming alliances among disparate cultures?
5. How does the Law endeavor to be the voice of the people?

The Star Spangled Banner

FRANCIS SCOTT KEY

As night fell on September 7, 1814, Francis Scott Key watched the British attack on Fort McHenry in Baltimore Harbor. Key did not know who had won the battle until the following morning. When he saw the United States' flag waving on the flagstaff, he was inspired to write the poem "The Star Spangled Banner."

Set to the tune of an old British drinking song, "The Star Spangled Banner" became an immediate hit but did not become the national anthem of the United States until 1931.

Oh, say can you see, by the dawn's early light,
What so proudly we hailed at the twilight's last gleaming?
Whose broad stripes and bright stars, through the perilous fight,
O'er the ramparts we watched, were so gallantly streaming?
And the rockets' red glare, the bombs bursting in air,
Gave proof through the night that our flag was still there.
O say, does that star-spangled banner yet wave
O'er the land of the free and the home of the brave?

On the, shore, dimly seen through the mists of the deep,
Where the foe's haughty host in dread silence reposes,
What is that which the breeze, o'er the towering steep,
As it fitfully blows, now conceals, now discloses?

Now it catches the gleam of the morning's first beam,
In full glory reflected now shines on the stream:
'Tis the star-spangled banner! O long may it wave
O'er the land of the free and the home of the brave.

And where is that band who so vauntingly swore
That the havoc of war and the battle's confusion
A home and a country should leave us no more?
Their blood has wiped out their foul footstep's pollution.
No refuge could save the hireling and slave
From the terror of flight, or the gloom of the grave:
And the star-spangled banner in triumph doth wave
O'er the land of the free and the home of the brave.

Oh! thus be it ever, when freemen shall stand
Between their loved homes and the war's desolation!
Blest with victory and peace, may the heaven-rescued land
Praise the Power that hath made and preserved us a nation.
Then conquer we must, for our cause it is just,
And this be our motto: "In God is our trust."
And the star-spangled banner forever shall wave
O'er the land of the free and the home of the brave!

1814

My Country 'Tis of Thee

SAMUEL F. SMITH

"My Country 'Tis of Thee," written by Reverend Samuel F. Smith in Andover, Massachusetts, was generally considered the national anthem of the United States through most of the nineteenth Century, even though its melody is copied from the British national anthem, "God Save the Queen." The hymn is also known by the name "America."

My country, 'tis of thee,
Sweet land of liberty,
Of thee I sing;
Land where my fathers died,

Land of the pilgrims' pride,
From every mountainside,
Let freedom ring!

My native country, thee,
Land of the noble free,
Thy name I love;
I love thy rocks and rills,
Thy woods and templed hills;
My heart with rapture thrills,
Like that above.

Let music swell the breeze,
And ring from all the trees,
Sweet freedom's song;
Let mortal tongues awake;
Let all that breathe partake;
Let rocks their silence break,
The sound prolong.

Our fathers' God, to Thee,
Author of liberty,
To Thee we sing;
Long may our land be bright
With freedom's holy light;
Protect us by Thy might,
Great God, our King.

1832

For Discussion and Writing

1. "The Star Spangled Banner" and "My Country 'Tis of Thee" express an evolving image of America. What are some of the themes concerning the nature of America and Americans common to both songs? What themes are prevalent in each song?
2. At different times, "My Country 'Tis of Thee" and "The Star Spangled Banner" have served as the national anthem of the United States. Which song is a better representation of your understanding of America? Why?
3. Think of three words that express the tone of each song. For example, three words that could express the tone of "The Star Spangled Banner" are "solemn," "formal," and "stirring." Can you think of other words that express the tone of "The Star Spangled Banner"? Of "My Country 'Tis of Thee"?

4. It's been said that the last line of "The Star Spangled Banner" is either "Gentlemen, start your engines" or "Play ball!" (depending on whether you are a racing or a baseball fan). Why is the national anthem played at sporting events, as well as at patriotic events like parades and memorials? What might be good settings for singing "My Country 'Tis of Thee"? What in the nature of a song makes it appropriate in particular situations?

From "Walker's Appeal, in Four Articles; Together with a Preamble, to the Coloured Citizens of the World, but in Particular, and Very Expressly, to Those of the United States of America"

DAVID WALKER

David Walker (1785–1830), an early black abolitionist, was born a free man but had many opportunities to observe the cruelty of slavery. His demand for immediate emancipation of all slaves was considered extreme at the time: Southern slaveholders offered a bounty for him dead or alive. Walker's Appeal reminds us that, from its earliest inception, the American Dream was denied to many.

Walker was found dead on his doorstep the same year the Appeal was published. The official cause of death was tuberculosis, but many believed he had actually been poisoned.

PREAMBLE

My dearly beloved Brethren and Fellow Citizens.

Having travelled over a considerable portion of these United States, and having, in the course of my travels, taken the most accurate observations of things as they exist—the result of my observations has warranted the full and unshaken conviction, that we, (coloured people of these United States,) are the most degraded, wretched, and abject set of beings that ever lived since the world began; and I pray God that none like us ever may live again until time shall be no more. They tell us of the Israelites in Egypt, the Helots in Sparta, and of the Roman Slaves, which last were made up from almost every nation under heaven, whose sufferings under those ancient and heathen nations, were, in comparison with ours, under this enlightened and Christian nation, no more than a cypher—or, in other words, those heathen nations of antiquity, had but little more among them than the name and form of slavery; while wretchedness and endless miseries were reserved, apparently in a phial, to be poured out upon our fathers, ourselves and our children, by *Christian* Americans. . . .

I am fully aware, in making this appeal to my much afflicted and suffering brethren, that I shall not only be assailed by those whose greatest earthly desires are, to keep us in abject ignorance and wretchedness, and who are of the firm conviction that Heaven has designed us and our children to be slaves and *beasts of burden* to them and their children. I say, I do not only expect to be held up to the public as an ignorant, impudent and restless disturber of the public peace, by such avaricious creatures, as well as a mover of insubordination—and perhaps put in prison or to death, for giving a superficial exposition of our miseries, and exposing tyrants. But I am persuaded, that many of my brethren, particularly those who are ignorantly in league with slaveholders or tyrants, who acquire their daily bread by the blood and sweat of their more ignorant brethren—and not a few of those too, who are too ignorant to see an inch beyond their noses, will rise up and call me cursed—Yea, the jealous ones among us will perhaps use more abject subtlety, by affirming that this work is not worth perusing, that we are well situated, and there is no use in trying to better our condition, for we cannot. I will ask one question here.—Can our condition be any worse?—Can it be more mean and abject? If there are any changes, will they not be for the better though they may appear for the worst at first? Can they get us any lower? Where can they get us? They are afraid to treat us worse, for they know well, the day they do it they are gone. But against all accusations which may or can be preferred against me, I appeal to Heaven for my motive in writing—who knows what my object is, if possible, to awaken in the breasts of my afflicted, degraded and slumbering brethren, a spirit of inquiry and investigation respecting our miseries and wretchedness in this *Republican Land of Liberty!!!!!!*

The sources from which our miseries are derived, and on which I shall comment, I shall not combine in one, but shall put them under distinct heads and expose them in their turn; in doing which, keeping truth on my side, and not departing from the strictest rules of morality, I shall endeavour to penetrate, search out, and lay them open for your inspection. If you cannot or will not profit by them, I shall have done *my* duty to you, my country and my God.

And as the inhuman system of *slavery*, is the *source* from which most of our miseries proceed, I shall begin with that *curse to nations*, which has spread terror and devastation through so many nations of antiquity, and which is raging to such a pitch at the present day in Spain and in Portugal. It had one tug in England, in France, and in the United States of America; yet the inhabitants thereof, do not learn wisdom, and erase it entirely from their dwellings and from all with whom they have to do. The fact is, the labour of slaves comes so cheap to the avaricious usurpers, and is (as they think) of such great utility to the country where it exists, that those who are actuated by sordid avarice only, overlook the evils, which will as sure as the Lord lives, follow after the good. In fact, they are so happy to keep in ignorance and degradation, and to receive the homage and the labour of the slaves, they forget that God rules in the armies of heaven and among the inhabitants of the earth, having his ears continually open to the cries, tears and groans of his oppressed people; and being a just and holy Being will at one day appear fully in behalf of the oppressed, and arrest the progress of the avaricious oppressors; for although the destruction of the oppressors God may not effect by the oppressed, yet the Lord our God will bring other destructions upon them—for not unfrequently will he cause them to rise up one against another, to be split and divided, and to oppress each other, and sometimes to open hostilities with sword in hand. Some may ask, what is the matter with this united and happy people?—Some say it is the cause of political usurpers, tyrants, oppressors, But has not the Lord an oppressed and suffering people among them? Does the Lord condescend to hear their cries and see their tears in consequence of oppression? Will he let the oppressors rest comfortably and happy always? Will he not cause the very children of the oppressors to rise up against them, and of times put them to death? "God works in many ways his wonders to perform.". . .

I saw a paragraph, a few years since, in a South Carolina paper, which, speaking of the barbarity of the Turks, it said "The Turks are the most barbarous people in the world—they treat the Greeks more like *brutes* than human beings." And in the same paper was an advertisement, which said: "Eight well built Virginia and Maryland *Negro fellows* and four *wenches* will positively be *sold* this day, *to the highest bidder*!" And what astonished me still more was, to see in this same *humane* paper!! the cuts of three men, with clubs and budgets on their backs, and an advertisement offering a considerable sum of money for their apprehension and delivery. I declare, it is really so amusing to hear the Southerners and Westerners of this country talk about *barbarity*, that it is positively, enough to make a man *smile*.

The sufferings of the Helots among the Spartans, were somewhat severe, it is true, but to say that theirs, were as severe as ours among the Americans, I do most strenuously deny—for instance, can any man show me an article on a page of ancient history which specifies, that, the Spartans chained, and handcuffed the Helots, and dragged them from their wives and children, children from their parents, mothers from their suckling babes, wives from their husbands, driving them from one end of the country to the other? Notice the Spartans were heathens, who lived long before our Divine Master made his appearance in the flesh. Can Christian Americans deny these barbarous cruelties? Have you not, Americans, having subjected us under you, added to these miseries, by insulting us in telling us to our face, because we are helpless, that we are not of the human family? I ask you, O! Americans, I ask you, in the name of the Lord, can you deny these charges. . . .

Are we MEN!!—I ask you, O my brethren! are we MEN? Did our Creator make us to be slaves to dust and ashes like ourselves? Are they not dying worms as well as we? Have they not to make their appearance before the tribunal of Heaven, to answer for the deeds done in the body, as well as we? Have we any other Master but Jesus Christ alone? Is he not their Master as well as ours?—What right then, have we to obey and call any other Master, but Himself? How we could be so *submissive* to a gang of men, whom we cannot tell whether they are as good as ourselves or not, I never could conceive. However, this is shut up with the Lord, and we cannot precisely tell—but I declare, we judge men by their works.

The whites have always been an unjust, jealous, unmerciful, avaricious and blood-thirsty set of beings, always seeking after power and authority.—We view them all over the confederacy of Greece, where they were first known to be any thing, (in consequence of education) we see them there, cutting each other's throats—trying to subject each other to wretchedness and misery—to effect which, they used all kinds of deceitful, unfair, and unmerciful means. We view them next in Rome, where the spirit of tyranny and deceit raged still higher. We view them in Gaul, Spain, and in Britain.—In fine, we view them all over Europe, together with what were scattered about in Asia and Africa, as heathens, and we see them acting more like devils than accountable men. But some may ask, did not the blacks of Africa, and the mulattoes of Asia, go on in the same way as did the whites of Europe. I answer, no—they never were half so avaricious, deceitful and unmerciful as the whites, according to their knowledge.

But we will leave the whites or Europeans as heathens, and take a view of them as Christians, in which capacity we see them as cruel, if not more so than ever. In fact, take them as a body, they are ten times more cruel, avaricious and unmerciful than ever they were; for while they were heathens, they were bad enough it is true, but it is positively a fact that they were not quite so audacious as to go and take vessel loads of men, women and children, and in cold blood, and through devilishness, throw them into the sea, and murder them in all kind of ways. While they were heathens, they were too ignorant for such barbarity. . . .

ARTICLE I. OUR WRETCHEDNESS IN CONSEQUENCE OF SLAVERY

My beloved brethren:—The Indians of North and of South America—the Greeks—the Irish, subjected under the king of Great [Britain?]—the Jews, that ancient people of the Lord—the inhabitants of the islands of the sea—in fine, all the inhabitants of the earth, (except however, the sons of Africa) are called *men*, and of course are, and ought to be free. But we, (coloured people) and our children are *brutes!!* and of course are, and *ought to be* SLAVES to the American people and their children forever!! to dig their mines and work their farms; and thus go on enriching them, from one generation to another with our *blood* and our *tears!!!!*

I promised in a preceding page to demonstrate to the satisfaction of the most incredulous, that we, (coloured people of these United States of America) are the *most wretched, degraded* and *abject* set of beings that *ever lived* since the world began, and that the white Americans having reduced us to the wretched state of *slavery*, treat us in that condition *more cruel* (they being an enlightened and Christian people,) than any heathen nation did any people whom it had reduced to our condition. These affirmations are so well confirmed in the minds of all unprejudiced men, who have taken the trouble to read histories, that they need no elucidation from me. But to put them beyond all doubt, I refer you in the first place to the children of Jacob, or of Israel in Egypt, under Pharaoh and his people. Some of my brethren do not know who Pharaoh and the Egyptians were—I know it to be a fact, that some of them take the Egyptians to have been a gang of *devils*, not knowing any better, and that they (Egyptians) having got possession of the Lord's people, treated them *nearly* as cruel as *Christian Americans* do us, at the present day. For the information of such, I would only mention that the Egyptians, were Africans or coloured people, such as we are—some of them yellow and others dark—a mixture of Ethiopians and the natives of Egypt—about the same as you see the coloured people of the United States at the present day.—I say, I call your attention then, to the children of Jacob, while I point out particularly to you his son, among the rest, in Egypt. . . .

"And Pharaoh said unto Joseph, see, I have set thee over all the land of Egypt.". . . .

Now I appeal to heaven and to earth, and particularly to the American people themselves, who cease not to declare that our condition is not *hard*, and that we are comparatively satisfied to rest in wretchedness and misery, under them and their children. Not, indeed, to show me a coloured President, a Governor, a Legislator, a Senator, a Mayor, or an Attorney at the Bar.—But to show me a man of colour, who holds the low office of Constable, or one who sits in a Juror Box, even on a case of one of his wretched brethren, throughout this great Republic!!—But let us pass Joseph the son of Israel a little farther in review, as he existed with that heathen nation.

"And Pharaoh called Joseph's name Zaphnathpaaneah; and 15
he gave him to wife Asenath the daughter of Potipherah priest of On. And Joseph went out over all the land of Egypt."

Compare the above, with the American institutions. Do they not institute laws to prohibit us from marrying among the whites? I would wish, candidly, however, before the Lord, to be understood, that I would not give a *pinch of snuff* to be married to any white person I ever saw in all the days of my life. And I do say it, that the black man, or man of colour, who will leave his own colour (provided he can get one, who is good for any thing) and marry a white woman, to be a double slave to her, just because she is *white*, ought to be treated by her as he surely will be, viz: as a NIGGER!!!! It is not, indeed, what I care about inter-marriages with the whites, which induced me to pass this subject in review; for the Lord knows, that there is a day coming when they will be glad enough to get into the company of the blacks, notwithstanding, we are, in this generation, levelled by them, almost on a level with the brute creation: and some of us they treat even worse than they do the brutes that perish. I only made this extract to show how much lower we are held, and how much more cruel we are treated by the Americans, than were the children of Jacob, by the Egyptians. . . .

But to prove farther that the condition of the Israelites was better under the Egyptians than ours is under the whites. I call upon the professing Christians, I call upon the philanthropist, I call upon the very tyrant himself, to show me a page of history, either sacred or profane, on which a verse can be found, which maintains, that the Egyptians heaped the *insupportable insult* upon the children of Israel, by telling them that they were not of the *human family*. Can the whites deny this charge? Have they not, after having reduced us to the deplorable condition of slaves under their feet, held us up as descending originally from the tribes of *Monkeys* or *Orang-Outangs*? O! my God! I appeal to every man of feeling—is not this insupportable? Is it not heaping the most gross insult upon our miseries, because they have got us under their feet and we cannot help ourselves? Oh! pity us we pray thee, Lord Jesus, Master.—Has Mr. Jefferson declared to the world, that we are inferior to the whites, both in the endowments of our bodies and our minds? It is indeed surprising, that a man of such great learning, combined with such excellent natural parts, should speak so of a set of men in chains. I do not know what to compare it to, unless, like putting one wild deer in an iron cage, where it will be secured, and hold another by the side of the same, then let it go, and expect the one in the cage to run as fast as the one at liberty. . . .

1830

For Discussion and Writing

1. Who is the audience for *Walker's Appeal*? How does his language address the sensibilities and perceptions of that audience? What place do biblical arguments hold in his *Appeal*?
2. In several places in the *Appeal*, Walker argues that slaveholders see blacks as brutes, not as men. He particularly criticizes Thomas Jefferson, the author of the Declaration of Independence and a slaveholder himself, with propagating that belief. How does David Walker argue in defense of the humanity of blacks?

3. Walker compares the slaves' state unfavorably with that of other oppressed peoples through history: the Israelites under the Egyptians, the Greeks under the Turks, the Helots under the Spartans. In what ways does he find the American slaves' situation to be worse than those earlier subjugations?
4. According to Walker, what element of the American Dream is the motivation behind slavery? Slavery is a good example of the way in which one group's pursuit of the American Dream can deny another group's realization of it. How did slaveholders justify their actions?

From "Democracy in America" (Democratie en Amerique)

ALEXIS DE TOCQUEVILLE

Alexis de Tocqueville (1805–59) based Democracy in America *on a visit he made to the United States from 1831–1832. This book was to become very influential and popular with its intended French audience as well as readers in England and the United States. His observations on American life and politics, while certainly colored by his preference for an aristocracy over a democracy, are quite astute, and many readers feel de Tocqueville accurately describes the society he observed while foreshadowing the social and political directions America's new democracy would take.*

Democratic laws generally tend to promote the welfare of the greatest possible number; for they emanate from the majority of the citizens, who are subject to error, but who cannot have an interest opposed to their own advantage. The laws of an aristocracy tend, on the contrary, to concentrate wealth and power in the hands of the minority; because an aristocracy, by its very nature, constitutes a minority. It may therefore be asserted, as a general proposition, that the purpose of a democracy in its legislation is more useful to humanity than that of an aristocracy. This, however, is the sum total of its advantages.

Aristocracies are infinitely more expert in the science of legislation than democracies ever can be. They are possessed of a self-control that protects them from the errors of temporary excitement; and they form far-reaching designs, which they know how to mature till a favorable opportunity arrives. Aristocratic government proceeds with the dexterity of art; it understands how to make the collective force of all its laws converge at the same time to a given point. Such is not the case with democracies, whose laws are almost always ineffective or inopportune. The means of democracy are therefore more imperfect than those of aristocracy, and the measures that it unwittingly adopts are frequently opposed to its own cause; but the object it has in view is more useful.

Let us now imagine a community so organized by nature or by its constitution that it can support the transitory action of bad laws, and that it can await, without destruction, the general tendency of its legislation: we shall then conceive how a democratic government, notwithstanding its faults, may be best fitted to produce the prosperity of this community. This is precisely what has occurred in the United States; and I repeat, what I have before remarked, that the great advantage of the Americans consists in their being able to commit faults which they may afterwards repair.

An analogous observation may be made respecting public officers. It is easy to perceive that American democracy frequently errs in the choice of the individuals to whom it entrusts the power of the administration; but it is more difficult to say why the state prospers under their rule. In the first place, it is to be remarked that if, in a democratic state, the governors have less honesty and less capacity than elsewhere, the governed are more enlightened and more attentive to their interests. As the people in democracies are more constantly vigilant in their affairs and more jealous of their rights, they prevent their representatives from abandoning that general line of conduct which their own interest prescribes. In the second place, it must be remembered that if the democratic magistrate is more apt to misuse his power, he possesses it for a shorter time. But there is yet another reason which is still more general and conclusive. It is no doubt of importance to the welfare of nations that they should be governed by men of talents and virtue; but it is perhaps still more important for them that the interests of those men should not differ from the interests of the community at large; for if such were the case, their virtues might become almost useless and their talents might be turned to a bad account. I have said that it is important that the interests of the persons in authority should not differ from or oppose the interests of the community at large; but I do not insist upon their having the same interests as the *whole* population, because I am not aware that such a state of things ever existed in any country. . . .

The men who are entrusted with the direction of public 5
affairs in the United States are frequently inferior, in both capacity and morality, to those whom an aristocracy would raise to power. But their interest is identified and mingled with that of the majority of their fellow citizens. They may frequently be faithless and frequently mistaken, but they will never systematically adopt a line of conduct hostile to the majority; and they cannot give a dangerous or exclusive tendency to the government. . . .

The English aristocracy is perhaps the most liberal that has ever existed, and no body of men has ever, uninterruptedly, furnished so many honorable and enlightened individuals to the government of a country. It cannot escape observation, however, that in the legislation of England the interests of the poor have often been sacrificed to the advantages of the rich, and the rights of the majority to the privileges of a few. The result is that England at the present day combines the extremes of good and evil fortune in the bosom of her society; and the miseries and privations of her poor almost equal her power and renown.

In the United States, where public officers have no class interests to promote, the general and constant influence of the government is beneficial, although the individuals who conduct it are frequently unskillful and sometimes contemptible. . . .

There is one sort of patriotic attachment which principally arises from that instinctive, disinterested, and undefinable feeling which connects the affections of man with his birthplace. This natural fondness is united with a taste for ancient customs and a reverence for traditions of the past; those who cherish it love their country as they love the mansion of their fathers. They love the tranquillity that it affords them; they cling to the peaceful habits that they have contracted within its bosom; they are attached to the reminiscences that it awakens; and they are even pleased by living there in a state of obedience. . . .

But there is another species of attachment to country which is more rational than the one I have been describing. It is perhaps less generous and less ardent, but it is more fruitful and more lasting: it springs from knowledge; it is nurtured by the laws; it grows by the exercise of civil rights; and, in the end, it is confounded with the personal interests of the citizen. A man comprehends the influence which the well-being of his country has upon his own; he is aware that the laws permit him to contribute to that prosperity, and he labors to promote it, first because it benefits him, and secondly because it is in part his own work. . . .

10 How does it happen that in the United States, where the inhabitants have only recently immigrated to the land which they now occupy, and brought neither customs nor traditions with them there; where they met one another for the first time with no previous acquaintance; where, in short, the instinctive love of country can scarcely exist; how does it happen that everyone takes as zealous an interest in the affairs of his township, his county, and the whole state as if they were his own? It is because everyone, in his sphere, takes an active part in the government of society.

The lower orders in the United States understand the influence exercised by the general prosperity upon their own welfare; simple as this observation is, it is too rarely made by the people. Besides, they are accustomed to regard this prosperity as the fruit of their own exertions. The citizen looks upon the fortune of the public as his own, and he labors for the good of the state, not merely from a sense of pride or duty, but from what I venture to term cupidity.

It is unnecessary to study the institutions and the history of the Americans in order to know the truth of this remark, for their manners render it sufficiently evident. As the American participates in all that is done in his country, he thinks himself obliged to defend whatever may be censured in it; for it is not only his country that is then attacked, it is himself. The consequence is that his national pride resorts to a thousand artifices and descends to all the petty tricks of personal vanity.

Nothing is more embarrassing in the ordinary intercourse of life than this irritable patriotism of the Americans. A stranger may be well inclined to praise many of the institutions of their country, but he begs permission to blame some things in it, a permission that is inexorably refused. America is therefore a free country in which, lest anybody should be hurt by your remarks, you are not allowed to speak freely of private individuals or of the state, of the citizens or of the authorities, of public or of private undertakings, or, in short, of anything at all except, perhaps, the climate and the soil; and even then Americans will be found ready to defend both as if they had co-operated in producing them. . . .

On passing from a free country into one which is not free the traveler is struck by the change; in the former all is bustle and activity; in the latter everything seems calm and motionless. In the one, amelioration and progress are the topics of inquiry; in the other, it seems as if the community wished only to repose in the enjoyment of advantages already acquired. Nevertheless, the country which exerts itself so strenuously to become happy is generally more wealthy and prosperous than that which appears so contented with its lot; and when we compare them, we can scarcely conceive how so many new wants are daily felt in the former, while so few seem to exist in the latter.

If this remark is applicable to those free countries which have 15
preserved monarchical forms and aristocratic institutions, it is still more so to democratic republics. In these states it is not a portion only of the people who endeavor to improve the state of society, but the whole community is engaged in the task; and it is not the exigencies and convenience of a single class for which provision is to be made, but the exigencies and convenience of all classes at once.

It is not impossible to conceive the surprising liberty that the Americans enjoy; some idea may likewise be formed of their extreme equality; but the political activity that pervades the United States must be seen in order to be understood. No sooner do you set foot upon American ground than you are stunned by a kind of tumult; a confused clamor is heard on every side, and a thousand simultaneous voices demand the satisfaction of their social wants. Everything is in motion around you; here the people of one quarter of a town are met to decide upon the building of a church; there the election of a representative is going on; a little farther, the delegates of a district are hastening to the town in order to consult upon some local improvements; in another place, the laborers of a village quit their plows to deliberate upon the project of a road or a public school. Meetings are called for the sole purpose of declaring their disapprobation of the conduct of the government; while in other assemblies citizens salute the authorities of the day as the fathers of their country. Societies are formed which regard drunkenness as the principal cause of the evils of the state, and solemnly bind themselves to give an example of temperance.

The great political agitation of American legislative bodies, which is the only one that attracts the attention of foreigners, is a mere episode, or a sort of continuation, of that universal movement which originates in the lowest classes of the people and extends successively to all the ranks of society. It is impossible to spend more effort in the pursuit of happiness. . . .

Democracy does not give the people the most skillful government, but it produces what the ablest governments are frequently unable to create: namely, an all-pervading and restless activity, a superabundant force, and an energy which is inseparable from it and which may, however unfavorable circumstances may be, produce wonders. These are the true advantages of democracy.

In the present age, when the destinies of Christendom seem to be in suspense, some hasten to assail democracy as a hostile power while it is yet growing; and others already adore this new deity which is springing forth from chaos. But both parties are imperfectly acquainted with the object of their hatred or their worship; they strike in the dark and distribute their blows at random.

We must first understand what is wanted of society and its government. Do you wish to give a certain elevation to the human mind and teach it to regard the things of this world with generous feelings, to inspire men with a scorn of mere temporal advantages, to form and nourish strong convictions and keep alive the spirit of honorable devotedness? Is it your object to refine the habits, embellish the manners, and cultivate the arts, to promote the love of poetry, beauty, and glory? Would you constitute a people fitted to act powerfully upon all other nations, and prepared for those high enterprises which, whatever be their results, will leave a name forever famous in history? If you believe such to be the principal object of society, avoid the government of the democracy, for it would not lead you with certainty to the goal.

But if you hold it expedient to divert the moral and intellectual activity of man to the production of comfort and the promotion of general well-being; if a clear understanding be more profitable to man than genius; if your object is not to stimulate the virtues of heroism, but the habits of peace; if you had rather witness vices than crimes, and are content to meet with fewer noble deeds, provided offenses be diminished in the same proportion; if, instead of living in the midst of a brilliant society, you are contented to have prosperity around you; if, in short, you are of the opinion that the principal object of a government is not to confer the greatest possible power and glory upon the body of the nation, but to ensure the greatest enjoyment and to avoid the most misery to each of the individuals who compose it—if such be your desire, then equalize the conditions of men and establish democratic institutions. . . .

1836

For Discussion and Writing

1. In this excerpt from *Democracy in America,* de Tocqueville compares American democracy with the aristocracies of England and France. His perspective as a strong supporter of the aristocracy is evident in his writing.

Find some sections in which his perspective is particularly clear, and identify other sections in which he seems to question his assumptions about the superiority of aristocratic government.

2. To what does de Tocqueville ascribe the remarkable patriotism (at one point he calls it "this irritable patriotism") of the American? Contemporary Americans disagree on the propriety of overt displays of patriotism. Where, how, and when do you believe it is appropriate to display patriotism?
3. How does de Tocqueville explain the great "bustle and activity" he sees in Americans' political lives? How does this energy "produce wonders?" To what extent can contemporary political life in America be characterized as "bustle and activity"? To what extent is it "producing wonders"?
4. De Tocqueville wrote *Democracy in America* for his fellow French citizens. In what specific ways does he address this audience?

Simple Gifts

Elder Joseph Brackett

Joseph Brackett (1797–1882) wrote "Simple Gifts" in 1797, while he was an Elder of the Shaker church in Maine. The Shakers, a Protestant denomination founded in 1772, were known for their active church services, which involved trembling, shouting, dancing and singing. "Simple Gifts" is generally sung to the tune of the hymn "Lord of the Dance."

Elder Brackett died on July 4, 1882, having reached the remarkable age of 105.

'Tis the gift to be simple, 'tis the gift to be free,
'Tis the gift to come down where we ought to be,
And when we find ourselves in the place just right,
'Twill be in the valley of love and delight.
When true simplicity is gain'd,
To bow and to bend we shan't be asham'd,
To turn, turn will be our delight,
Till by turning, turning we come round right.

1848

America the Beautiful

KATHARINE LEE BATES

A trip to the top of Pikes Peak, Colorado, inspired Katharine Lee Bates (1859–1929) to write "America the Beautiful." Bates was a professor of English literature at Wellesley College for many years. Although efforts were made to declare "America the Beautiful" the national anthem, President Herbert Hoover settled the dispute by declaring the "Star Spangled Banner" the national anthem in 1931.

O beautiful for spacious skies,
For amber waves of grain
For purple mountain majesties
Above the fruited plain!

America! America!
God shed His grace on thee,
And crown thy good with brotherhood
From sea to shining sea!

O beautiful for pilgrim feet
Whose stern impassion'd stress
A thoroughfare for freedom beat
Across the wilderness.

America! America!
God mend thine ev'ry flaw,
Confirm thy soul in self-control,
Thy liberty in law.

O beautiful for heroes prov'd
In liberating strife,
Who more than self their country loved,
And mercy more than life.

America! America!
May God thy gold refine
Till all success be nobleness,
And ev'ry gain divine.

O beautiful for patriot dream
That sees beyond the years
Thine alabaster cities gleam
Undimmed by human tears.

America! America!
God shed His grace on thee,
And crown thy good with brotherhood
From sea to shining sea.

1895

Lift Ev'ry Voice and Sing

James Weldon Johnson

A high school principal, diplomat, poet, and novelist, James Weldon Johnson (1871–1938) wrote "Lift Ev'ry Voice and Sing" in 1900 to commemorate the birthday of Abraham Lincoln. The song became very popular in the black community, and has often been called the "Black National Anthem."

Lift every voice and sing, till earth and Heaven ring,
Ring with the harmonies of liberty;
Let our rejoicing rise, high as the listening skies,
Let it resound loud as the rolling sea.
Sing a song full of the faith that the dark past has taught us,
Sing a song full of the hope that the present has brought us;
Facing the rising sun of our new day begun,
Let us march on till victory is won.

Stony the road we trod, bitter the chastening rod,
Felt in the days when hope unborn had died;
Yet with a steady beat, have not our weary feet,
Come to the place for which our fathers sighed?
We have come over a way that with tears has been watered,
We have come, treading our path through the blood of the slaughtered;

Out from the gloomy past, till now we stand at last
Where the white gleam of our bright star is cast.

God of our weary years, God of our silent tears,
Thou Who hast brought us thus far on the way;
Thou Who hast by Thy might, led us into the light,
Keep us forever in the path, we pray.
Lest our feet stray from the places, our God, where we met
  Thee.
Lest our hearts, drunk with the wine of the world, we forget
  Thee.
Shadowed beneath Thy hand, may we forever stand,
True to our God, true to our native land.

1900

This Land is Your Land

Woody Guthrie

Born in Okemah, Oklahoma, in 1912, Woody Guthrie (1912–1967) became one of the best-known and most imitated American folk musicians. Disturbed by the poverty he observed among those fleeing the Dust Bowl, he became a lifelong socialist, trade unionist, and champion of the working man. His music has been performed by Joan Baez, Bruce Springsteen, and Ani Difranco, as well as by his son, Arlo Guthrie, a famous folk musician and singer in his own right.

Chorus:

This land is your land, This land is my land,
From California to the New York island;
From the redwood forest to the Gulf Stream waters,
This land was made for you and me.

As I was walking that ribbon of highway,
I saw above me that endless skyway:
I saw below me that golden valley:
This land was made for you and me.

Chorus

I've roamed and rambled, and I followed my footsteps
To the sparkling sands of her diamond deserts;
And all around me a voice was sounding:
This land was made for you and me.

Chorus

When the sun came shining, and I was strolling,
And the wheat fields waving and the dust clouds rolling,
As the fog was lifting a voice come chanting:
This land was made for you and me.

Chorus

As I went walking, I saw a sign there,
And on the sign, it said—"No Trespassing."
But on the other side; it didn't say nothing.
That sign was made for you and me.

Chorus

In the shadow of the steeple I saw my people,
By the relief office, I seen my people;
As they stood there hungry, I stood there asking
Is this land made for you and me?

Chorus (2x)

1940

For Discussion and Writing

1. "Simple Gifts," "America the Beautiful," "Lift Ev'ry Voice and Sing," and "This Land is Your Land" all reference some of the overriding themes of the American Dream. What are some of these themes?
2. Trace the nature of faith and hope in the American Dream as it is expressed from "Simple Gifts" in 1848 to "This Land is Your Land" in 1940.
3. Note the difference in tone between the first three and the last two verses of "This Land is Your Land." What might have accounted for the concerns expressed in the last two verses of Guthrie's song?

4. While Johnson and Guthrie cannot be called "founders" in the usual sense of the word, they are both participants in an essential process of the American Dream: the right to dissent, to revise the dream to line up with what seems real. What inequities in the American Dream does Johnson address? Guthrie?

Chapter 1: For Further Research and Writing

1. What is your interpretation of the American Dream? What are its major themes? Based on your reading of the selections in Chapter 1, what were the major themes of the American Dream as expressed by the Founders? How does your vision of the American Dream connect with that of the Founders—which elements are similar and which are different? How can you account for any differences between the two?
2. Chapter 1 presents a cross-section of early Americans' ideas, but it is far from complete in representing the ideas of all the thinkers or writers of that time. Access material from two or more of the following authors or texts, and write an essay commenting on what they added to the concept of the American Dream:
   - William Bradford
   - Cotton Mather
   - *The Federalist Papers*
   - St. Jean de Crèvecoeur
   - Benjamin Franklin (particularly his autobiography)
   - Phyllis Wheatley
3. Trace one of the basic themes of the American Dream as it is discussed by 3–5 of the authors presented in Chapter 1. You might consider one of these themes: unity, liberty, tolerance, equality, opportunity, prosperity, security. How, in your opinion, has contemporary society succeeded in making the theme you have chosen a reality? How has it failed?
4. Write a rhetorical analysis of one of the selections in this chapter. Do not summarize the selection, although you will need to discuss the major arguments the author makes. Include in your analysis discussion of the following:
   a) How does the author represent himself/herself to the reader? Does the author seem to be writing to an equal? A friend? A subordinate?
   b) What assumptions does the author seem to be making about the audience?
   c) What evidence does the author present? To what extent is the author's evidence based on fact and logic? On emotion?
   d) How does the author's language contribute to or detract from the force of the argument?

CHAPTER 2

Dreams Deferred

The readings in this chapter present the voices of those for whom the American Dream was neither definitive nor certain. From slavery's role as a "peculiar institution" seen radically differently by its defenders and critics, to the status of newly freed slaves and constantly relocated American Indians, to the Civil Rights era and the awakening of American women, the American Dream was faced with constant challenges and questions about its ability to be truly attainable—and about the price asked for its attainment.

While following these readings, watch for the different approaches taken by these writers as they express their particular challenges to the idea of the Dream. Frederick Douglass and Martin Luther King, for instance, share a note of praise and hope in their messages—at least for a time—but then depart radically in the ways they present the rest of their messages. Some writers borrow the structures of famous documents well known to American readers, and others depend heavily on the emotional impact that words and images in their messages will have on the audience. (It will be helpful to keep in mind that the idea of a *United States of America* was first expressed in a document that listed grievances against an oppressive king, and that explained why those wrongs could no longer be tolerated on a moral basis.) In all cases, the writers have a clear idea of the American Dream as it *could be*, and to bring readers around to sharing this vision, they must first depict the dream as it currently exists: as something promised, but not yet granted. It is, as Langston Hughes put it in poetic terms, a "dream deferred."

The Seneca Falls Declaration

ELIZABETH CADY STANTON AND SUSAN B. ANTHONY

The 1848 women's rights convention in Seneca Falls, New York, was held partly as a result of one organizer having been refused permission to attend an abolitionist meeting conducted exclusively by men. This document, which women's rights advocates turned to as their foundation well into the early twentieth century when women finally gained the right to vote, was drafted and approved at the 1848 convention. Unlike the 1966 Statement of the National Organization for Women, *the* Declaration *did not articulate or reject particular beliefs for women, but it made clear that the nation was facing an extensive list of grievances from its female citizens.*

✦

THE DECLARATION OF SENTIMENTS

When, in the course of human events, it becomes necessary for one portion of the family of man to assume among the people of the earth a position different from that which they have hitherto occupied, but one to which the laws of nature and of nature's God entitle them, a decent respect to the opinions of mankind requires that they should declare the causes that impel them to such a course.

We hold these truths to be self-evident: that all men and women are created equal; that they are endowed by their Creator with certain inalienable rights; that among these are life, liberty, and the pursuit of happiness; that to secure these rights governments are instituted, deriving their just powers from the consent of the governed. Whenever any form of government becomes destructive of these ends, it is the right of those who suffer from it to refuse allegiance to it, and to insist upon the institution of a new government, laying its foundation on such principles, and organizing its powers in such form, as to them shall seem most likely to effect their safety and happiness. Prudence, indeed, will dictate that governments long established should not be changed for light and transient causes; and accordingly all experience hath shown that mankind are more disposed to suffer, while evils are sufferable, than to right themselves by abolishing the forms to which they are accustomed.

But when a long train of abuses and usurpations, pursuing invariably the same object, evinces a design to reduce them under absolute despotism, it is their duty to throw off such government, and to provide new guards for their future security. Such has been the patient sufferance of the women under this government, and such is now the necessity which constrains them to demand the equal station to which they are entitled. The history of mankind is a history of repeated injuries and usurpations on the part of man toward woman, having in direct object the establishment of an absolute tyranny over her. To prove this, let facts be submitted to a candid world.

The history of mankind is a history of repeated injuries and usurpations on the part of man toward woman, having in direct object the establishment of an absolute tyranny over her. To prove this, let facts be submitted to a candid world.

He has never permitted her to exercise her inalienable right to the elective franchise.

He has compelled her to submit to laws, in the formation of which she had no voice.

He has withheld from her rights which are given to the most ignorant and degraded men—both natives and foreigners.

Having deprived her of this first right of a citizen, the elective franchise, thereby leaving her without representation in the halls of legislation, he has oppressed her on all sides.

He has made her, if married, in the eye of the law, civilly dead.

He has taken from her all right in property, even to the wages she earns.

He has made her, morally, an irresponsible being, as she can commit many crimes with impunity, provided they be done in the presence of her husband. In the covenant of marriage, she is compelled to promise obedience to her husband, he becoming, to all intents and purposes, her master—the law giving him power to deprive her of her liberty, and to administer chastisement.

He has so framed the laws of divorce, as to what shall be the proper causes, and in case of separation, to whom the guardianship of the children shall be given, as to be wholly regardless of the happiness of women—the law, in all cases, going upon a flase supposition of the supremacy of man, and giving all power into his hands.

After depriving her of all rights as a married woman, if single, and the owner of property, he has taxed her to support a government which recognizes her only when her property can be made profitable to it.

He has monopolized nearly all the profitable employments, and from those she is permitted to follow, she receives but a scanty remuneration. He closes against her all the avenues to wealth and distinction which he considers most honorable to himself. As a teacher of theology, medicine, or law, she is not known.

He has denied her the facilities for obtaining a thorough education, all colleges being closed against her.

He allows her in church, as well as state, but a subordinate position, claiming apostolic authority for her exclusion from the ministry, and, with some exceptions, from any public participation in the affairs of the church.

He has created a false public sentiment by giving to the world a different code of morals for men and women, by which moral delinquencies which exclude women from society, are not only tolerated, but deemed of little account in man.

He has usurped the prerogative of Jehovah himself, claiming it as his right to assign for her a sphere of action, when that belongs to her conscience and to her God.

He has endeavored, in every way that he could, to destroy her confidence in her own powers, to lessen her self-respect, and to make her willing to lead a dependent and abject life.

Now, in view of this entire disfranchisement of one-half the people of this country, their social and religious degradation—in view of the unjust laws above mentioned, and because women do feel themselves aggrieved, oppressed, and fraudulently deprived of their most sacred rights, we insist that they have immediate admission to all the rights and privileges which belong to them as citizens of the United States.

1848

For Discussion and Writing

1. What famous document does this declaration imitate in its style and structure? What effect were the authors hoping for in adopting that other document's style?
2. The authors write than men have "made [women], if married, in the eyes of the law, civilly dead." What specific circumstances and conditions are they referring to?
3. Why would the claim that men have "usurped the prerogative of Jehovah himself" have been a serious and effective charge in 1848?
4. The authors portray "[t]he history of mankind" as a "history of repeated injuries and usurpations on the part of man toward woman." Write an essay

that explains some of the key events and attitudes in world history that would support this charge.

5. In an essay, compare and contrast the specific grievances of the women's movement in 1848 with those it published in the National Organization for Women's 1966 Statement of Purpose, found elsewhere in this chapter.

Speech of 1851

Chief Seattle

Chief Seattle was a leader of the Salish tribe near Puget Sound in Washington, and the following speech is attributed to him on the event of that tribe having agreed to a treaty selling two million acres of land to the U.S. government for $150,000. Many versions of this speech exist on the Internet and elsewhere, and one of the most well-known versions of it, much more poetic than the one here, was never delivered by Chief Seattle at all. Rather, it was written by a Hollywood screenwriter in the 1970s. The version here is believed to be the most accurate, even though its published transcription, attributed to a White settler, first appeared several decades after the chief delivered the speech.

✦

Yonder sky that has wept tears of compassion upon my people for centuries untold, and which to us appears changeless and eternal, may change. Today is fair. Tomorrow it may be overcast with clouds. My words are like the stars that never change. Whatever Seattle says, the great chief at Washington can rely upon with as much certainty as he can upon the return of the sun or the seasons. The white chief says that Big Chief at Washington sends us greetings of friendship and goodwill. This is kind of him for we know he has little need of our friendship in return. His people are many. They are like the grass that covers vast prairies. My people are few. They resemble the scattering trees of a storm-swept plain. The great, and I presume—good, White Chief sends us word that he wishes to buy our land but is willing to allow us enough to live comfortably. This indeed appears just, even generous, for the Red Man no longer has rights that he need respect, and the offer may be wise, also, as we are no longer in need of an extensive country.

There was a time when our people covered the land as the waves of a wind-ruffled sea cover its shell-paved floor, but that time long since passed away with the greatness of tribes that are now but a mournful memory. I will not dwell on, nor mourn over, our untimely decay, nor reproach my paleface brothers with hastening it, as we too may have been somewhat to blame.

Youth is impulsive. When our young men grow angry at some real or imaginary wrong, and disfigure their faces with black paint, it denotes that their hearts are black, and that they are often cruel and relentless, and our old men and old women are unable to restrain them. Thus it has ever been. Thus it was when the white man began to push our forefathers ever westward. But let us hope that the hostilities between us may never return. We would have everything to lose and nothing to gain. Revenge by young men is considered gain, even at the cost of their own lives, but old men who stay at home in times of war, and mothers who have sons to lose, know better.

Our good father in Washington—for I presume he is now our father as well as yours, since King George has moved his boundaries further north—our great and good father, I say, sends us word that if we do as he desires he will protect us. His brave warriors will be to us a bristling wall of strength, and his wonderful ships of war will fill our harbors, so that our ancient enemies far to the northward—the Haidas and Tsimshians—will cease to frighten our women, children, and old men. Then in reality he will be our father and we his children. But can that ever be? Your God is not our God! Your God loves your people and hates mine! He folds his strong protecting arms lovingly about the paleface and leads him by the hand as a father leads an infant son. But, He has forsaken His Red children, if they really are His. Our God, the Great Spirit, seems also to have forsaken us. Your God makes your people wax stronger every day. Soon they will fill all the land. Our people are ebbing away like a rapidly receding tide that will never return. The white man's God cannot love our people or He would protect them. They seem to be orphans who can look nowhere for help. How then can we be brothers? How can your God become our God and renew our prosperity and awaken in us dreams of returning greatness? If we have a common Heavenly Father He must be partial, for He came to His paleface children. We never saw Him. He gave you laws but had no word for His red children whose teeming multitudes once filled this vast continent as stars fill the firmament. No; we are two distinct races with separate origins and separate destinies. There is little in common between us.

5 To us the ashes of our ancestors are sacred and their resting place is hallowed ground. You wander far from the graves of your

ancestors and seemingly without regret. Your religion was written upon tablets of stone by the iron finger of your God so that you could not forget. The Red Man could never comprehend or remember it. Our religion is the traditions of our ancestors—the dreams of our old men, given them in solemn hours of the night by the Great Spirit; and the visions of our sachems, and is written in the hearts of our people.

Your dead cease to love you and the land of their nativity as soon as they pass the portals of the tomb and wander away beyond the stars. They are soon forgotten and never return. Our dead never forget this beautiful world that gave them being. They still love its verdant valleys, its murmuring rivers, its magnificent mountains, sequestered vales and verdant lined lakes and bays, and ever yearn in tender fond affection over the lonely hearted living, and often return from the happy hunting ground to visit, guide, console, and comfort them.

Day and night cannot dwell together. The Red Man has ever fled the approach of the White Man, as the morning mist flees before the morning sun. However, your proposition seems fair and I think that my people will accept it and will retire to the reservation you offer them. Then we will dwell apart in peace, for the words of the Great White Chief seem to be the words of nature speaking to my people out of dense darkness.

It matters little where we pass the remnant of our days. They will not be many. The Indian's night promises to be dark. Not a single star of hope hovers above his horizon. Sad-voiced winds moan in the distance. Grim fate seems to be on the Red Man's trail, and wherever he will hear the approaching footsteps of his fell destroyer and prepare stolidly to meet his doom, as does the wounded doe that hears the approaching footsteps of the hunter.

A few more moons, a few more winters, and not one of the descendants of the mighty hosts that once moved over this broad land or lived in happy homes, protected by the Great Spirit, will remain to mourn over the graves of a people once more powerful and hopeful than yours. But why should I mourn at the untimely fate of my people? Tribe follows tribe, and nation follows nation, like the waves of the sea. It is the order of nature, and regret is useless. Your time of decay may be distant, but it will surely come, for even the White Man whose God walked and talked with him as friend to friend, cannot be exempt from the common destiny. We may be brothers after all. We will see.

We will ponder your proposition and when we decide we will let you know. But should we accept it, I here and now make this condition that we will not be denied the privilege without molestation of visiting at any time the tombs of our ancestors, friends, and children. Every part of this soil is sacred in the estimation of my people. Every hillside, every valley, every plain and grove, has been hallowed by some sad or happy event in days long vanished. Even the rocks, which seem to be dumb and dead as the swelter in the sun along the silent shore, thrill with memories of stirring events connected with the lives of my people, and the very dust upon which you now stand responds more lovingly to their footsteps than yours, because it is rich with the blood of our ancestors, and our bare feet are conscious of the sympathetic touch. Our departed braves, fond mothers, glad, happy hearted maidens, and even the little children who lived here and rejoiced here for a brief season, will love these sombre solitudes and at eventide they greet shadowy returning spirits. And when the last Red Man shall have perished, and the memory of my tribe shall have become a myth among the White Men, these shores will swarm with the invisible dead of my tribe, and when your children's children think themselves alone in the field, the store, the shop, upon the highway, or in the silence of the pathless woods, they will not be alone. In all the earth there is no place dedicated to solitude. At night when the streets of your cities and villages are silent and you think them deserted, they will throng with the returning hosts that once filled them and still love this beautiful land. The White Man will never be alone.

1851

For Discussion and Writing

1. In how many places does Seattle employ nature imagery? How does that imagery affect the message he's conveying?
2. Why does the speech end with such a strong emphasis on death and absence?
3. In the fourth paragraph, Seattle makes an abrupt shift in focus from the "good father in Washington" to a "God [who] loves your people and hates mine." What is the connection between these two "fathers," and what is Seattle hoping to illustrate by making the comparison?
4. Near the middle of the speech, Seattle notes the contrasting ways that Indians and Whites interact with, and conceptualize, their dead. What is significant about the differences he describes? If the White conception of ancestors were more like the Indian one, what might be different in the scenario prompting Seattle's speech?

5. Chief Seattle says that "Revenge by young men is considered gain . . . but old men who stay at home in times of war, and mothers who have sons to lose, know better." Can you relate to this point? How is this point still relevant today, and how can we relate to it?

From "What to the Slave is the Fourth of July?"

FREDERICK DOUGLASS

Frederick Augustus Washington Bailey, better known by the name he chose after escaping from slavery, is considered a giant of American letters. Teaching himself to read and write as a teenager, Frederick Douglass discovered books that unlocked feelings and gave voice to passions that had previously had no words to describe them. Armed with a strong speaking voice and a masterful grasp of literacy, Douglass was a tireless speaker on the lecture circuit in the northern United States in the years leading up to the Civil War, advocating for the abolition of slavery. To back up the eloquent words, he also participated in the Underground Railroad from his home in Rochester, New York, helping hundreds of slaves to freedom in the north. In the 1852 speech excerpted here, Douglass makes what many considered at the time to be one of the most moving arguments ever presented on behalf of American slaves.

✦

This, for the purpose of this celebration, is the 4th of July. It is the birthday of your National Independence, and of your political freedom. This, to you, is what the Passover was to the emancipated people of God. It carries your minds back to the day, and to the act of your great deliverance; and to the signs, and to the wonders, associated with that act, and that day. This celebration also marks the beginning of another year of your national life; and reminds you that the Republic of America is now 76 years old. I am glad, fellow-citizens, that your nation is so young. Seventy-six years, though a good old age for a man, is but a mere speck in the life of a nation. Three score years and ten is the allotted time for individual men; but nations number their years by thousands.

According to this fact, you are, even now, only in the beginning of your national career, still lingering in the period of childhood.

I repeat, I am glad this is so. There is hope in the thought, and hope is much needed, under the dark clouds which lower above the horizon. The eye of the reformer is met with angry flashes, portending disastrous times; but his heart may well beat lighter at the thought that America is young, and that she is still in the impressible stage of her existence. May he not hope that high lessons of wisdom, of justice and of truth, will yet give direction to her destiny?

Were the nation older, the patriot's heart might be sadder, and the reformer's brow heavier. Its future might be shrouded in gloom, and the hope of its prophets go out in sorrow. There is consolation in the thought that America is young. Great streams are not easily turned from channels, worn deep in the course of ages. They may sometimes rise in quiet and stately majesty, and inundate the land, refreshing and fertilizing the earth with their mysterious properties. They may also rise in wrath and fury, and bear away, on their angry waves, the accumulated wealth of years of toil and hardship. They, however, gradually flow back to the same old channel, and flow on as serenely as ever. But, while the river may not be turned aside, it may dry up, and leave nothing behind but the withered branch, and the unsightly rock, to howl in the abyss-sweeping wind, the sad tale of departed glory. As with rivers, so with nations.

Fellow-citizens, I shall not presume to dwell at length on the associations that cluster about this day. The simple story of it is that, 76 years ago, the people of this country were British subjects. The style and title of your "sovereign people" (in which you now glory) was not then born. You were under the British Crown. Your fathers esteemed the English Government as the home government; and England as the fatherland. This home government, you know, although a considerable distance from your home, did, in the exercise of its parental prerogatives, impose upon its colonial children, such restraints, burdens and limitations, as, in its mature judgment, it deemed wise, right and proper.

5 But, your fathers, who had not adopted the fashionable idea of this day, of the infallibility of government, and the absolute character of its acts, presumed to differ from the home government in respect to the wisdom and the justice of some of those burdens and restraints. They went so far in their excitement as to pronounce the measures of government unjust, unreasonable, and oppressive, and altogether such as ought not to be quietly submitted to. I scarcely need say, fellow-citizens, that my opinion of those measures fully accords with that of your fathers. Such a declaration of agreement on my part would not be worth much to

anybody. It would, certainly, prove nothing, as to what part I might have taken, had I lived during the great controversy of 1776.

To say now that America was right, and England wrong, is exceedingly easy. Everybody can say it; the dastard, not less than the noble brave, can flippantly discant on the tyranny of England towards the American Colonies. It is fashionable to do so; but there was a time when to pronounce against England, and in favor of the cause of the colonies, tried men's souls. They who did so were accounted in their day, plotters of mischief, agitators and rebels, dangerous men. To side with the right, against the wrong, with the weak against the strong, and with the oppressed against the oppressor! here lies the merit, and the one which, of all others, seems unfashionable in our day. The cause of liberty may be stabbed by the men who glory in the deeds of your fathers. But, to proceed.

Feeling themselves harshly and unjustly treated by the home government, your fathers, like men of honesty, and men of spirit, earnestly sought redress. They petitioned and remonstrated; they did so in a decorous, respectful, and loyal manner. Their conduct was wholly unexceptionable. This, however, did not answer the purpose. They saw themselves treated with sovereign indifference, coldness and scorn. Yet they persevered. They were not the men to look back.

As the sheet anchor takes a firmer hold, when the ship is tossed by the storm, so did the cause of your fathers grow stronger, as it breasted the chilling blasts of kingly displeasure. The greatest and best of British statesmen admitted its justice, and the loftiest eloquence of the British Senate came to its support. But, with that blindness which seems to be the unvarying characteristic of tyrants, since Pharaoh and his hosts were drowned in the Red Sea, the British Government persisted in the exactions complained of. The madness of this course, we believe, is admitted now, even by England; but we fear the lesson is wholly lost on our present rulers.

Oppression makes a wise man mad. Your fathers were wise men, and if they did not go mad, they became restive under this treatment. They felt themselves the victims of grievous wrongs, wholly incurable in their colonial capacity. With brave men there is always a remedy for oppression. Just here, the idea of a total separation of the colonies from the crown was born! It was a startling idea, much more so, than we, at this distance of time, regard it. The timid and the prudent (as has been intimated) of that day, were, of course, shocked and alarmed by it. . . .

On the second of July, 1776, the old Continental Congress, to 10
the dismay of the lovers of ease, and the worshipers of property,

clothed that dreadful idea with all the authority of national sanction. They did so in the form of a resolution; and as we seldom hit upon resolutions, drawn up in our day, whose transparency is at all equal to this, it may refresh your minds and help my story if I read it.

"Resolved, That these united colonies are, and of right, ought to be free and Independent States; that they are absolved from all allegiance to the British Crown; and that all political connection between them and the State of Great Britain is, and ought to be, dissolved."

Citizens, your fathers made good that resolution. They succeeded; and to-day you reap the fruits of their success. The freedom gained is yours; and you, therefore, may properly celebrate this anniversary. The 4th of July is the first great fact in your nation's history—the very ring-bolt in the chain of your yet undeveloped destiny.

Pride and patriotism, not less than gratitude, prompt you to celebrate and to hold it in perpetual remembrance. I have said that the Declaration of Independence is the ring-bolt to the chain of your nation's destiny; so, indeed, I regard it. The principles contained in that instrument are saving principles. Stand by those principles, be true to them on all occasions, in all places, against all foes, and at whatever cost. . . .

The coming into being of a nation, in any circumstances, is an interesting event. But, besides general considerations, there were peculiar circumstances which make the advent of this republic an event of special attractiveness. The whole scene, as I look back to it, was simple, dignified and sublime. The population of the country, at the time, stood at the insignificant number of three millions. The country was poor in the munitions of war. The population was weak and scattered, and the country a wilderness unsubdued. There were then no means of concert and combination, such as exist now. Neither steam nor lightning had then been reduced to order and discipline. From the Potomac to the Delaware was a journey of many days. Under these, and innumerable other disadvantages, your fathers declared for liberty and independence and triumphed.

Fellow Citizens, I am not wanting in respect for the fathers of this republic. The signers of the Declaration of Independence were brave men. They were great men too—great enough to give fame to a great age. It does not often happen to a nation to raise, at one time, such a number of truly great men. The point from which I am compelled to view them is not, certainly, the most favorable; and yet I cannot contemplate their great deeds with less than admiration. They were statesmen, patriots and heroes, and for the good they did, and the principles they contended for, I will unite with you to honor their memory.

They loved their country better than their own private interests; and, though this is not the highest form of human excellence, all will concede that it is a rare virtue, and that when it is exhibited, it ought to command respect. He who will, intelligently, lay down his life for his country, is a man whom it is not in human nature to despise. Your fathers staked their lives, their fortunes, and their sacred honor, on the cause of their country. In their admiration of liberty, they lost sight of all other interests.

They were peace men; but they preferred revolution to peaceful submission to bondage. They were quiet men; but they did not shrink from agitating against oppression. They showed forbearance; but that they knew its limits. They believed in order; but not in the order of tyranny. With them, nothing was "settled" that was not right. With them, justice, liberty and humanity were "final"; not slavery and oppression. You may well cherish the memory of such men. They were great in their day and generation. Their solid manhood stands out the more as we contrast it with these degenerate times.

How circumspect, exact and proportionate were all their movements! How unlike the politicians of an hour! Their statesmanship looked beyond the passing moment, and stretched away in strength into the distant future. They seized upon eternal principles, and set a glorious example in their defence. Mark them!

Fully appreciating the hardship to be encountered, firmly believing in the right of their cause, honorably inviting the scrutiny of an on-looking world, reverently appealing to heaven to attest their sincerity, soundly comprehending the solemn responsibility they were about to assume, wisely measuring the terrible odds against them, your fathers, the fathers of this republic, did, most deliberately, under the inspiration of a glorious patriotism, and with a sublime faith in the great principles of justice and freedom, lay deep the corner-stone of the national superstructure, which has risen and still rises in grandeur around you. . . .

Fellow-citizens, pardon me, allow me to ask, why am I called 20
upon to speak here to-day? What have I, or those I represent, to do with your national independence? Are the great principles of political freedom and of natural justice, embodied in that Declaration of Independence, extended to us? and am I, therefore, called upon to bring our humble offering to the national altar, and

to confess the benefits and express devout gratitude for the blessings resulting from your independence to us?

. . . I am not included within the pale of this glorious anniversary! Your high independence only reveals the immeasurable distance between us. The blessings in which you, this day, rejoice, are not enjoyed in common. The rich inheritance of justice, liberty, prosperity and independence, bequeathed by your fathers, is shared by you, not by me. The sunlight that brought life and healing to you, has brought stripes and death to me. This Fourth [of] July is yours, not mine. You may rejoice, I must mourn. To drag a man in fetters into the grand illuminated temple of liberty, and call upon him to join you in joyous anthems, were inhuman mockery and sacrilegious irony. Do you mean, citizens, to mock me, by asking me to speak to-day? If so, there is a parallel to your conduct. And let me warn you that it is dangerous to copy the example of a nation whose crimes, lowering up to heaven, were thrown down by the breath of the Almighty, burying that nation in irrecoverable ruin! I can to-day take up the plaintive lament of a peeled and woe-smitten people!

Fellow-citizens; above your national, tumultuous joy, I hear the mournful wail of millions! whose chains, heavy and grievous yesterday, are, to-day, rendered more intolerable by the jubilee shouts that reach them. If I do forget, if I do not faithfully remember those bleeding children of sorrow this day, "may my right hand forget her cunning, and may my tongue cleave to the roof of my mouth!" To forget them, to pass lightly over their wrongs, and to chime in with the popular theme, would be treason most scandalous and shocking, and would make me a reproach before God and the world. My subject, then fellow-citizens, is AMERICAN SLAVERY. I shall see this day, and its popular characteristics, from the slave's point of view. Standing, there, identified with the American bondman, making his wrongs mine, I do not hesitate to declare, with all my soul, that the character and conduct of this nation never looked blacker to me than on this 4th of July!

Whether we turn to the declarations of the past, or to the professions of the present, the conduct of the nation seems equally hideous and revolting. America is false to the past, false to the present, and solemnly binds herself to be false to the future. Standing with God and the crushed and bleeding slave on this occasion, I will, in the name of humanity which is outraged, in the name of liberty which is fettered, in the name of the constitution and the Bible, which are disregarded and trampled upon, dare to call in question and to denounce, with all the emphasis I can command, everything that serves to perpetuate slavery—the great sin and shame of America! "I will not equivocate; I will not excuse;" I will use the severest language I can command; and yet not one word shall escape me that any man, whose judgment is not blinded by prejudice, or who is not at heart a slaveholder, shall not confess to be right and just.

But I fancy I hear some one of my audience say, it is just in this circumstance that you and your brother abolitionists fail to make a favorable impression on the public mind. Would you argue more, and denounce less, would you persuade more, and rebuke less, your cause would be much more likely to succeed. But, I submit, where all is plain there is nothing to be argued. What point in the anti-slavery creed would you have me argue? On what branch of the subject do the people of this country need light? Must I undertake to prove that the slave is a man? That point is conceded already. Nobody doubts it. The slaveholders themselves acknowledge it in the enactment of laws for their government. They acknowledge it when they punish disobedience on the part of the slave. There are seventy-two crimes in the State of Virginia, which, if committed by a black man, (no matter how ignorant he be), subject him to the punishment of death; while only two of the same crimes will subject a white man to the like punishment. What is this but the acknowledgement that the slave is a moral, intellectual and responsible being? The manhood of the slave is conceded. It is admitted in the fact that Southern statute books are covered with enactments forbidding, under severe fines and penalties, the teaching of the slave to read or to write. When you can point to any such laws, in reference to the beasts of the field, then I may consent to argue the manhood of the slave. When the dogs in your streets, when the fowls of the air, when the cattle on your hills, when the fish of the sea, and the reptiles that crawl, shall be unable to distinguish the slave from a brute, there will I argue with you that the slave is a man!

For the present, it is enough to affirm the equal manhood of the negro race. Is it not astonishing that, while we are ploughing, planting and reaping, using all kinds of mechanical tools, erecting houses, constructing bridges, building ships, working in metals of brass, iron, copper, silver and gold; that, while we are reading, writing and cyphering, acting as clerks, merchants and secretaries, having among us lawyers, doctors, ministers, poets, authors, editors, orators and teachers; that, while we are engaged in all manner of enterprises common to other men, digging gold in California, capturing the whale in the Pacific, feeding sheep and cattle on the hill-side, living, moving, acting, thinking, planning, living in families as husbands, wives and children, and, above all, confessing and worshipping the Christian's God, and looking hopefully for life and immortality beyond the grave, we are called upon to prove that we are men!

Would you have me argue that man is entitled to liberty? That he is the rightful owner of his own body? You have already declared it. Must I argue the wrongfulness of slavery? Is that a question for Republicans? Is it to be settled by the rules of logic and argumentation, as a matter beset with great difficulty, involving a doubtful application of the principle of justice, hard to be understood? How should I look to-day, in the presence of Americans, dividing, and subdividing a discourse, to show that men have a natural right to freedom? speaking of it relatively, and positively, negatively, and affirmatively. To do so, would be to make myself ridiculous, and to offer an insult to your understanding. There is not a man beneath the canopy of heaven, that does not know that slavery is wrong for him.

What, am I to argue that it is wrong to make men brutes, to rob them of their liberty, to work them without wages, to keep them ignorant of their relations to their fellow men, to beat them with sticks, to flay their flesh with the lash, to load their limbs with irons, to hunt them with dogs, to sell them at auction, to sunder their families, to knock out their teeth, to burn their flesh, to starve them into obedience and submission to their masters? Must I argue that a system thus marked with blood, and stained with pollution, is wrong? No! I will not. I have better employments for my time and strength, than such arguments would imply.

What, to the American slave, is your 4th of July? I answer: a day that reveals to him, more than all other days in the year, the gross injustice and cruelty to which he is the constant victim. To him, your celebration is a sham; your boasted liberty, an unholy license; your national greatness, swelling vanity; your sounds of rejoicing are empty and heartless; your denunciations of tyrants, brass fronted impudence; your shouts of liberty and equality, hollow mockery; your prayers and hymns, your sermons and thanksgivings, with all your religious parade, and solemnity, are, to him, mere bombast, fraud, deception, impiety, and hypocrisy—a thin veil to cover up crimes which would disgrace a nation of savages. There is not a nation on the earth guilty of practices, more shocking and bloody, than are the people of these United States, at this very hour.

1852

For Discussion and Writing

1. Where does the key turn take place in this address, from one of praise for the United States to one of condemnation?
2. Frederick Douglass is considered one of the greatest orators (speakers) of the nineteenth century. What features of his content or delivery do you see in this address to support that definition?
3. How does Douglass manage to speak out against injustice without alienating his audience and making them feel that they are the subject of his attack?
4. Douglass makes clear why slaves are not participants in the July 4th celebration. At which point in the nation's history do you think the slaves' descendants could fully celebrate and have an equal share in the American Dream?
5. Write an essay comparing Douglass's address with Malcolm X's "Ballot or the Bullet" speech from 1964, found through an internet search as explained elsewhere in this chapter. On what main points does the latter speaker repeat complaints first voiced in the 1852 speech? Are they repeated exactly, or have they changed during that century?

From *The Planter's Northern Bride*

CAROLINE LEE HENTZ

Caroline Lee Hentz is a controversial figure in nineteenth century literature. Derided by Nathaniel Hawthorne as one of the female writers he labeled a "scribbling mob," Hentz did nonetheless make a contribution to women's recognition for their writing abilities. For better or worse, her 1854 novel The Planter's Northern Bride, *excerpted here, is her most famous (or perhaps notorious) publication. Written as a direct rebuttal to Harriet Beecher Stowe's* Uncle Tom's Cabin, *Lentz's work represents the "plantation novel" genre—books whose sole purpose was to counter abolitionist literature (especially slave narratives) by defending slavery and depicting the abolitionist "cruel and immoral" view of slavery as inaccurate. Although* The Planter's Northern Bride *is almost laughably obvious as blatant propaganda today, many readers of the mid-1800s did not see it that way.*

✦

. . . When we have seen the dark and horrible pictures drawn of slavery and exhibited to a gazing world, we have wondered if we were one of those favoured individuals to whom the fair side of life is ever turned, or whether we were created with a moral blindness, incapable of distinguishing its lights and shadows. One thing is certain, and if we were on judicial oath we would repeat it, that during our residence in the South, we have never witnessed one scene of cruelty or oppression, never beheld a chain or a manacle, or the infliction of a punishment more severe than parental authority would be justified in applying to filial disobedience or transgression. This is not owing to our being placed in a limited sphere of observation, for we have seen and studied domestic, social, and plantation life, in Carolina, Alabama, Georgia, and Florida. We have been admitted into close and familiar communion with numerous families in each of these States, not merely as a passing visitor, but as an indwelling guest, and we have never been pained by an inhuman exercise of authority, or a wanton abuse of power.

On the contrary, we have been touched and gratified by the exhibition of affectionate kindness and care on one side, and loyal and devoted attachment on the other. We have been especially struck with the cheerfulness and contentment of the slaves, and their usually elastic and buoyant spirits. From the abundant opportunities we have had of judging, we give it as our honest belief, that the negroes of the South are the happiest labouring class on the face of the globe; even subtracting from their portion of enjoyment all that can truly be said of their trials and sufferings. The fugitives who fly to the Northern States are no proof against the truth of this statement. They have most of them been made disaffected by the influence of others—tempted by promises which are seldom fulfilled[.] Even in the garden of Eden, the seeds of discontent and rebellion were sown; surely we need not wonder that they sometimes take root in the beautiful groves of the South.

In the large cities we have heard of families who were cruel to their slaves, as well as unnaturally severe in the discipline of their children. (Are there no similar instances at the North?) But the indignant feeling which any known instance of inhumanity calls forth at the South, proves that they are not of common occurrence.

We have conversed a great deal with the coloured people, feeling the deepest interest in learning their own views of their peculiar situation, and we have almost invariably been delighted and affected by their humble devotion to their master's family, their child-like, affectionate reliance on their care and protection, and above all, with their genuine cheerfulness and contentment.

This very morning, since commencing these remarks, our sympathies have been strongly moved by the simple eloquence of a negro woman in speaking of her former master and mistress, who have been dead for many years.

"Oh!" said she, her eyes swimming with tears, and her voice choking with emotion, "I loved my master and mistress like my own soul. If I could have died in their stead, I would gladly done it. I would have gone into the grave and brought them up, if the Lord had let me do it. Oh! they were so good—so kind. All on us black folks would 'ave laid down our lives for 'em at any minute."

"Then you were happy?" we said; "you did not sigh to be free?"

"No, mistress, that I didn't. I was too well off for that. I wouldn't have left my master and mistress for all the freedom in the world. I'd left my own father and mother first. I loved 'em better than I done them. I loved their children too. Every one of 'em has been babies in my arms—and I loved 'em a heap better than I done my own, I want to stay with 'em as long as I live, and I know they will take care of me when I get too old to work."

These are her own words. We have not sought this simple instance of faithful and enduring love. It came to us as if in corroboration of our previous remarks, and we could not help recording it. . . .

• • •

There might have been a dozen men seated around the table, some whose dress and manners proclaimed that they were gentlemen, others evidently of a coarser grain. They all looked up at the entrance of Moreland, who, with a bow, such as the courteous stranger is always ready to make, took his seat, while Albert placed himself behind his master's chair.

"Take a seat," said Mr. Grimby, the landlord, looking at Albert. "There's one by the gentleman. Plenty of room for us all."

"My boy will wait," cried Mr. Moreland with unconscious haughtiness, while his pale cheek visibly reddened. "I would thank you to leave the arrangement of such things to myself."

"No offence, I hope, sir," rejoined Mr. Grimby. "We look upon everybody here as free and equal. This is a free country, and when folks come among us we don't see why they can't conform to our ways of thinking. There's a proverb that says, 'When you're with the Romans, it's best to do as the Romans do.' "

"Am I to understand," said Mr. Moreland, fixing his eye deliberately on his Indian-visaged host, "that you wish my servant to sit down with yourself and these gentlemen?"

15 "To be sure I do," replied the landlord, winking his small black eye knowingly at his left-hand neighbour. "I don't see why he isn't as good as the rest of us. I'm an enemy to all distinctions myself, and I'd like to bring everybody round to my opinion."

"Albert!" cried his master, "obey the landlord's wishes. I want no supper; take my seat and see that you are well attended to."

"Mars. Russell," said the mulatto, in a confused and deprecating tone.

"Do as I tell you," exclaimed Mr. Moreland, in a tone of authority, which, though tempered by kindness, Albert understood too well to resist. As Moreland passed from the room, a gentleman, with a very prepossessing countenance and address, who was seated on the opposite side of the table, rose and followed him.

"I am sorry you have had so poor a specimen of Northern politeness," said the gentleman, accosting Moreland, with a slight embarrassment of manner. "I trust you do not think we all endorse such sentiments."

20 "I certainly must make you an exception, sir," replied Moreland, holding out his hand with involuntary frankness; "but I fear there are but very few. This is, however, the first direct attack I have received, and I hardly knew in what way to meet it. I have too much self-respect to place myself on a level with a man so infinitely my inferior. That he intended to insult me, I know by his manner. He knows our customs at home, and that nothing could be done in more positive violation of them than his unwarrantable proposition."

They had walked out in the open air while they were speaking, and continued their walk through the poplar avenue, through whose stiff and stately branches the first stars of evening were beginning to glisten.

"I should think you would fear the effect of these things on your servant," said the gentleman, "that it would make him insolent and rebellious. Pardon me, sir, but I think you were rather imprudent in bringing him with you, and exposing him to the influences which must meet him on every side. You will not be surprised, after the instance which has just occurred, when I tell you, that, in this village, you are in the very hot-bed of fanaticism; and that a Southern planter, accompanied by his slave, can meet but little sympathy, consideration, or toleration; I fear there will be strong efforts made to induce your boy to leave you."

"I fear nothing of that kind," answered Moreland. "If they can bribe him from me, let him go. I brought him far less to minister to my wants than to test his fidelity and affection. I believe them proof against any temptation or assault; if I am deceived I wish to know it, though the pang would be as severe as if my own brother should lift his hand against me."

"Indeed! I did not imagine that the feelings were ever so deeply interested. While I respect your rights, and resent any ungentlemanlike infringement of them, as in the case of our landlord, I cannot conceive how beings, who are ranked as goods and chattels, things of bargain and traffic, can ever fill the place of a friend or brother in the heart."

"Nevertheless, I assure you, that next to our own kindred, we look upon our slaves as our best friends."

As they came out of the avenue into the open street, they perceived the figure of a woman, walking with slow steps before them, bearing a large bundle under her arm; she paused several times, as if to recover breath, and once she stopped and leaned against the fence, while a dry, hollow cough rent her frame.

"Nancy," said the gentleman, "is that you? You should not be out in the night air." The woman turned round, and the starlight fell on a pale and wasted face.

"I can't help it," she answered, "I can't hold out any longer, I can't work any more; I ain't strong enough to do a single chore now; and Mr. Grimby says he hadn't got any room for me to lay by in. My wages stopped three weeks ago. He says there's no use in my hanging on any longer, for I'll never be good for anything any more."

"Where are you going now?" said the gentleman.

"Home!" was the reply, in a tone of deep and hopeless despondency, "Home, to my poor old mother. I've supported her by my wages ever since I've been hired out; that's the reason I haven't laid up any. God knows."

Here she stopped, for her words were evidently choked by an awful realization of the irremediable misery of her condition. Moreland listened with eager interest. His compassion was awakened, and so were other feelings. Here was a problem he earnestly desired to solve, and he determined to avail himself of the opportunity thrown in his path.

"How far is your home from here?" he asked.

"About three-quarters of a mile."

"Give me your bundle—I'll carry it for you, you are too feeble; nay, I insist upon it."

Taking the bundle from the reluctant hand of the poor woman, he swung it lightly upward and poised it on his left shoulder. His companion turned with a look of unfeigned surprise towards the elegant and evidently high-bred stranger, thus courteously relieving poverty and weakness of an oppressive burden.

"Suffer me to assist you," said he. "You must be very unaccustomed to services of this kind; I ought to have anticipated you."

"I am not accustomed to do such things for myself," answered Moreland, "because there is no occasion; but it only makes me more willing to do them for others. You look upon us as very self-indulging beings, do you not?"

"We think your institutions calculated to promote the growth of self-indulgence and selfishness. The virtues that resist their opposing influences must have more than common vitality."

"We, who know the full length and breadth of our responsibilities, have less time than any other men for self-indulgence. We feel that life is too short for the performance of our duties, made doubly arduous and irksome by the misapprehension and prejudice of those who ought to know us better and judge us more justly and kindly. My good woman, do we walk too fast?"

"Oh, no, sir. I so long to get home, but I am so ashamed to have you carry that bundle."

He had forgotten the encumbrance in studying the domestic problem, presented to him for solution. Here was a poor young woman, entirely dependent on her daily labour for the support of herself and aged mother, incapacitated by sickness from ministering to their necessities, thrown back upon her home, without the means of subsistence: in prospective, a death of lingering torture for herself, for her mother a life of destitution or a shelter in the almshouse. For every comfort, for the bare necessaries of life, they must depend upon the compassion of the public; the attendance of a physician must be the work of charity, their existence a burden on others. . . .

Moreland, whose moral perceptions were rendered very acute by observation, drew a contrast in his own mind, between the Northern and Southern labourer, when reduced to a state of sickness and dependence. He brought his own experience in comparison with the lesson of the present hour, and thought that the sick and dying negro, retained under his master's roof, kindly nursed and ministered unto, with no sad, anxious lookings forward into the morrow for the supply of nature's wants, no fears of being cast into the pauper's home, or of being made a member of that unhappy family, consecrated by no head, hallowed by no domestic relationship, had in contrast a far happier lot. In the latter case there was no sickness, without its most horrible concomitant, poverty, without the harrowing circumstances connected with public charity, or the capricious influence of private compassion. It is true, the nominal bondage of the slave was wanting, but there was the bondage of poverty, whose iron chains are heard clanking in every region of God's earth, whose dark links are wrought in the forge of human suffering, eating slowly into the quivering flesh, till they reach and dry up the life-blood of the heart. It has often been said that there need be no such thing as poverty in this free and happy land; that here it is only the offspring of vice and intemperance; that the avenues of wealth and distinction are open to all, and that all who choose may arrive at the golden portals of success and honour, and enter boldly in. Whether this be true or not, let the thousand toiling operatives of the Northern manufactories tell; let the poor, starving seamstresses, whose pallid faces mingle their chill, wintry gleams with the summer glow and splendour of the Northern cities, tell; let the free negroes, congregated in the suburbs of some of our modern Babylons, lured from their homes by hopes based on sand, without forethought, experience, or employment, without sympathy, influence, or caste, let them also tell.

When Moreland reached the low, dark-walled cottage which Nancy pointed out as her home, he gave her back her bundle, and at the same time slipped a bill into her hand, of whose amount she could not be aware. But she knew by the soft, yielding paper the nature of the gift, and something whispered her that it was no niggard boon.

"Oh, sir," she cried, "you are too good. God bless you, sir, over and over again!"

She stood in the doorway of the little cabin, and the dull light within played luridly on her sharpened and emaciated features. Her large black eyes were burning with consumption's wasting fires, and a deep red, central spot in each concave cheek, like the flame of the magic cauldron, was fed with blood alone. Large tears were now sparkling in those glowing flame-spots, but they did not extinguish their wasting brightness. "Poor creature!" thought Moreland. "Her day of toil is indeed over. There is nothing left for her but to endure and to die. She has learned to labour, she must now learn to wait."

As he turned from the door, resolving to call again before he left the village, he saw his companion step back and speak to her, extending his hand at the same time. Perceiving that he was actuated by the Christian spirit, which does not wish the left hand to know what the right hand doeth, he walked slowly on, through an atmosphere perfumed by the delicious but oppressive fragrance of the blossoming lilacs, that lent to this obscure habitation a certain poetic charm. . . .

When they returned to the inn, they found Albert waiting at the door, with a countenance of mingled vexation and triumph.

The landlord and several other men were standing near him, and had evidently been engaged in earnest conversation. The sudden cessation of this, on the approach of Mr. Moreland, proved that he had been the subject of it, and from the manner in which they drew back as he entered the passage, he imagined their remarks were not of the most flattering nature.

"Well, Albert, my boy," said he, when they were alone in his chamber, "I hope you relished your supper."

"Please, Mars. Russell, don't do that again. I made 'em wait on me this time, but it don't seem right. Besides, I don't feel on an equality with 'em, no way. They are no gentlemen."

Moreland laughed.

"What were they talking to you about so earnestly as I entered?" asked he.

"About how you treated me and the rest of us. Why, Mars. Russell, they don't know nothing about us. They want to know if we don't wear chains at home and manacles about our wrists. One asked if you didn't give us fodder to eat. Another wanted to strip off my coat, to see if my back wa'n't all covered with scars. I wish you'd heard what I told 'em. Master, I wish you'd heard the way I give it to 'em."

"I have no doubt you did me justice, Albert. My feelings are not in the least wounded, though my sense of justice is pained. Why, I should think the sight of your round, sleek cheeks, and sound, active limbs would be the best argument in my favour. They must believe you thrive wonderfully on fodder."

"What you think one of 'em said, Mars. Russell? They say you fatten me up, you dress me up, and carry me 'bout as a show-boy, to make folks think you treat us all well, but that the niggers at home are treated worse than dogs or cattle, a heap worse. I tell 'em it's all one big lie. I tell 'em you're the best."

"Never mind, Albert. That will do. I want to think."

Albert never ventured to intrude on his master's thinking moments, and, turning away in respectful silence, he soon stretched himself on the carpet and sunk in a profound sleep. In the mean time Moreland waded through a deep current of thought, that swelled as it rolled, and oft times it was turbid and foaming, and sometimes it seemed of icy chillness. He was a man of strong intellect and strong passions; but the latter, being under the control of principle, gave force and energy and warmth to a character which, if unrestrained, they would have defaced and laid waste. He was a searcher after truth, and felt ready and brave enough to plunge into the cold abyss, where it is said to be hidden, or to encounter the fires of persecution, the thorns of prejudice, to hazard everything, to suffer everything, rather than relinquish the hope of attaining it. He pondered much on the condition of mankind, its inequalities and wrongs. He thought of the poor and subservient in other lands, and compared them with our own. He thought of the groaning serfs of Russia; the starving sons of Ireland; the squalid operatives of England, its dark, subterranean workshops, sunless abodes of want, misery, and sin, its toiling millions, doomed to drain their hearts' best blood to add to the splendours and luxuries of royalty and rank; of the free hirelings of the North, who, as a class, travail in discontent and repining, anxious to throw off the yoke of servitude, sighing for an equality which exists only in name; and then he turned his thoughts homeward, to the enslaved children of Africa, and, taking them as a class, as a distinct race of beings, he came to the irresistible conclusion, that they were the happiest subservient race that were found on the face of the globe. He did not seek to disguise to himself the evils which were inseparably connected with their condition, or that man too oft abused the power he owned; but in view of all this, in view of the great, commanding truth, that wherever civilized man exists, there is the dividing line of the high and the low, the rich and the poor, the thinking and the labouring, in view of the God-proclaimed fact that "all Creation toileth and groaneth together," and that labour and suffering are the solemn sacraments of life, he believed that the slaves of the South were blest beyond the pallid slaves of Europe, or the anxious, care-worn labourers of the North.

With this conviction he fell asleep, and in his dreams he still tried to unravel the mystery of life, and to reconcile its inequalities with the justice and mercy of an omnipotent God. . . .

1854

For Discussion and Writing

1. If you were writing a one-paragraph description of Mr. Moreland's qualities, what would those qualities be? What scenes does the author provide to support your observations?
2. What are the definitions of propaganda? How do those definitions fit this example of a "plantation novel"?
3. What issues does the author hope northern readers will recognize about "their own" people and region? Does she hope to show that the South is better than the North, or merely that it is equal?
4. Consider the various depictions of slaves in this excerpt. What do those depictions reveal as the most important elements of an American Dream for slaves? What does this say about the way the writer sees the slaves as human beings?

5. In an essay, explain whether a writer can make an important contribution to literature even if her or his writing is severely biased.

Graduating Address at Yale College, 1887

Yan Phou Lee

When the California wilderness stopped producing endless supplies of wealth for prospectors and miners, and the railroads had successfully laid track across the country, American sentiment began to turn against the Chinese immigrants who had formerly been welcomed as laborers in both industries. They were now seen as a "Yellow Peril" that threatened to take away jobs held by native-born Americans, and as tensions and outright hostilities between individuals in the U.S. increased, the relationship between their countries worsened in equal measure. The Chinese Exclusion Act of 1882 *called for a complete suspension of Chinese immigration, and many of the immigrants who had not yet received citizenship were sent back to China. A young student from Yale University, Yan Phou Lee, nonetheless escaped from his homeland and returned to the U.S. to continue his education. In his commencement speech, he offered strong criticism of anti-Chinese immigration laws and the social climate that had produced them.*

The torrents of hatred and abuse which have periodically swept over the Chinese industrial class in America had their sources in the early California days. They grew gradually in strength, and, uniting in one mighty stream, at last broke the barriers with which justice, humanity and the Constitution of the Republic had until then restrained their fury.

The catastrophe was too terrible, and has made too deep an impression to be easily forgotten. Even if Americans are disposed to forget, the Chinese will not fail to keep the sad record of faith unkept, of persecution permitted by an enlightened people, of rights violated without redress in a land where all are equal before the law.

Sad it is that in a Christian community only a feeble voice here and there has been raised against this public wrong; while the enemies of the Chinese laborer may be counted by the millions. Yet these men, having everything their own way, are still dissatisfied and cannot rest secure until all the Chinese laborers have been driven out or killed off with the connivance of a perverted public opinion. Is it not high time for good men to say to the enemy of industry and order, "Halt! thus far shalt though go, and no farther"? For be assured that after the Chinese have all departed, those men who are determined to get high wages for doing nothing will turn against other peaceful sons of toil; and who would venture to say that there will be absolute safety for the native American? Mob-rule knows no respect for persons; the Chinese were attacked first simply because they were the weakest. I do not deny that the anti-Chinese agitation has some *show* of reason. But its strength rests on three erroneous assumptions, by proving the groundlessness of which the whole superstructure of fallacy and falsehood can be made to totter.

First, it is assumed that the work to be done and the fund for labor's remuneration are fixed quantities, and that if the Chinese are employed so much will be taken from other laborers. It is sufficient to reply that no economist holds that view.

5 Secondly, it is assumed that the Pekin [Beijing] authorities are anxious to get rid of their redundant population. Nothing can be more absurd. They have been always, and are still, averse to the emigration of their subjects; so much so that they yielded only to the inducements and concessions offered by this Government, which are embodied in the Burlingame Treaty. Another proof is the readiness with which they consented to the limitation of Chinese immigration when the Angell Treaty was negotiated.

Thirdly, it is assumed that China's four hundred millions are only waiting for an opening to "inundate" this country. This is soberly asserted and has the effect of the Gorgon-head; for who is not stunned at the bare mention of this appalling and impending disaster? It would be terrible if it were possible—if it could be true. But there is no cause for apprehension. The immigration of my compatriots has been exclusively from Canton and the region around it within a radius of a hundred miles. The population of this district is estimated at 5,000,000. Not a single immigrant has hailed from any other part of the Empire. The Mongolization of America, therefore, is an event as far off as the Millennium. For after twenty-five years of unrestricted immigration, your patriotic agitators could muster up only 200,000 Chinese laborers in all the

States and Territories. Now place this figure side by side with the 3,000,000 of immigrant princes from the "English Poland," which has never had more than 8,000,000 inhabitants at any one time, and you will be struck with the contrast.

What reason can we give why so few comparatively come from China? The Chinese are by nature and from habit gregarious, but not migratory. They dislike to cut adrift from the ties of kindred, the associations of home, the traditions of fatherland. The belief that their welfare in the future life depends on the proper burial of their remains in home-soil, followed by sorrowing children and tearful widow, curbs their desire to go abroad, even with the hope of bettering their condition. But as only the poorest are tempted to lead a life of adventure, and as the good Emperor does not pay their passage money, the number that *can* leave their native land is very small. Thus you will find that Chinese immigrants are usually poor on landing, for they bring no votes in their pockets which can immediately be turned into money, and so they must rely upon their countrymen who have preceded them for assistance. . . .

In every such conflict might is right; the weakest goes to the wall. Two parties were bidding for the Pacific vote—that of great moral principles as well as that of no principles. The Chinese came in like cloth between the blades of the scissors. . . . When 80,000 offices were at stake, and the hoodlums of California had to be petted, it was not hard to make the Chinese out to be *undesirable* immigrants and to hoodwink the public with charges against them which are false, or which may be preferred against all immigrants. Sand-lotters were scandalized by the alleged immoral practices of the Asiatics; were in trembling and fear lest their Christianity should suffer by contact with Chinese paganism. I believe the cesspool once complained of the influx of muddy water. Californians prohibited the Chinese from becoming citizens and then accused them of failure to become naturalized. People in general were staggered at the imminent danger of the Mongolization of American and at the same time found fault with the Chinese for not making the United States their home. . . .

But why pursue this theme further? The bill was passed which excluded both skilled as well as unskilled Chinese laborers, though the Court of Pekin [Beijing] diplomatically understood that the restriction was to affect common workmen alone. Natives of China are forbidden to become citizens of this Republic, which takes to its bosom the off-scouring, the garbage, and the dynamite of Europe. Never had there been seen such pandering to the worst passion of an insignificant faction!

Were it not for the tragic events which trod on the heels of the 10
Chinese Immigration Bill, one might be inclined to laugh at the absurdities in the bill itself. If the law is faithfully executed (and to be worth anything it must be), all Americans born in China are disenfranchised, and all Chinese natives of British colonies, like Hong Kong and India, have free access to this country. But who could laugh in the midst of indignant tears? By passing a discriminating law against an already persecuted class, the Central Government yielded to the demands of the mob, and to that extent countenanced its violence and lawlessness. The Anti-Chinese Act is a cause of all the outrages and massacres that have been since committed in Rock Springs and Denver, in Portland, San Francisco and other parts, which, if they had been perpetrated in China against Americans, would have resounded from Bedloe's Island (whereon stands the Statue of Liberty) to the Golden Gate. But the criminals in these cases were not punished, and even the pitiful indemnity was voted down until Congress could not withhold it from very shame.

I have stated facts which are well known. It is not necessary to exaggerate. I now ask you Christian people of America whether you have not failed in your duties as lovers of justice and fatherland, in *not* enforcing your opinions in public and in private, as well as in church as in State. I ask those who gallantly sided with the strong against the weak, whether they do not think they have done enough for glory and personal ambition?

If there is an avenging Deity, (and we believe there is), ought you not to beware of the retribution which is sure to overtake a nation that permits the cold-blooded murder of innocent strangers within its gates to go unpunished?

1887

For Discussion and Writing

1. What does Yan Phou Lee mean when he says that "the cesspool once complained of the influx of muddy water"?
2. What are the three basic problems with anti-Chinese legislation, as Lee defines them?
3. In several places, Lee mentions the issue of voting. What role did a right to vote play in the buildup of tensions between Americans—especially Californians—and Chinese immigrants?

4. Lee's primary focus here is to criticize and condemn anti-Chinese legislation and its effects, but what definition of the American Dream do you see implied within the larger message?
5. Looking carefully at the full address, what specific kinds of appeals is Lee using to persuade his audience? What emotions does he hope to rouse, and in response to what core American values?
6. Conduct research into the Angel Island detention center in California in the early 1900s. Then conduct research into the internment camps for Japanese-American citizens during World War II. In an essay, explain what connections you see between these facilities and the popular and political sentiments behind them.

From *How the Other Half Lives*

Jacob Riis

Born in Denmark in 1849, Jacob Riis experienced first-hand the effects of poverty when he emigrated to the United States from Denmark in his early 20s. Before finding work as a crime reporter, Riis often stayed in the "poor houses" of New York, places with squalid conditions that motivated his later work as a "muckraker" journalist whose focus was on exposing the plight of the urban poor. His photo exposé, How the Other Half Lives, *startled the nation into awareness through its stark visual and verbal depictions of impoverished lives.*

Of the harvest of tares, sown in iniquity and reaped in wrath, the police returns tell the story. The pen that wrote the "Song of the Shirt" is needed to tell of the sad and toil-worn lives of New York's working women. The cry echoes by night and by day through its tenements:

> Oh, God! that bread should be so dear,
> And flesh and blood so cheap!

Six months have not passed since at a great public meeting in this city, the Working Women's Society reported: "It is a known fact that men's wages cannot fall below a limit upon which they can exist, but woman's wages have no limit, since the paths of shame are always open to her. It is simply impossible for any woman to live without assistance on the low salary a saleswoman earns, without depriving herself of real necessities. . . . It is inevitable that they must in many instances resort to evil." It was only a few brief weeks before that verdict was uttered, that the community was shocked by the story of a gentle and refined woman who, left in direst poverty to earn her own living alone among strangers, threw herself from her attic window, preferring death to dishonor. "I would have done any honest work, even to scrubbing," she wrote, drenched and starving, after a vain search for work in a driving storm. She had tramped the streets for weeks on her weary errand, and the only living wages that were offered her were the wages of sin. The ink was not dry upon her letter before a woman in an East Side tenement wrote down her reason for self-murder: "Weakness, sleeplessness, and yet obliged to work. My strength fails me. Sing at my coffin: 'Where does the soul find a home and rest?' " Her story may be found as one of two typical "cases of despair" in one little church community, in the *City Mission Society's Monthly* for last February. It is a story that has many parallels in the experience of every missionary, every police reporter and every family doctor whose practice is among the poor.

It is estimated that at least one hundred and fifty thousand women and girls earn their own living in New York; but there is reason to believe that this estimate falls far short of the truth when sufficient account is taken of the large number who are not wholly dependent upon their own labor, while contributing by it to the family's earnings. These alone constitute a large class of the women wage-earners, and it is characteristic of the situation that the very fact that some need not starve on their wages condemns the rest to that fate. The pay they are willing to accept all have to take. What the "everlasting law of supply and demand," that serves as such a convenient gag for public indignation, has to do with it, one learns from observation all along the road of inquiry into these real woman's wrongs. To take the case of the saleswomen for illustration: The investigation of the Working Women's Society disclosed the fact that wages averaging from $2 to $4.50 a week were reduced by excessive fines, "the employers placing a value upon time lost that is not given to services rendered." A little girl, who received two dollars a week, made cash-sales amounting to $167 in a single day, while the receipts of a fifteen-dollar male clerk in the same department footed up only $125; yet for some trivial mistake the girl was fined sixty cents out of her two dollars. The practice prevailed in some stores of dividing the fines between the superintendent and the time-keeper at the end of the year. In one instance they amounted to $3,000, and "the superintendent was heard to charge the time-keeper with not being strict enough in his duties." One of the causes for fine in a certain large store was sitting down. The law requiring seats for saleswomen, generally ignored, was obeyed faithfully in this establishment. The seats were there, but the girls were fined when found using them.

Cash-girls receiving $1.75 a week for work that at certain seasons lengthened their day to sixteen hours were sometimes required to pay for their aprons. A common cause for discharge from stores in which, on account of the oppressive heat and lack of ventilation, "girls fainted day after day and came out looking like corpses," was too long service. No other fault was found with the discharged saleswomen than that they had been long enough in the employ of the firm to justly expect an increase of salary. The reason was even given with brutal frankness, in some instances.

5 These facts give a slight idea of the hardships and the poor pay of a business that notoriously absorbs child-labor. The girls are sent to the store before they have fairly entered their teens, because the money they can earn there is needed for the support of the family. If the boys will not work, if the street tempts them from home, among the girls at least there must be no drones. To keep their places they are told to lie about their age and to say that they are over fourteen. The precaution is usually superfluous. The Women's Investigating Committee found the majority of the children employed in the stores to be under age, but heard only in a single instance of the truant officers calling. In that case they came once a year and sent the youngest children home; but in a month's time they were all back in their places, and were not again disturbed. When it comes to the factories, where hard bodily labor is added to long hours, stifling rooms, and starvation wages, matters are even worse. The Legislature has passed laws to prevent the employment of children, as it has forbidden saloon-keepers to sell them beer, and it has provided means of enforcing its mandate, so efficient, that the very number of factories in New York is *guessed* at as in the neighborhood of twelve thousand. Up till this summer, a single inspector was charged with the duty of keeping the run of them all, and of seeing to it that the law was respected by the owners.

Sixty cents is put as the average day's earnings of the 150,000, but into this computation enters the stylish "cashier's" two dollars a day, as well as the thirty cents of the poor little girl who pulls threads in an East Side factory, and, if anything, the average is probably too high. Such as it is, however, it represents board, rent, clothing, and "pleasure" to this army of workers. Here is the case of a woman employed in the manufacturing department of a Broadway house. It stands for a hundred like her own. She averages three dollars a week. Pays $1.50 for her room; for breakfast she has a cup of coffee; lunch she cannot afford. One meal a day is her allowance. This woman is young, she is pretty. She has "the world before her." Is it anything less than a miracle if she is guilty of nothing worse than the "early and improvident marriage," against which moralists exclaim as one of the prolific causes of the distress of the poor? Almost any door might seem to offer welcome escape from such slavery as this. "I feel so much healthier since I got three square meals a day," said a lodger in one of the Girls' Homes. Two young sewing-girls came in seeking domestic service, so that they might get enough to eat. They had been only half-fed for some time, and starvation had driven them to the one door at which the pride of the American-born girl will not permit her to knock, though poverty be the price of her independence.

The tenement and the competition of public institutions and farmers' wives and daughters, have done the tyrant shirt to death, but they have not bettered the lot of the needle-women. The sweater of the East Side has appropriated the flannel shirt. He turns them out to-day at forty-five cents a dozen, paying his Jewish workers from twenty to thirty-five cents. One of these testified before the State Board of Arbitration, during the shirtmakers' strike, that she worked eleven hours in the shop and four at home, and had never in the best of times made over six dollars a week. Another stated that she worked from 4 o'clock in the morning to 11 at night. These girls had to find their own thread and pay for their own machines out of their wages. The white shirt has gone to the public and private institutions that shelter large numbers of young girls, and to the country. There are not half as many shirtmakers in New York to-day as only a few years ago, and some of the largest firms have closed their city shops. The same is true of the manufacturers of underwear. One large Broadway firm has nearly all its work done by farmers' girls in Maine, who think themselves well off if they can earn two or three dollars a week to pay for a Sunday silk, or the wedding outfit, little dreaming of the part they are playing in starving their city sisters. Literally, they sew "with double thread, a shroud as well as a shirt." Their pin-money sets the rate of wages for thousands of poor sewing-girls in New York. The average earnings of the worker on under-wear to-day do not exceed the three dollars which her competitor among the Eastern hills is willing to accept as the price of her play. The shirtmaker's pay is better only because the very finest custom work is all there is left for her to do.

Calico wrappers at a dollar and a half a dozen—the very expert sewers able to make from eight to ten, the common run five or six—neckties at from 25 to 75 cents a dozen, with a dozen as a good day's work, are specimens of women's wages. And yet people persist in wondering at the poor quality of work done in the tenements! Italian cheap labor has come of late also to possess this poor field, with the sweater in its train. There is scarce a branch of woman's work outside of the home in which wages, long since at low-water mark, have not fallen to the point of actual starvation. A case was brought to my notice recently by a woman doctor, whose heart as well as her life-work is with the poor, of a widow with two little children she found at work in an East Side attic, making paper-bags. Her father, she told the doctor, had made good wages at it; but she received only five cents for six hundred of the little three-cornered bags, and her fingers had to be very swift and handle the paste-brush very deftly to bring her earnings up to twenty-five and thirty cents a day. She paid four dollars a month for her room. The rest went to buy food for her-self and the children. The physician's purse, rather than her skill, had healing for their complaint.

I have aimed to set down a few dry facts merely. They carry their own comment. Back of the shop with its weary, grinding toil—the home in the tenement, of which it was said in a report of the State Labor Bureau: "Decency and womanly reserve can-not be maintained there—what wonder so many fall away from virtue?" Of the outlook, what? Last Christmas Eve my business took me to an obscure street among the West Side tenements. An old woman had just fallen on the doorstep, stricken with paraly-sis. The doctor said she would never again move her right hand or foot. The whole side was dead. By her bedside, in their cheer-less room, sat the patient's aged sister, a hopeless cripple, in dumb despair. Forty years ago the sisters had come, five in num-ber then, with their mother, from the North of Ireland to make their home and earn a living among strangers. They were lace embroiderers and found work easily at good wages. All the rest had died as the years went by. The two remained and, firmly resolved to lead an honest life, worked on though wages fell and fell as age and toil stiffened their once nimble fingers and dimmed their sight. Then one of them dropped out, her hands palsied and her courage gone. Still the other toiled on, resting neither by night nor by day, that the sister might not want. Now that she too had been stricken, as she was going to the store for the work that was to keep them through the holidays, the battle was over at last. There was before them starvation, or the poorhouse. And the proud spirits of the sisters, helpless now, quailed at the outlook.

These were old, with life behind them. For them nothing was left but to sit in the shadow and wait. But of the thousands, who are travelling the road they trod to the end, with the hot blood of youth in their veins, with the love of life and of the beautiful world to which not even sixty cents a day can shut their eyes—who is to blame if their feet find the paths of shame that are "always open to them?" The very paths that have effaced the saving "limit," and to which it is declared to be "inevitable that they must in many instances resort." Let the moralist answer. Let the wise economist apply his rule of supply and demand, and let the answer be heard in this city of a thousand charities where justice goes begging.

To the everlasting credit of New York's working-girl let it be said that, rough though her road be, all but hopeless her battle with life, only in the rarest instances does she go astray. As a class she is brave, virtuous, and true. New York's army of profligate women is not, as in some foreign cities, recruited from her ranks. She is as plucky as she is proud. That "American girls never whimper" became a proverb long ago, and she accepts her lot uncomplainingly, doing the best she can and holding her cherished independence cheap at the cost of a meal, or of half her daily ration, if need be. The home in the tenement and the traditions of her childhood have neither trained her to luxury nor predisposed her in favor of domestic labor in preference to the shop. So, to the world she presents a cheerful, uncomplaining front that sometimes deceives it. Her courage will not be without its reward. Slowly, as the conviction is thrust upon society that woman's work must enter more and more into its planning, a better day is dawning. The organization of working girls' clubs, unions, and societies with a community of interests, despite the obstacles to such a movement, bears testimony to it, as to the devotion of the unselfish women who have made their poorer sister's cause their own, and will yet wring from an unfair world the justice too long denied her.

For Discussion and Writing

1. What is the "path of shame," "fall away from virtue," and "dishonor" that Riis alludes to but never fully describes? What is the effect of his describing the situation this way rather than stating it clearly?
2. What is the author's attitude toward the "country girls" of Maine in contrast to their "city sisters"?
3. Is the condition of the women Riis describes here mainly an economic, political, or social issue? Why?
4. What effect does the author's tone of praise and encouragement at the end have on his earlier depictions of hopelessness and despair?
5. After conducting basic research on immigrants and homelessness in urban centers in the early 1900s, explain why Riis would describe the elderly sisters' choice of "starvation or the poor-house" as something that made them "quail at the outlook."

From *The Souls of Black Folk*

W. E. B. Du Bois

In 1903, W. E. B. Du Bois wrote that "the problem of the twentieth century is the problem of the color-line"—an observation that still reverberates in the twenty-first century. The events of the last century bear out Du Bois' prediction, but he worked tirelessly to eradicate racism. By publishing Black artists and scholars through his NAACP magazine, The Crisis, *and through historical and sociological research that remains influential today, Du Bois hoped to show that American Blacks were worthy of full citizenship. The first African American to earn a Ph.D. at Harvard University, Du Bois went on to a distinguished career as a scholar, educator, poet, and activist. Toward the end of his life, Du Bois came to believe that America would never achieve racial equality, and he became instead a citizen of Ghana in 1963 at the age of 95, where he died just months later.*

✦

BETWEEN me and the other world there is ever an unasked question: unasked by some through feelings of delicacy; by others through the difficulty of rightly framing it. All, nevertheless, flutter round it. They approach me in a half-hesitant sort of way, eye me curiously or compassionately, and then, instead of saying directly, How does it feel to be a problem? they say, I know an excellent colored man in my town; or, I fought at Mechanicsville; or, Do not these Southern outrages make your blood boil? At these I smile, or am interested, or reduce the boiling to a simmer, as the occasion may require. To the real question, How does it feel to be a problem? I answer seldom a word.

And yet, being a problem is a strange experience,—peculiar even for one who has never been anything else, save perhaps in babyhood and in Europe. It is in the early days of rollicking boyhood that the revelation first bursts upon one, all in a day, as it were. I remember well when the shadow swept across me. I was a little thing, away up in the hills of New England, where the dark Housatonic winds between Hoosac and Taghkanic to the sea. In a wee wooden schoolhouse, something put it into the boys' and girls' heads to buy gorgeous visiting-cards—ten cents a package—and exchange. The exchange was merry, till one girl, a tall newcomer, refused my card,—refused it peremptorily, with a glance. Then it dawned upon me with a certain suddenness that I was different from the others; or like, mayhap, in heart and life and longing, but shut out from their world by a vast veil. I had thereafter no desire to tear down that veil, to creep through; I held all beyond it in common contempt, and lived above it in a region of blue sky and great wandering shadows. That sky was bluest when I could beat my mates at examination-time, or beat them at a foot-race, or even beat their stringy heads. Alas, with the years all this fine contempt began to fade; for the worlds I longed for, and all their dazzling opportunities, were theirs, not mine. But they should not keep these prizes, I said; some, all, I would wrest from them. Just how I would do it I could never decide: by reading law, by healing the sick, by telling the wonderful tales that swam in my head,—some way. With other black boys the strife was not so fiercely sunny: their youth shrunk into tasteless sycophancy, or into silent hatred of the pale world about them and mocking distrust of everything white; or wasted itself in a bitter cry, Why did God make me an outcast and a stranger in mine own house? The shades of the prison-house closed round about us all: walls strait and stubborn to the whitest, but relentlessly narrow, tall, and unscalable to sons of night who must plod darkly on in resignation, or beat unavailing palms against the stone, or steadily, half hopelessly, watch the streak of blue above.

After the Egyptian and Indian, the Greek and Roman, the Teuton and Mongolian, the Negro is a sort of seventh son, born with a veil, and gifted with second-sight in this American world,—a world which yields him no true self-consciousness, but only lets him see himself through the revelation of the other world. It is a peculiar sensation, this double-consciousness, this sense of always looking at one's self through the eyes of others, of measuring one's soul by the tape of a world that looks on in amused contempt and pity. One ever feels his two-ness,—an American, a Negro; two souls, two thoughts, two unreconciled strivings; two warring ideals in one dark body, whose dogged strength alone keeps it from being torn asunder.

The history of the American Negro is the history of this strife,—this longing to attain self-conscious manhood, to merge his double self into a better and truer self. In this merging he wishes neither of the older selves to be lost. He would not Africanize America, for America has too much to teach the world and Africa. He would not bleach his Negro soul in a flood of white Americanism, for he knows that Negro blood has a message for the world. He simply wishes to make it possible for a man to be both a Negro and an American, without being cursed and spit upon by his fellows, without having the doors of Opportunity closed roughly in his face.

5 This, then, is the end of his striving: to be a co-worker in the kingdom of culture, to escape both death and isolation, to husband and use his best powers and his latent genius. These powers of body and mind have in the past been strangely wasted, dispersed, or forgotten. The shadow of a mighty Negro past flits through the tale of Ethiopia the Shadowy and of Egypt the Sphinx. Throughout history, the powers of single black men flash here and there like falling stars, and die sometimes before the world has rightly gauged their brightness. Here in America, in the few days since Emancipation, the black man's turning hither and thither in hesitant and doubtful striving has often made his very strength to lose effectiveness, to seem like absence of power, like weakness. And yet it is not weakness,—it is the contradiction of double aims. The double-aimed struggle of the black artisan—on the one hand to escape white contempt for a nation of mere hewers of wood and drawers of water, and on the other hand to plough and nail and dig for a poverty-stricken horde—could only result in making him a poor craftsman, for

he had but half a heart in either cause. By the poverty and ignorance of his people, the Negro minister or doctor was tempted toward quackery and demagogy; and by the criticism of the other world, toward ideals that made him ashamed of his lowly tasks. The would-be black savant was confronted by the paradox that the knowledge his people needed was a twice-told tale to his white neighbors, while the knowledge which would teach the white world was Greek to his own flesh and blood. The innate love of harmony and beauty that set the ruder souls of his people a-dancing and a-singing raised but confusion and doubt in the soul of the black artist; for the beauty revealed to him was the soul-beauty of a race which his larger audience despised, and he could not articulate the message of another people. This waste of double aims, this seeking to satisfy two unreconciled ideals, has wrought sad havoc with the courage and faith and deeds of ten thousand thousand people,—has sent them often wooing false gods and invoking false means of salvation, and at times has even seemed about to make them ashamed of themselves.

The Nation has not yet found peace from its sins; the freedman has not yet found in freedom his promised land. Whatever of good may have come in these years of change, the shadow of a deep disappointment rests upon the Negro people,—a disappointment all the more bitter because the unattained ideal was unbounded save by the simple ignorance of a lowly people.

The first decade was merely a prolongation of the vain search for freedom, the boon that seemed ever barely to elude their grasp,—like a tantalizing will-o'-the-wisp, maddening and misleading the headless host. The holocaust of war, the terrors of the Ku-Klux Klan, the lies of carpet-baggers, the disorganization of industry, and the contradictory advice of friends and foes, left the bewildered serf with no new watchword beyond the old cry for freedom. As the time flew, however, he began to grasp a new idea. The ideal of liberty demanded for its attainment powerful means, and these the Fifteenth Amendment gave him. The ballot, which before he had looked upon as a visible sign of freedom, he now regarded as the chief means of gaining and perfecting the liberty with which war had partially endowed him. And why not? Had not votes made war and emancipated millions? Had not votes enfranchised the freedmen? Was anything impossible to a power that had done all this? A million black men started with renewed zeal to vote themselves into the kingdom. So the decade flew away, the revolution of 1876 came, and left the half-free serf weary, wondering, but still inspired. Slowly but steadily, in the following years, a new vision began gradually to replace the dream of political power,—a powerful movement, the rise of another ideal to guide the unguided, another pillar of fire by night after a clouded day. It was the ideal of "book-learning"; the curiosity, born of compulsory ignorance, to know and test the power of the cabalistic letters of the white man, the longing to know. Here at last seemed to have been discovered the mountain path to Canaan; longer than the highway of Emancipation and law, steep and rugged, but straight, leading to heights high enough to overlook life.

A people thus handicapped ought not to be asked to race with the world, but rather allowed to give all its time and thought to its own social problems. But alas! while sociologists gleefully count his bastards and his prostitutes, the very soul of the toiling, sweating black man is darkened by the shadow of a vast despair. Men call the shadow prejudice, and learnedly explain it as the natural defence of culture against barbarism, learning against ignorance, purity against crime, the "higher" against the "lower" races. To which the Negro cries Amen! and swears that to so much of this strange prejudice as is founded on just homage to civilization, culture, righteousness, and progress, he humbly bows and meekly does obeisance. But before that nameless prejudice that leaps beyond all this he stands helpless, dismayed, and well-nigh speechless; before that personal disrespect and mockery, the ridicule and systematic humiliation, the distortion of fact and wanton license of fancy, the cynical ignoring of the better and the boisterous welcoming of the worse, the all-pervading desire to inculcate disdain for everything black, from Toussaint to the devil,—before this there rises a sickening despair that would disarm and discourage any nation save that black host to whom "discouragement" is an unwritten word.

Merely a concrete test of the underlying principles of the great republic is the Negro Problem, and the spiritual striving of the freedmen's sons is the travail of souls whose burden is almost beyond the measure of their strength, but who bear it in the name of an historic race, in the name of this the land of their fathers' fathers, and in the name of human opportunity.

1903

For Discussion and Writing

1. What does Du Bois mean by "the Veil"?
2. What impact did the author's experience with a grade school Valentine's Day card have on his later statement that "one ever feels his two-ness"?
3. Du Bois writes that after 1876, "a new vision" of literacy slowly replaced the old "dream of political power." Was political power possible for the former slaves without first striving for literacy skills? What does the author mean by "the power of the cabalistic letters of the white man"?
4. Based on this writing, what does Du Bois see as most necessary if former slaves and their descendants are to achieve the American Dream?
5. This excerpt was written in 1903. In an essay, explain what you see as the most significant difference between it and Malcolm X's speech (found through an Internet search as explained elsewhere in this chapter) 61 years later. Had the main issues expressed by Du Bois improved, become worse, stayed the same, or merely shifted in the time that passed?

Keep Your Eyes on the Prize

Traditional Civil Rights Song

"Keep Your Eyes on the Prize," alternately known as "Hold On" and "Gospel Plow," is a tune dating back to before World War I. Its lyrics, however, were composed at the start of the Civil Rights era in the 1950s, and the stanza mentioning "that big Greyhound" refers to the buses that transported the Freedom Riders of that later era from city to city. It is a song that calls for steadfast resolution toward a common goal of equal rights for all, and its calls for patience and even love in the face of adversity reflect the "nonviolent non-cooperation" sentiments of the time well.

Paul and Silas bound in jail
Had no money for to go their bail
Keep your eyes on the prize, hold on.

Paul and Silas began to shout
Jail door opened and they walked out
Keep your eyes on the prize, hold on.

Freedom's name is mighty sweet
Soon one day we're gonna meet
Keep your eyes on the prize, hold on.

Got my hand on the gospel plow
Wouldn't take nothin' for my journey now
Keep your eyes on the prize, hold on.

The only chain that we can stand
Is that chain of hand in hand
Keep your eyes on the prize, hold on.

The only thing that we did wrong
Stayed in the wilderness a day too long
Keep your eyes on the prize, hold on.

But the one thing we did right
Was the day we started to fight
Keep your eyes on the prize, hold on.

We're gonna board that big Greyhound
Carryin' love from town to town
Keep your eyes on the prize, hold on.

We're gonna ride for civil rights
We're gonna ride for both black and white
Keep your eyes on the prize, hold on.

Traditional

For Discussion and Writing

1. Who were the Biblical figures, Paul and Silas, and what might their connections be to the sentiments of the song?
2. What does the song refer to in the words, "Stayed in the wilderness a day too long"?
3. What is the "gospel" in the fourth stanza, and what is it plowing? How?
4. In his speech, found through an Internet search as explained elsewhere in this chapter, Malcolm X accused leading proponents of Civil Rights of doing "too much singing and not enough swinging." Do you think the ideas expressed in this song are too weak to make an impact?
5. What is a particular prize in your conception of the American Dream? What must you do in order to "keep your eyes on the prize"?

New York Fire Kills 148: Girl Victims Leap to Death from Factory

CHICAGO SUNDAY TRIBUNE

The great influx of immigrants who arrived in the United States between 1880 and1920 seeking the "streets paved with gold" and a chance to live the promise of America provided thousands of workers to the burgeoning industries of New England and beyond.

Immigrant women and girls sought paid work to help their families rise from poverty, often sewing garments twelve or more hours a day, six days a week in sweatshops for meager pay. Most factories and sweatshops were poorly ventilated, crowded, unsanitary, and unsafe. Though activists organized strikes for better pay and work conditions, few immigrants dared complain for fear of losing their jobs. Most believed that they were doing what was expected of them as new Americans. Tragic workplace accidents were not unusual; one of the most infamous was the horrific fire at the Triangle Shirtwaist Factory in New York City in 1911. The doors of the factory on the 9th and 10th floors were routinely locked because owners assumed their workers would steal fabric and other materials. Though the owners were acquitted of wrongdoing, the Triangle Fire led to significant workplace safety reforms, most of which are still in effect today.

✦

Chicago Sunday Tribune, March 26, 1911, p. 1.

NEW YORK FIRE KILLS 148: GIRL VICTIMS LEAP TO DEATH FROM FACTORY

One hundred and forty-eight persons nine-tenths of them girls and young women are known to have been killed in a fire which burned out the ten story factory building at the northwest corner of Washington place and Green street, just off Washington square, this afternoon.

One hundred and forty-one of them were instantly killed, either by leaps from the windows and down elevator shafts, or by being smothered. Seven died in the hospitals.

Falling Bodies Hurt Rescuers

Women and girl machine operators jumped from the eighth, ninth, and tenth floors in groups of twos and threes into life nets and their bodies spun downward from the high windows of the building so close together that the few nets soon were broken and the firemen and passersby who helped hold them were crushed to the pavement by the rain of falling bodies.

Within a few minutes after the first cry of fire had been yelled on the eighth floor of the building, fifty-three were lying half nude, on the pavement. Bare legs in some cases were burned a dark brown and waists and skirts in tatters showed that they had been torn in the panic within the building before the girls got to the windows to jump to death.

The mangled bodies lay there with the spill of the water which the firemen soon were pouring from water towers and hose into the building, soaking them. There was no time to clear away the dead in the street. Inside the building the firemen believed there still were dozens upon dozens of girls and men and they wasted no time upon those whom they knew to be dead.

Bodies Lie in Piles

It was more than an hour and a half before the firemen could enter the floor where the fire started, the eighth, and they came back then with word that a glance showed fifty dead bodies on the floor alone.

In the elevator shaft was a pile of bodies estimated conservatively at twenty-five bodies of girls who had jumped down the elevator shaft after the elevator had made its last trip.

Some of the girls, in jumping, smashed through the sidewalk vault lights on the Washington place side of the building. The bodies that continued to crash upon the vault light finally made a hole in it about five feet in diameter. Just at dusk firemen and policemen were pulling many half nude and burned corpses from this hole.

Croker Staggered by Sights

Inside the building on the three top floors the sights were even more awful. When Fire Chief Croker could make his way into these three floors he saw a tragedy that utterly staggered him that sent him, a man used to viewing horrors, back and down into the street with quivering lips.

The floors were black with smoke. And then he saw as the smoke drifted away bodies burned to bare bone. There were skeletons bending over sewing machines, the victims having been killed as they worked. Other piles of skeletons lay before every door and elevator shaft where the sufferers fell in their effort to escape.

"The worst fire in a New York building," said Chief Croker as he came out among the ambulances and fire apparatus again, "since the burning of the Brooklyn theater in the 70's."

Found Living Among Dead

More than an hour after the last of the girls had jumped policemen who had approached the building to gather up the bodies and stretch them out on the opposite side of Greene street found one girl, Bertha Weintrout, the last girl to leap from the ninth floor, still breathing. Two or three dead bodies were piled alongside her, and as the policemen were moving those away they heard the girl sigh. The police yelled for a doctor, and the girl, still bleeding and dripping wet was hurried to St. Vincent's hospital.

A man who has an office on the third floor of the building in Washington place, across from the burned building, said he looked up upon hearing shrieks and saw a girl climb out of a window on the ninth floor of the Asch building, where the fire occurred. At this time the man, who refused to give his name, says there was no sign of smoke or flame. The girl stood for a moment. Then she jumped. She whirled over and over, a streak of black gown and white underclothing, for nine floors and crashed into the sidewalk.

Leap to their Death

About the same time Dr. Ralph Fralick, 119 Waverley place, was walking across Washington Square park toward the building and started on a run as he saw the heads of screaming girls at the window sills of the ninth floor.

They stood for a time, the doctor says, on the little ledge. Then a girl jumped and another and another. Some of them fell straight as a plummet and smashed through the vault lights of the street into the basement under the sidewalk. Most of them turned many times, shrieking as they fell.

One girl, the doctor says, deliberately took off her hat and laid on the ledge before she jumped.

Man Pushes Many Out

But the greater number were jumping from the east side of the corner building and landing burned and crushed in Green street. Here one man ran from window to window, picked up girls bodily, and dropped them to the pavement. Either he thought the nets were there to catch them or he believed this was the easiest way.

When he had dropped the last girl within reach he climbed on to the sill and jumped straight out, with a hand raised as a bridge jumper holds his arm upward to balance himself.

20 All the girls had jumped from the Greene street side of the building and it seemed that the ninth floor ledge on this side was clear when two girls clambered out upon it. One of them seemed self-poised; at least her movements were slow and deliberate. With her was a younger girl shrieking and twisting with fright.

Tries to Save Companion

The crowd yelled to the two not to jump. The older girl placed both arms around the younger and pulled her back on the ledge toward the brick wall and tried to press her close to the wall. But the younger girl twisted her head and shoulders loose from the protecting embrace, took a step or two to the right and jumped.

After her younger companion had died the girl who was left stood back against the wall motionless, and for a moment she held her hands rigid against her thighs, her head tilted upward and looking toward the sky. Smoke began to trickle out of the broken window a few inches to her left. She began to raise her arms then and make slow gestures as if she were addressing a crowd above her. A tongue of flame licked up along the window sill and singed her hair and then out of the smoke which was beginning to hide her from view she jumped, feet foremost, falling, without turning, to the street. It was the Bertha Weintrout, whom the police found still breathing an hour later under the cataracts spilling from ledge to ledge upon the dead who lay around her.

About 200 other employees, mostly women, in the meantime had got out on the roof of the building, crazy with fright. Across the small court at the back of the building are the rear windows of the New York University Law school.

Law Students Save Many

At the first cry from the burning building, two of the law students, Charles T. Kremer and Elias Kanter, led a party of students to the roof of the law school building, [which] is a story higher than the building where the fire occurred. Kanter and the other students dragged two short ladders to the roof of the law school and by making a sort of extension ladder of the two short ones Kremer got down on to the roof of the burning building and tried to get the girls into orderly line and send them up the ladder to where his school fellows were waiting to grab them to safety.

The students got 150 women, girls, and men away from the burning building in this way.

Many Fight for Safety

At the other end of the roof from the students' ladders, fifty men and women were fighting with one another to climb the five feet to the roof of an adjoining building at the corner of Waverly place and Greene street. The law students say that the men bit and kicked the women and girls for a chance to climb to the other roof and safety.

Kremer, when the last of the group nearest the law school had been saved, climbed down the ladder to the roof of the burning building and went down the roof scuttle to the top floor.

He could see only one girl, who ran shrieking toward him with her hair burning. She had come up from the floor beneath and as she came to Kremer she fainted in his arms. He smothered the sparks in her hair with his hands and then tried to carry her up the narrow ladder to the roof. But because she was unconscious he had to wrap long strands of her hair around his hand and drag her to fresh air in the way. His friend Kanter helped him to get the girl up the ladder to the law school roof and safety.

1911

For Discussion and Writing

1. What does the Triangle Factory tragedy suggest about how business owners viewed poor and immigrant laborers?
2. Given the conditions of the Triangle factory, how realistic is attaining the American Dream for industrial workers?
3. How do workplace safety regulations contribute to the fulfillment of the American Dream?
4. How do the accounts of survivors and specific details about the dead add to the story?
5. In an essay, compare the style and content of this story with that of "The *Pineros*." What techniques do the two articles share? How do the writers make the stories vivid for readers? Given that they are written nearly one hundred years apart, are there any noticeable differences in prose style?

The Ballot or the Bullet (Text through Internet Search)

Malcolm X

Malcolm Little discovered Islam while serving prison time for a burglary charge. Changing his last name to a simple "X" as a way to deny his "slave name," Malcolm X quickly moved up the hierarchy of the Nation of Islam, led by Elijah Muhummad, after being paroled and becoming a minister in the NOI. Although unfairly and inaccurately remembered today for two sound bites—"by any means necessary" and "the white man is the devil"—that have been removed from their proper context, Malcolm X did generate a great deal of controversy toward the end of his short life, especially after a highly publicized split from his former mentor, Elijah Muhummad. During an address in New York, gunmen rushed the stage and shot the newly conciliatory minister fifteen times at close range, killing him. One of his most famous speeches was delivered to a supportive crowd in Detroit in April 1964. To find the text of this speech, simply enter "Malcolm X Ballot Or Bullet" into a Google search. The speech transcript has been reproduced on hundreds of Web sites.

For Discussion and Writing

1. Having read the speech, how would you define Black Nationalism?
2. At the end of his speech, Malcolm X says, "We don't see any American Dream; we've experienced only the American nightmare." In how many ways has he offered evidence to support this statement?
3. If Malcolm X had lived to the present day and were offering a follow-up to this speech, what might he say has improved since 1964? Remained the same? Worsened?
4. How can many of the principles expressed in this speech be applied to the phenomenon of outsourcing, the closing of American workplaces and opening of facilities in other countries?
5. Conduct research and write an essay on the state of business ownership and/or leadership by African Americans in the twenty-first century.

From "The American Dream"

Dr. Martin Luther King, Jr.

Perhaps no other African American figure looms as large in the country's history as Dr. Martin Luther King. The esteemed Civil Rights leader's life is a core feature of Black History Month each February, and his life's work has been recognized through the dedication of a Federal holiday in his name. Often overshadowed by his involvement in Civil Rights is his simpler role as a Baptist minister—a "called and ordained servant of the Word" whose words rivaled those of Frederick Douglass in the nineteenth century as models of masterful eloquence that could move audiences to reflection and action. In this sermon excerpt, given at Ebenezer Baptist Church in Atlanta, Georgia, in 1965, Dr. King examines the role and meaning of the American Dream in the lives of not just the congregation, but the entire nation.

✦

. . . This morning I was riding to the airport in Washington, D.C., and on the way to the airport the limousine passed by the Jefferson monument, and Reverend Andrew Young, my executive assistant, said to me, "It's quite coincidental that we would be passing by the Jefferson Monument on Independence Day." You can get so busy in life that you forget holidays and other days, and it had slipped my mind altogether that today was the Fourth of July. And I said to him, "It is coincidental and quite significant, and I think when I get to Atlanta and go to my pulpit, I will try to preach a sermon in the spirit of the founding fathers of our nation and in the spirit of the Declaration of Independence." And so this morning I would like to use as a subject from which to preach: "The American Dream."

It wouldn't take us long to discover the substance of that dream. It is found in those majestic words of the Declaration of Independence, words lifted to cosmic proportions: "We hold these truths to be self-evident, that all men are created equal, that they are endowed by God, Creator, with certain inalienable Rights, that among these are Life, Liberty, and the pursuit of Happiness." This is a dream. It's a great dream.

The first saying we notice in this dream is an amazing universalism. It doesn't say "some men," it says "all men." It doesn't say "all white men," it says "all men," which includes black men. It does not say "all Gentiles," it says "all men," which includes Jews. It doesn't say "all Protestants," it says "all men," which includes Catholics. It doesn't even say "all theists and believers," it says "all men," which includes humanists and agnostics.

Then that dream goes on to say another thing that ultimately distinguishes our nation and our form of government from any totalitarian system in the world. It says that each of us has certain basic rights that are neither derived from or conferred by the state. In order to discover where they came from, it is necessary to move back behind the dim mist of eternity. They are God-given, gifts from His hands. Never before in the history of the world has a sociopolitical document expressed in such profound, eloquent, and unequivocal language the dignity and the worth of human personality. The American dream reminds us, and we should think about it anew on this Independence Day, that every man is an heir of the legacy of dignity and worth.

Now ever since the founding fathers of our nation dreamed this dream in all of its magnificence—to use a big word that the psychiatrists use—America has been something of a schizophrenic personality, tragically divided against herself. On the one hand we have proudly professed the great principles of democracy, but on the other hand we have sadly practiced the very opposite of those principles.

5 But now more than ever before, America is challenged to realize its dream, for the shape of the world today does not permit our nation the luxury of an anemic democracy. And the price that America must pay for the continued oppression of the Negro and other minority groups is the price of its own destruction. For the hour is late. And the clock of destiny is ticking out. We must act now before it is too late.

And so it is marvelous and great that we do have a dream, that we have a nation with a dream; and to forever challenge us; to forever give us a sense of urgency; to forever stand in the midst of the "isness" of our terrible injustices; to remind us of the "oughtness" of our noble capacity for justice and love and brotherhood.

This morning I would like to deal with some of the challenges that we face today in our nation as a result of the American dream. First, I want to reiterate the fact that we are challenged more than ever before to respect the dignity and the worth of all human personality. We are challenged to really believe that all men are created equal. And don't misunderstand that. It does not mean that all men are created equal in terms of native endowment, in terms of intellectual capacity—it doesn't mean that. There are certain bright stars in the human firmament in every field. It doesn't mean that every musician is equal to a Beethoven or Handel, a Verdi or a Mozart. It doesn't mean that every physicist is equal to an Einstein. It does not mean that every literary figure in history is equal to Aeschylus and Euripides, Shakespeare and Chaucer. It does not mean that every philosopher is equal to Plato, Aristotle, Immanuel Kant, and Friedrich Hegel. It doesn't mean that. There are individuals who do excel and rise to the heights of genius in their areas and in their fields. What it does mean is that all men are equal in intrinsic worth.

You see, the founding fathers were really influenced by the Bible. The whole concept of the *imago dei*, as it is expressed in Latin, the "image of God," is the idea that all men have something within them that God injected. Not that they have substantial unity with God, but that every man has a capacity to have fellowship with God. And this gives him a uniqueness, it gives him worth, it gives him dignity. And we must never forget this as a nation: there are no gradations in the image of God. Every man from a treble white to a bass black is significant on God's keyboard, precisely because every man is made in the image of God. One day we will learn that. We will know one day that God made us to live together as brothers and to respect the dignity and worth of every man. . . .

And I tell you this morning, my friends, the reason we got to solve this problem here in America: Because God somehow called America to do a special job for mankind and the world. Never before in the history of the world have so many racial groups and so many national backgrounds assembled together in one nation. And somehow if we can't solve the problem in America the world can't solve the problem, because America is the world in miniature and the world is America writ large. And God set us out with all of the opportunities. He set us between two great oceans; made it possible for us to live with some of the great natural resources of the world. And there he gave us through the minds of our forefathers a great creed: "We hold these truths to be self-evident, that all men are created equal. . . ."

Are we really taking this thing seriously? "All men are created 10
equal." And that means that every man who lives in a slum today is just as significant as John D., Nelson, or any other Rockefeller. Every man who lives in the slum is just as significant as Henry Ford. All men are created equal, and they are endowed by their

Creator with certain inalienable rights, rights that can't be separated from you. Go down and tell them, "You may take my life, but you can't take my right to life. You may take liberty from me, but you can't take my right to liberty. You may take from me the desire, you may take from me the propensity to pursue happiness, but you can't take from me my right to pursue happiness. We hold these truths to be self-evident, that all men are created equal and endowed by their Creator with certain inalienable Rights and among these are Life, Liberty, and the pursuit of Happiness."

Now there's another thing that we must never forget. If we are going to make the American dream a reality, we are challenged to work in an action program to get rid of the last vestiges of segregation and discrimination. This problem isn't going to solve itself, however much people tell us this. However much the Uncle Toms and Nervous Nellies in the Negro communities tell us this, this problem isn't just going to work itself out. History is the long story of the fact that privileged groups seldom give up their privileges without strong resistance, and they seldom do it voluntarily. And so if the American dream is to be a reality, we must work to make it a reality and realize the urgency of the moment. And we must say now is the time to make real the promises of democracy. Now is the time to get rid of segregation and discrimination. Now is the time to make Georgia a better state. Now is the time to make the United States a better nation. We must live with that, and we must believe that.

And I would like to say to you this morning what I've tried to say all over this nation, what I believe firmly: that in seeking to make the dream a reality we must use and adopt a proper method. I'm more convinced than ever before that nonviolence is the way. I'm more convinced than ever before that violence is impractical as well as immoral. If we are to build right here a better America, we have a method as old as the insights of Jesus of Nazareth and as modern as the techniques of Mohandas K. Gandhi. We need not hate; we need not use violence. We can stand up before our most violent opponent and say: "We will match your capacity to inflict suffering by our capacity to endure suffering. We will meet your physical force with soul force. Do to us what you will and we will still love you. We cannot in all good conscience obey your unjust laws, because non-cooperation with evil is as much a moral obligation as is cooperation with good, and so throw us in jail. We will go in those jails and transform them from dungeons of shame to havens of freedom and human dignity.

Send your hooded perpetrators of violence into our communities after midnight hours and drag us out on some wayside road and beat us and leave us half-dead, and as difficult as it is, we will still love you. Somehow go around the country and use your propaganda agents to make it appear that we are not fit culturally, morally, or otherwise for integration, and we will still love you. Threaten our children and bomb our homes, and as difficult as it is, we will still love you.

But be assured that we will ride you down by our capacity to suffer. One day we will win our freedom, but we will not only win freedom for ourselves, we will so appeal to your heart and your conscience that we will win you in the process." And our victory will be a double victory.

Oh yes, love is the way. Love is the only absolute. More and more I see this. I've seen too much hate to want to hate myself; hate is too great a burden to bear. I've seen it on the faces of too many sheriffs of the South—I've seen hate. In the faces and even the walk of too many Klansmen of the South, I've seen hate. Hate distorts the personality. Hate does something to the soul that causes one to lose his objectivity. The man who hates can't think straight; the man who hates can't reason right; the man who hates can't see right; the man who hates can't walk right. And I know now that Jesus is right, that love is the way. And this is why John said, "God is love," so that he who hates does not know God, but he who loves at that moment has the key that opens the door to the meaning of ultimate reality. So this morning there is so much that we have to offer to the world.

We have a great dream. It started way back in 1776, and God 15
grant that America will be true to her dream.

About two years ago now, I stood with many of you who stood there in person and all of you who were there in spirit before the Lincoln Monument in Washington. As I came to the end of my speech there, I tried to tell the nation about a dream I had. I must confess to you this morning that since that sweltering August afternoon in 1963, my dream has often turned into a nightmare; I've seen it shattered. I saw it shattered one night on Highway 80 in Alabama when Mrs. Viola Liuzzo was shot down. I had a nightmare and saw my dream shattered one night in Marion, Alabama, when Jimmie Lee Jackson was shot down. I saw my dream shattered one night in Selma when Reverend Reeb was clubbed to the ground by a vicious racist and later died. And oh, I continue to see it shattered as I walk through the Harlems of our nation and see sometimes ten and fifteen Negroes trying to live in one or two rooms. I've been down to the Delta of Mississippi since then, and I've seen my dream shattered as I met hundreds of people who didn't earn more than six or seven hundred dollars a week. I've seen my dream shattered as I've walked the streets of Chicago and seen Negroes, young men and women, with a sense of utter hopelessness because they can't find any jobs. And they see life as a long and desolate corridor with no exit signs. And not only Negroes at this point. I've seen my dream shattered because I've been through Appalachia, and I've seen my white brothers along with Negroes living in poverty. And I'm concerned about white poverty as much as I'm concerned about Negro poverty.

So yes, the dream has been shattered, and I have had my nightmarish experiences, but I tell you this morning once more that I haven't lost the faith. I still have a dream that one day all of God's children will have food and clothing and material well-being for their bodies, culture and education for their minds, and freedom for their spirits.

I still have a dream this morning: one day all of God's black children will be respected like his white children.

1965

For Discussion and Writing

1. Based on this sermon, what is Martin Luther King's definition of the American Dream?
2. Why is Dr. King convinced that nonviolence is the right way to end segregation and discrimination? What proof does he offer that it will eventually achieve its goals?
3. One well-known feature of Dr. King's sermons and speeches was his use of metaphors to amplify his points. Two early examples in this sermon are "the clock of destiny" and the black and white keys on "God's keyboard." How many other metaphors are at work in this sermon? What do they lend to the paragraphs and sections where they appear?
4. Why is Dr. King's work acknowledged and his life celebrated by the United States government, while Malcolm X's is not? Examine the ideologies behind a society's decisions to acknowledge or disregard specific historical figures.
5. In an essay, explain what you see as the three most significant differences between Dr. King's sermon here and Malcolm X's "Ballot or Bullet" speech, found through an Internet search as explained elsewhere in this chapter, regarding African Americans and the American Dream.

The Ten-Point Program

THE BLACK PANTHER PARTY FOR SELF-DEFENSE

Founded in 1966 in California as the Black Panther Party for Self-Defense, the Black Panthers began as a group dedicated to feeding the hungry, protecting children, and caring for the sick in their communities. (See also Dr. Tolbert Small in this chapter.) As civil unrest in the United States increased with the ongoing Vietnam War as its backdrop, the Black Panther Party (BPP) likewise became more militant, especially after marching, fully armed but peacefully, on the California State Assembly to demonstrate their knowledge of gun ownership laws. The Federal government, through the FBI's "COINTEL" program, gave the BPP "Public Enemy #1" status and began a series of covert actions to dismantle the party. Many of the group's leaders were involved in legal issues and some were killed, and by the mid-1970s the BPP was an "organization" only in name.

OCTOBER 1966 BLACK PANTHER PARTY PLATFORM AND PROGRAM

WHAT WE WANT
WHAT WE BELIEVE

1. We want freedom. We want power to determine the destiny of our Black Community.

We believe that black people will not be free until we are able to determine our destiny.

2. We want full employment for our people.

We believe that the federal government is responsible and obligated to give every man employment or a guaranteed income. We believe that if the white American businessmen will not give full employment, then the means of production should be taken from the businessmen and placed in the community so that the people of the community can organize and employ all of its people and give a high standard of living.

3. We want an end to the robbery by the white man of our Black 5
Community.

We believe that this racist government has robbed us and now we are demanding the overdue debt of forty acres and two mules. "Forty acres and two mules" was promised 100 years ago as restitution for slave labor and mass murder of black people. We will accept the payment as currency which will be distributed to our many communities. The Germans are now aiding the Jews in Israel for the genocide of the Jewish people. The Germans murdered six million Jews. The American racist has taken part in the slaughter of over twenty million black people; therefore, we feel that this is a modest demand that we make.

4. We want decent housing, fit for shelter of human beings.

We believe that if the white landlords will not give decent housing to our black community, then the housing and the land should be made into cooperatives so that our community, with government aid, can build and make decent housing for its people.

5. We want education for our people that exposes the true nature of this decadent American society. We want education that teaches us our true history and our role in the present-day society.

We believe in an educational system that will give to our people a knowledge of self. If a man does not have knowledge of himself and his position in society and the world, then he has little chance to relate to anything else.

6. We want all black men to be exempt from military service.

We believe that Black people should not be forced to fight in the military service to defend a racist government that does not protect us. We will not fight and kill other people of color in the world who, like black people, are being victimized by the white racist government of America. We will protect ourselves from the force and violence of the racist police and the racist military, by whatever means necessary.

7. We want an immediate end to police brutality and murder of black people.

We believe we can end police brutality in our black community by organizing black self-defense groups that are dedicated to defending our black community from racist police oppression and brutality. The Second Amendment to the Constitution of the United States gives a right to bear arms. We therefore believe that all black people should arm themselves for self-defense.

8. We want freedom for all black men held in federal, state, county and city prisons and jails.

We believe that all black people should be released from the many jails and prisons because they have not received a fair and impartial trial.

9. We want all black people when brought to trial to be tried in court by a jury of their peer group or people from their black communities, as defined by the Constitution of the United States.

We believe that the courts should follow the United States Constitution so that black people will receive fair trials. The 14th Amendment of the U.S. Constitution gives a man a right to be tried by his peer group. A peer is a person from a similar economic, social, religious, geographical, environmental, historical and racial background. To do this the court will be forced to select a jury from the black community from which the black defendant came. We have been, and are being tried by all-white juries that have no understanding of the "average reasoning man" of the black community.

10. We want land, bread, housing, education, clothing, justice and peace. And as our major political objective, a United Nations-supervised plebiscite to be held throughout the black colony in which only black colonial subjects will be allowed to participate for the purpose of determining the will of black people as to their national destiny.

When in the course of human events, it becomes necessary 20
for one people to dissolve the political bands which have connected them with another, and to assume, among the powers of the earth, the separate and equal station to which the laws of nature and nature's God entitle them, a decent respect to the opinions of mankind requires that they should declare the causes which impel them to the separation.

We hold these truths to be self evident, that all men are created equal; that they are endowed by their Creator with certain unalienable rights; that among these are life, liberty, and the pursuit of happiness. That, to secure these rights, governments are instituted among men, deriving their just powers from the consent of the governed; that, whenever any form of government becomes destructive of these ends, it is the right of the people to alter or to abolish it, and to institute a new government, laying its foundation on such principles, and organizing its powers in such form, as to them shall seem most likely to effect their safety and happiness. Prudence, indeed, will dictate that governments long established should not be changed for light and transient causes; and accordingly, all experience hath shown, that mankind are more disposed to supper, while evils are sufferable, than to right themselves by abolishing the forms to which they are accustomed. But, when a long train of abuses and usurpations, pursuing invariable the same object, evinces a design to reduce them under absolute despotism, it is their right, it is their duty, to throw off such government, and to provide new guards for their future security.

For Discussion and Writing

1. What is the source of the language that ends this Program's tenth point? Why is it significant in light of the ten points that have been raised?
2. What contradictions might lie between the desires expressed in points two and four, and those expressed in points six and ten?
3. If a key skill in any bargaining campaign is to ask for more than what is reasonably expected, so that the other side has room to counter-negotiate, then which of these ten points might the Black Panther Party have been willing to abandon if other points were won? Which points would be considered essential?
4. Taking the ten-point program as a whole, which main elements of the American Dream are most grievously missing from Black experience at the time of this writing, in the view of the document's writers?
5. Conduct extensive research, using a variety of credible sources, on the Black Panthers' history and its conflict with the United States government. What inroads, if any, did the group make for African Americans?

The National Organization for Women's 1966 Statement of Purpose

Betty Friedan

Over a hundred years after the Seneca Falls Declaration *was written, the National Organization for Women (NOW) issued this "Statement of Purpose," written by Betty Friedan. Whereas the 1848* Declaration *had served as a list of grievances, meant to illustrate the extensive inequality of women's rights as citizens in contrast to men's, the 1966 document offered a combination of stated beliefs, historical overviews, and firm rejections of particular social ideologies. While the document excerpted here is not as bleak as its nineteenth-century counterpart, it is clear that NOW in 1966 saw much work left to be done.*

✦

We, men and women who hereby constitute ourselves as the National Organization for Women, believe that the time has come for a new movement toward true equality for all women in America, and toward a fully equal partnership of the sexes, as part of the world-wide revolution of human rights now taking place within and beyond our national borders.

The purpose of NOW is to take action to bring women into full participation in the mainstream of American society now, exercising all the privileges and responsibilities thereof in truly equal partnership with men.

We believe the time has come to move beyond the abstract argument, discussion and symposia over the status and special nature of women which has raged in America in recent years; the time has come to confront, with concrete action, the conditions that now prevent women from enjoying the equality of opportunity and freedom of choice which is their right, as individual Americans, and as human beings.

NOW is dedicated to the proposition that women, first and foremost, are human beings, who, like all other people in our society, must have the chance to develop their fullest human potential. We believe that women can achieve such equality only by accepting to the full the challenges and responsibilities they share with all other people in our society, as part of the decision-making mainstream of American political, economic and social life.

5 We organize to initiate or support action, nationally, or in any part of this nation, by individuals or organizations, to break through the silken curtain of prejudice and discrimination against women in government, industry, the professions, the churches, the political parties, the judiciary, the labor unions, in education, science, medicine, law, religion and every other field of importance in American society.

Enormous changes taking place in our society make it both possible and urgently necessary to advance the unfinished revolution of women toward true equality, now. With a life span lengthened to nearly 75 years it is no longer either necessary or possible for women to devote the greater part of their lives to child-rearing; yet childbearing and rearing which continues to be a most important part of most women's lives—still is used to justify barring women from equal professional and economic participation and advance.

Today's technology has reduced most of the productive chores which women once performed in the home and in mass-production industries based upon routine unskilled labor. This same technology has virtually eliminated the quality of muscular strength as a criterion for filling most jobs, while intensifying American industry's need for creative intelligence. In view of this new industrial revolution created by automation in the mid-twentieth century, women can and must participate in old and new fields of society in full equality—or become permanent outsiders.

Despite all the talk about the status of American women in recent years, the actual position of women in the United States has declined, and is declining, to an alarming degree throughout the 1950's and 60's. Although 46.4% of all American women between the ages of 18 and 65 now work outside the home, the overwhelming majority—75%—are in routine clerical, sales, or factory jobs, or they are household workers, cleaning women, hospital attendants. About two-thirds of Negro women workers are in the lowest paid service occupations. Working women are becoming increasingly—not less—concentrated on the bottom of the job ladder. As a consequence full-time women workers today earn on the average only 60% of what men earn, and that wage gap has been increasing over the past twenty-five years in every major industry group. In 1964, of all women with a yearly income, 89% earned under $5,000 a year; half of all full-time year round women workers earned less than $3,690; only 1.4% of full-time year round women workers had an annual income of $10,000 or more.

Further, with higher education increasingly essential in today's society, too few women are entering and finishing college or going on to graduate or professional school. Today, women earn only one in three of the B.A.'s and M.A.'s granted, and one in ten of the Ph.D.'s.

10 In all the professions considered of importance to society, and in the executive ranks of industry and government, women are losing ground. Where they are present it is only a token handful. Women comprise less than 1% of federal judges; less than 4% of all lawyers; 7% of doctors. Yet women represent 51% of the U.S. population. And, increasingly, men are replacing women in the top positions in secondary and elementary schools, in social work, and in libraries—once thought to be women's fields. . . .

WE DO NOT ACCEPT the token appointment of a few women to high-level positions in government and industry as a substitute for serious continuing effort to recruit and advance women according to their individual abilities. To this end, we urge American government and industry to mobilize the same resources of ingenuity and command with which they have solved problems of far greater difficulty than those now impeding the progress of women.

WE BELIEVE that this nation has a capacity at least as great as other nations, to innovate new social institutions which will enable women to enjoy the true equality of opportunity and responsibility in society, without conflict with their responsibilities as mothers and homemakers. In such innovations, America does not lead the Western world, but lags by decades behind many European countries. We do not accept the traditional assumption that a woman has to choose between marriage and motherhood, on the one hand, and serious participation in industry or the professions on the other. We question the present expectation that all normal women will retire from job or profession for 10 or 15 years, to devote their full time to raising children, only to reenter the job market at a relatively minor level. This, in itself, is a deterrent to the aspirations of women, to their acceptance into management or professional training courses, and to the very possibility of equality of opportunity or real choice, for all but a few women. Above all, we reject the assumption that these problems are the unique responsibility of each individual woman, rather than a basic social dilemma which society must solve. True equality of opportunity and freedom of choice for women requires such practical, and possible innovations as a nationwide network of child-care centers, which will make it unnecessary for women to retire completely from society until their children are grown, and national programs to provide retraining for women who have chosen to care for their children full-time. . . .

WE REJECT the current assumptions that a man must carry the sole burden of supporting himself, his wife, and family, and that a woman is automatically entitled to lifelong support by a man upon her marriage, or that marriage, home and family are primarily woman's world and responsibility—hers, to dominate—his to support. We believe that a true partnership between the sexes demands a different concept of marriage, an equitable sharing of the responsibilities of home and children and of the economic burdens of their support. We believe that proper recognition should be given to the economic and social value of homemaking and child-care. To these ends, we will seek to open a reexamination of laws and mores governing marriage and divorce, for we believe that the current state of "half-equity" between the sexes discriminates against both men and women, and is the cause of much unnecessary hostility between the sexes.

WE BELIEVE that women must now exercise their political rights and responsibilities as American citizens. They must refuse to be segregated on the basis of sex into separate-and-not-equal ladies' auxiliaries in the political parties, and they must demand representation according to their numbers in the regularly constituted party committees—at local, state, and national levels—and in the informal power structure, participating fully in the selection of candidates and political decision-making, and running for office themselves.

15 IN THE INTERESTS OF THE HUMAN DIGNITY OF WOMEN, we will protest, and endeavor to change, the false image of women now prevalent in the mass media, and in the texts, ceremonies, laws, and practices of our major social institutions. Such images perpetuate contempt for women by society and by women for themselves. We are similarly opposed to all policies and practices—in church, state, college, factory, or office—which, in the guise of protectiveness, not only deny opportunities but also foster in women self-denigration, dependence, and evasion of responsibility, undermine their confidence in their own abilities and foster contempt for women. . . .

WE BELIEVE THAT women will do most to create a new image of women by acting now, and by speaking out in behalf of their own equality, freedom, and human dignity—not in pleas for special privilege, nor in enmity toward men, who are also victims of the current, half-equality between the sexes—but in an active, self-respecting partnership with men. By so doing, women will develop confidence in their own ability to determine actively, in partnership with men, the conditions of their life, their choices, their future and their society.

1966

For Discussion and Writing

1. Much of this document presents statistical information meant to illustrate gender-based inequalities. Would this argument technique—appeals to logic and mathematical evidence—have been effective in 1848?
2. The women's rights movement and NOW have been portrayed by some media commentators as overly aggressive, unreasonable, and hostile to the

conventions of marriage and children. What, if anything, in this document might lead those commentators to such conclusions?

3. How does Friedan attempt to balance the issues of family and work for women? Are the expectations placed on business and government reasonable ones?
4. On its web site, NOW precedes this document with a disclaimer: "This is a historical document . . . [t]he words are those of the 1960s, and do not reflect current language or NOW's current priorities." What sections of the document might be the main motivation for the group to disclaim in this way?
5. In the Statement, Betty Friedan asks the audience to compare the social standing of women to that of Black Americans, who in 1966 were also struggling to gain full equality. What specific aspects of the American Dream were both groups clamoring for most vocally?

Trail of Broken Treaties—20-Point Proposal

AMERICAN INDIAN MOVEMENT

In 1972, several Indian groups from the U.S. and Canada, including the American Indian Movement (AIM), formed a caravan that traveled from the American West to Washington, D.C., where the travelers presented the proposal they had drafted along their journey. When the U.S. government failed to treat the proposal seriously, the caravan's members took over the Bureau of Indian Affairs (BIA) building and held it for six days, gathering national media attention for their cause and for the complaints articulated in this excerpt from the Proposal.

We want to have a new RELATIONSHIP with you . . . an HONEST one!

"TRAIL OF BROKEN TREATIES": FOR RENEWAL OF CONTRACTS—RECONSTRUCTION OF INDIAN COMMUNITIES & SECURING AN INDIAN FUTURE IN AMERICA!

RESTORATION OF CONSTITUTIONAL TREATY-MAKING AUTHORITY

The U.S. President should propose by executive message, and the Congress should consider and enact legislation, to repeal the provision in the 1871 Indian Appropriations Act which withdrew federal recognition from Indian Tribes and Nations as political entities, which could be contracted by treaties with the United States, in order that the President may resume the exercise of his full constitutional authority for acting in the matters of Indian Affairs—and in order that Indian Nations may represent their own interests in the manner and method envisioned and provided in the Federal Constitution.

ESTABLISHMENT OF TREATY COMMISSION TO MAKE NEW TREATIES

The President should impanel and the Congress establish, within next year, a Treaty Commission to contract a security and assistance treaty of treaties, with Indian people to negotiate a national commitment to the future of Indian people for the last quarter of the Twentieth Century. Authority should be granted to allow tribes to contract by separate and individual treaty, multi-tribal or regional groupings or national collective, respecting general or limited subject matter and provide that no provisions of existing treaty agreements may be withdrawn or in any manner affected without the explicit consent and agreement of any particularly related Indian Nation.

COMMISSION TO REVIEW TREATY COMMITMENTS & VIOLATIONS

The President should immediately create a multi-lateral, Indian and non-Indian Commission to review domestic treaty commitments and complaints of chronic violations and to recommend or act for corrective actions including the imposition of mandatory sanctions or interim restraints upon violative activities, and including formulation of legislation designed to protect the jeopardized Indian rights and eliminate the unending patterns of prohibitively complex lawsuits and legal defenses—which habitually have produced indecisive and interment results, only too frequently forming guidelines for more court battles, or additional challenges and attacks against Indian rights. (Indians have paid attorneys and lawyers more than $40,000,000 since 1962. Yet many Indian people are virtually imprisoned in the nation's courtrooms in being forced constantly to defend their rights, while many tribes are forced to maintain a multitude of suits in numerous jurisdictions relating to the same or a single issue, or a few similar issues. There is less need for more attorney assurances than there is for institution of protections that reduce violations and minimize the possibilities for attacks upon Indian rights.)

LAND REFORM AND RESTORATION OF A 110-MILLION ACRE NATIVE LAND BASE

The next Congress and Administration should commit themselves 5
and effect a national commitment implemented by statutes or executive and administrative actions, to restore a permanent non-diminishing Native American land base of not less than 110-million acres by July 4, 1976. This land base and its separate parts, should be vested with the recognized rights and conditions of being perpetually non-taxable except by autonomous and sovereign Indian authority, and should never again be permitted to be alienated from Native American or Indian ownership and control.

A. Priorities In Restoration of the Native American Land Base

When Congress acted to delimit the President's authority and the Indian Nations' powers for making treaties in 1871, approximately 135,000,000 acres of land and territory had been secured to Indian ownership against cession or relinquishment. This acreage did not include the 1867 treaty-secured recognition of land title and rights of Alaskan Natives, nor millions of acres otherwise retained by Indians in what were to become "unrelated" treaties of Indian land cession as in California; nor other land areas authorized to be set aside for Indian Nations contracted by, but never benefiting from their treaties. When the Congress, in 1887, under the General Allotment Act and other measures of the period and "single system of legislation," delegated treaty-assigned Presidential responsibilities to the Secretary of the Interior and his Commissioner of Indian Affairs and agents in the Bureau of Indian Affairs, relating to the government of Indian relations under the treaties for the 135 million acres, collectively held, immediately became subject to loss. The 1887 Act provided for the sale of "surplus" Indian lands—and contained a formula for the assignment or allocation of land tracts to Indian individuals, dependent partly on family size, which would have allowed an average-sized allotment of 135 acres to one million Indians—at a time when the number of tribally-related Indians was less than a quarter million or fewer than 200,000. The Interior Department efficiently managed the loss of 100-million acres of Indian land, and its transfer to non-Indian ownership (frequently by homestead, not direct purchase) in little more then the next quarter century. When Congress prohibited further allotments to Indian individuals, by its 1934 Indian Reorganization Act, it effectively determined that future generations of Indian people would be "land-less Indians" except by heirship and inheritance. . . .

D. Repeal of the Menominee, Klamath, and Other Termination Acts

The Congress should act immediately to repeal the Termination Acts of the 1950s and 1960s and restore ownership of the several million acres of land to the Indian people involved, perpetually non-alienable and tax-exempt. The Indians' rights to autonomous self-government and sovereign control of their resources and development should be reinstated. Repeal of the terminal legislation would also advance a commitment towards a collective 110-million acre land base for Native Americans—when added to the near 55-million acres already held by Indians, apart from the additional 40-million acres allocated in Alaska. (The impact of termination and its various forms have never been understood fully by the American people, the Congress, and many Indian people. Few wars between nations have ever accomplished as much as the total dispossession of a people of their rights and resources as have the total victories and total surrenders legislated by the Termination Laws. . . .)

REVISION OF 25 U.S.C. 163; RESTORATION OF RIGHTS TO INDIANS TERMINATED BY ENROLLMENT AND REVOCATION OF PROHIBITIONS AGAINST "DUAL BENEFITS" REPEAL OF STATE LAWS ENACTED UNDER PUBLIC LAW 280 (1953)

State enactments under the authority conferred by the Congress In Public Law 280 has posed the most serious threat to Indian sovereignty and local self-government of any measure in recent decades. Congress must now nullify those State statutes. Represented as a "law enforcement" measure, PL280 robs Indian communities of the core of their governing authority and operates to convert reservation areas into refuges from responsibilities, where many people, not restricted by race, can take full advantage of a veritable vacuum of controlling law, or law which commands its first respect for justice by encouraging an absence of offenses. These States' acceptance of condition for their own statehood in their Enabling Acts—that they forever disclaim sovereignty and jurisdiction over Indian lands and Indian people—should be binding upon them and that restrictive condition upon their sovereignty be reinstated. They should not be permitted further to gain from the conflict of interest engaged by such States' participation in enactment of Public Law 280—at the expense of the future of Indian people in their own communities, as well as our present welfare and well-being.

RESUME FEDERAL PROTECTIVE JURISDICTION FOR OFFENSES AGAINST INDIANS

The Congress should enact, the Administration support and seek passage of, new provisions under Titles 18 and 25 of the U.S. Code, which shall extend the protective jurisdiction of the United States over Indian persons wherever situated in its territory and the territory of the several States, outside of Indian Reservations or Country, and provide the prescribed offenses of violence against Indian persons shall be federal crimes, punishable by prescribed penalties through prosecutions in the federal judiciary, and enforced in arrest actions by the Federal Bureau of Investigation. U.S. Marshals, and other commissioned police agents of the United States—who shall be compelled to act upon the commission of such crimes, and upon any written complaint or sworn request alleging an offense, which by itself would be deemed probable cause for arresting actions.

ABOLITION OF THE BUREAU OF INDIAN AFFAIRS BY 1976

A New Structure: The Congress working through the proposed 10
Senate-House "Joint Committee on Reconstruction of Indian Relations and Programs," in formulation of an Indian Community Reconstruction Act should direct that the Bureau of Indian Affairs shall be abolished as an agency on or before July 4, 1976; to provide for an alternative structure of government for sustaining and revitalizing the Indian-federal relationship between the President and

the Congress of the United States, respectively, and the respective Indian Nations and Indian people at last consistent with constitutional criteria, national treaty commitments, and Indian sovereignty, and provide for transformation and transition into the new system as rapidly as possible prior to abolition of the BIA. . . . The Congress, with assent of the Courts, has developed its constitutional mandate to "regulate Indian commerce" into a doctrine of absolute control and total power over the lives of Indians—through failing to give these concerns the time and attention that the responsibilities of such power demand. The Congress restricted the highest authority of the President for dealing with Indian matters and affairs, then abandoned Indian people to the lowest levels of bureaucratic government for administration of its part-time care and asserted all-powerful control. The constitution maintained Indian people in citizenship and allegiance to our own Nations, but the Congress and the Bureau of Indian Affairs has converted this constitutional standard into the most bastardized forms of acknowledged autonomy and "sovereign self-governing control"—scarcely worthy of the terms, if remaining divested of their meaning.

PROTECTION OF INDIANS' RELIGIOUS FREEDOM AND CULTURAL INTEGRITY

The Congress shall proclaim its insistence that the religious freedom and cultural integrity of Indian people shall be respected and protected throughout the United States, and provide that Indian religion and culture, even in regenerating or renaissance or developing stages, or when manifested in the personal character and treatment of one's own body, shall not be interfered with, disrespected, or denied. (No Indian shall be forced to cut their hair by any institution or public agency or official, including military authorities or prison regulation, for example.) It should be an insistence by Congress that implies strict penalty for its violation.

HEALTH, HOUSING, EMPLOYMENT, ECONOMIC DEVELOPMENT, AND EDUCATION

The Congress and Administration and proposed Indian Community Reconstruction Office must allow for the most creative, if demanding and disciplined forms of community development and purposeful initiatives. The proposed $15,000,000,000 budget for the 1970s remainder could provide for completed construction of

100,000 now housing units; create more than 100,000 new permanent, income and tribal revenue-producing jobs on reservations and lay foundation for as many more in years following; meet all the economic and industrial development needs of numerous communities; and make education at all levels, and provide health services or medical care to all Indians as a matter of entitlement and fulfilled right. Yet, we now find most Indians unserved and programs not keeping pace with growing problems under a billion dollar plus budget annually—approximately a service cost of $10,000 per reservation Indian family per year, or $100,000 in this decade. Our fight is not over a $50-million cutback in a mismanaged and misdirected budget, and cannot be ended with restoration of that then invisible amount—but over the part that it, any and all amounts, have come to play in a perennial billion-dollar indignity upon the lives of Indian people, our aged, our young, our parents, and our children. Death remains a standard cure for environmentally induced diseases afflicting many Indian children without adequate housing facilities, heating systems, and pure water sources. Their delicate bodies provide their only defense and protection—and too often their own body processes become allies to the quickening of their deaths as with numerous cases of dysentery and diarrhea. Still, more has been spent on hotel bills for Indian-related problem-solving meetings, conferences, and conventions, than has been spent on needed housing in recent years. More is being spent from federal and tribal fund sources on such decision-making activities than is being committed to assist but two-thirds of Indian college students having desperate financial need. Rather, few decisions are made, and less problems solved, because there has developed an insensitivity to conscience which has eliminated basic standards of accountability. Indian communities have been fragmented in governmental, social, and constitutional functions as they have become restructured or destructured to accommodate the fragmentation in governmental programming and contradictions in federal policies. There is a need to reintegrate these functions into the life and fabric of the communities. . . .

1972

For Discussion and Writing

1. How might the level and style of language in this document be described? Why do you suppose the document was written this way?

2. The authors provide extensive details and examples to support and illustrate their grievances—but what core issues keep reappearing as the list of grievances unfolds?
3. This document was presented in 1972, at a time when the Vietnam War, Civil Rights, youth unrest, and many other social upheavals were taking place at once. To what extent do you think this cultural background affected the Federal government's refusal to take the Indians seriously and try to work with their requests?
4. How many aspects of an American Dream does this document identify as missing from American Indian lives? Do the authors want the "classic" Dream, or does their version of it differ?
5. Compare this document to the "Black Panther Party Platform and Program" in this chapter. In how many ways do the grievances and demands of the BPP align with those of AIM?

America

Dr. Tolbert Small

The great-grandson of a slave, Dr. Tolbert Small was born in rural Mississippi and raised in the Black Bottom section of Detroit. Having encountered blatant quota racism as a minority in his medical education, Dr. Small joined the Black Panther Party in 1968 and served as the group's physician for three years. At the urging of BPP co-founder Bobby Seale, Dr. Small headed the group's Sickle Cell Anemia Foundation; later he founded and ran the Harriet Tubman Clinic in East Oakland, California, a position that has allowed him to speak out on behalf of the millions of Americans who lack sufficient health insurance.

✦

America

We are America:
We who mop the floors,
We who pick the cotton,
We who farm the valleys.

We are America:
The sharecropper who plowed his mule,
The ironworker who forged his steel,
The women who bore our children.

We are America:
    The Chinese men who built the railroads,
    The Yiddish men who passed through Ellis Island,
    The Redmen who lived here first.

We are America:
    The slaves who chopped and picked your cotton,
    The Black faces who nursed your babies and scrubbed
      your floors.
    Though we were the other America,
We are still America.

We are America:
    We pray to Christ,
    We pray to Allah,
    We pray to Jehovah,
    We pray for humanity.

We are America.

2000

For Discussion and Writing

1. The fourth stanza of this poem mentions the "other America." Is the entire poem only in tribute to those who are marginalized?
2. By ending the poem with repetition of the words "we pray," what does the poet accomplish in advancing his message?
3. Which lines of the poem are especially well connected to Dr. Small's role in championing those without adequate health care?
4. If the poem were to include a line about you or your family, how would it read? Why would that line be significant in showing your role as part of America?

Chapter 2: For Further Research and Writing

1. How do the depictions of an American Dream differ in this chapter from those in Chapter 1—Founders' Dream/Dreamers Found? Given the passage of time from the original conception and creation of a new separate nation and the times covered by this chapter, how has the Dream shifted and taken new form? Could the original founders have envisioned these changes? Did their documents and ideas aid, or inhibit, a gradual widening of the Dream's

meaning to appeal to those who had previously been considered only peripheral to the idea of America?

2. Focusing on one of the many groups represented by these readings, find two additional documents written around the same time on the same issue (e.g. ending slavery, creating equal rights for women) that express differing viewpoints to those expressed here. How do those writers construct their arguments in contrast to the techniques and strategies shown in the writings from this chapter? Placing yourself as a participant in the issue's debate at the time, which side would you find more convincing based on its presentation of the argument?
3. As with Chapter 1, trace one of the themes of the American Dream as represented by a writer in this chapter. Has the Dream been made accessible since the time of writing? Fully, partially, or even less so than before? What has happened since the time of writing to create the current state of this issue for these groups or individuals?
4. Plan a research project around the American Indian Movement (AIM) and the Black Panther Party to track each group's origins and its overall conflict with the United States government. What was it about each group that the government found most threatening? What could these groups have done differently in order to be received with less hostility? Consider other political groups that have been more successful at creating lasting changes of attitudes and practices: given their success, what would you say should be the most important considerations when speaking truth to power?

CHAPTER 3

Streets Paved With Gold

Most civilizations have cherished "origin" stories, passed down through the ages, that establish a people's special status apart from other nations. The many tribes of indigenous peoples had such stories about the land now called the United States of America long before any white people set foot on its shores. Generations of Penobscot Indians learned that the Great Spirit made the land they were born on especially for them, and that they were his chosen people. When word began to spread across Europe of a bountiful, ostensibly uninhabited land across the sea, the symbolic "new world" took shape as hope for a better life to hundreds of millions of people.

As immigrants arrived and established themselves, they wrote to relatives in the old country about the "land of milk and honey," where anyone who worked hard could become rich. Everyone heard the fabulous rags-to-riches tales like that of Andrew Carnegie, who came to the United States from Scotland at age 13. Soon after his arrival he went to work in a factory for $1.20 a week, and eventually he became the richest man in the world. Such stories gave hope to the "huddled masses yearning to breathe free," in the words of poet Emma Lazarus.

Africans did not come to America willingly of course, but the descendants of slaves sought the same American Dream as immigrants who chose to come. As Reconstruction failed in the South and Jim Crow law took hold, black Americans moved north in search of better jobs, schools, and homes in a movement known as the Great Migration.

Americans—native-born and immigrant alike—have generally assumed that all are equally free to achieve their dreams of economic and social success if they work diligently. This belief forms the bedrock of American ideology, but the waking reality of America has never been as golden as the dream.

The following selections provide personal stories and theories that illuminate the many ways in which people pursue and view the American Dream. They are arranged chronologically, though discerning readers will find thematic threads. Few of the writers in this chapter explicitly refer to the founders' ideals, for instance, but the inherent promises of the Declaration of Independence loom large in the hopes and expectations of many, if not all, of these writers. As you read these selections, notice the variety of forms the American Dream takes, as well as the similarities. How might these writers define their American Dream? Do any of them critique it?

From *A New Home—Who'll Follow?*

Caroline Kirkland

Difficult as it is to imagine today, in the early years of the republic, the states of Kentucky, Ohio, and Michigan were frontier territory, vast and uncharted. Offers of cheap land fed the desires of many whites to move away from the increasingly crowded eastern seaboard to seek their fortunes.

William and Caroline Kirkland, an educated couple from New York City, were lured by the seemingly limitless possibilities of the west, and moved to the frontier town of Detroit in 1835. Two years later, they purchased 800 acres in southeastern Michigan territory and founded the town of Pinckney. Their new life provided rich material for Caroline's book, which was published to popular acclaim—and insulted her neighbors—in 1839. Kirkland's book provides an unusually intimate glimpse of the day-to-day lives of well-to-do Easterners who struck out for the wilderness.

When we first took our delighted abode in the "framed house," a palace of some twenty by thirty feet, flanked by a shanty kitchen, and thatched with oak shingles,—a sober neighbor, who having passed most of his life in the country, is extremely philosophical on the follies of civilization, took my husband to task on the appearance of the ghost of a departed parlor carpet, which he said was "introducing luxury." Whether from this bad example, I cannot tell, but it is certain that our neighbors are many of them beginning to perceive that carpets "save trouble." Women are the most reasonable beings in the world; at least, I am sure nobody ever catches a woman without an unanswerable reason for anything she wishes to do. Mrs. Micah Balwhidder only wanted a silver tea pot, because, as all the world knows, tea tastes better out of silver; and Mrs. Primrose loved her crimson paduasoy, merely because her husband had happened to say it became her.

Of the mingled mass of our country population, a goodly and handsome proportion—goodly as to numbers, and handsome as to cheeks and lips, and thews and sinews, consists of young married people just beginning the world; simple in their habits, moderate in their aspirations, and hoarding a little of old-fashioned romance, unconsciously enough, in the secret nooks of their rustic hearts. These find no fault with their bare loggeries. With a shelter and a handful of furniture they have enough. If there is the wherewithal to spread a warm supper for "th' old man" when he comes in from work, the young wife forgets the long, solitary, *wordless* day, and asks no greater happiness than preparing it by the help of such materials and such utensils as would be looked at with utter contempt in a comfortable kitchen; and then the youthful pair sit down and enjoy it together, with a zest that the *"orgies parfaites"* of the epicure can never awaken. What lack they that this world can bestow? They have youth, and health, and love and hope, occupation and amusement, and when you have added "meat, clothes, and fire," what more has England's fair young queen? These people are contented, of course.

There is another class of settlers neither so numerous nor so happy; people, who have left small farms in the eastward States, and come to Michigan with the hope of acquiring property at a more rapid rate. They have sold off, perhaps at considerable pecuniary disadvantage the home of their early married life; sacrificed the convenient furniture which had become necessary to daily comfort, and only awake when it is too late, to the fact that it kills old vines to tear them from their clinging-places. These people are much to be pitied, the women especially.

> The ladies first
> 'Gin murmur—as becomes the softer sex.

Woman's little world is overclouded for lack of the old familiar means and appliances. The husband goes to his work with the same axe or hoe which fitted his hand in his old woods and fields, he tills the same soil, or perhaps a far richer and more hopeful one—he gazes on the same book of nature which he has read from his infancy, and sees only a fresher and more glowing page; and he returns to his home with the sun, strong in heart and full of self-congratulation on the favorable change in his lot. But he finds the home-bird drooping and disconsolate. *She* has been looking in vain for the reflection of any of the cherished features of her own dear fire-side. She has found a thousand deficiencies which her rougher mate can scarce be taught to feel as evils. What cares he if the time honored cupboard is meagerly represented by a few oak-boards lying on pegs and called shelves? His tea-equipage shines as it was wont—the biscuits can hardly stay on the brightly glistening plates. Will he find fault with the clay-built oven, or even the tin "reflector"? His bread never was better baked. What does he want with the great old cushioned rocking-chair? When he is tired he goes to bed, for he is never tired till bed-time. Women are the grumblers in Michigan, and they have some apology. Many of them have made sacrifices for which they were not at all prepared, and which detract largely from their every day stores of comfort. The conviction of good accruing on a large scale does not prevent the wearing sense of minor deprivations.

5 Another large class of emigrants is composed of people of broken fortunes, or who have been unsuccessful in past undertakings. These like or dislike the country on various grounds, as their peculiar condition may vary. Those who are fortunate or industrious look at their new home with a kindly eye. Those who learn by experience that idlers are no better off in Michigan than elsewhere, can find no term too virulent in which to express their angry disappointment. The profligate and unprincipled lead stormy and uncomfortable lives anywhere; and Michigan, *now* at least, begins to regard such characters among her adopted children, with a stern and unfriendly eye, so that the few who may have come among us, hoping for the unwatched and unbridled license which we read of in regions nearer to the setting sun, find themselves marked and shunned as in the older world.

As women feel sensibly the deficiencies of the "salvage" state, so they are the first to attempt the refining process, the introduction of those important nothings on which so much depends. Small additions to the more delicate or showy part of the household gear are accomplished by the aid of some little extra personal exertion. "Spinning money" buys a looking-glass perhaps, or "butter money" a nice cherry table. Eglantines and wood-vine, or wild-cucumber, are sought and transplanted to shade the windows. Narrow beds round the house are bright with balsams and Sweet Williams, four o'clocks, poppies and marigolds; and if "th' old man" is good natured, a little gate takes the place of the great awkward *bars* before the door. By and bye a few apple-trees are set out; sweet briars grace the door yard, and lilacs and currant-bushes; all by female effort—at least I have never yet happened to see it otherwise where these improvements have been made at all. They are not all accomplished by her own hand indeed, but hers is the moving spirit, and if she do her "spiriting gently," and has anything but a Caliban for a minister, she can scarcely fail to throw over the real homeliness of her lot something of the magic of that IDEAL which has been truly sung—

> Nymph of our soul, and brightener of our being;
> She makes the common waters musical—
> Binds the rude night-winds in a silver thrall,
> Bids Hybla's thyme and Tempe's violet dwell
> Round the green marge of her moon-haunted cell.

• • •

This shadowy power, or power of shadows, is the "arch-vanquisher of time and care" every where; but most of all needed in the waveless calm of a strictly woodland life, and there most enjoyed. The lovers of "unwritten poetry" may find it in the daily talk of our rustic neighbors—in their superstitions—in the remedies which they propose for every ill of humanity, the ideal makes the charm of their life as it does that of all the world's, peer and poet, woodcutter and serving-maid.

After allowing due weight to the many disadvantages and trials of a new-country life, it would scarce be fair to pass without notice the compensating power of a feeling, inherent as I believe, in our universal nature, which rejoices in that freedom from the restraints of pride and ceremony which is found only in a new country. To borrow from a brilliant writer of our own, "I think we have an instinct, dulled by civilization, which is like the caged eaglet's, or the antelope's that is reared in the Arab's tent; an instinct of nature that scorns boundary and chain; that yearns to the free desert; that would have the earth like the sky, unappropriated and open; that rejoices in immeasurable liberty of foot and dwelling-place, and springs passionately back to its freedom, even after years of subduing method and spirit-breaking confinement!"

This "instinct," so beautifully noticed by Willis, is what I would point to as the compensating power of the wilderness. Those who are "to the manor born" feel this most sensibly, and pity with all their simple hearts the walled-up denizens of the city. And the transplanted ones—those who have been used to no forests but "forests of chimneys," though "the parted bosom clings to wonted home," soon learn to think nature no step-mother, and to discover many redeeming points even in the half-wild state at first so uncongenial.

10 That this love of unbounded and *unceremonious* liberty is a natural and universal feeling, needs no argument to show; I am only applying it on a small scale to the novel condition in which I find myself in the woods of Michigan. I ascribe much of the placid contentment, which seems the heritage of rural life, to the constant familiarity with woods and waters—

> All that the genial ray of morning gilds,
> And all that echoes to the song of even;
> All the mountain's sheltering bosom yields,
> And all the dread magnificence of heaven—

To the harmony which the Creator has instituted between the animate and inanimate works of His hands.

Authorities crowd upon me, and I must be allowed to close my chapter with a favorite paragraph from Hazlitt.

> "The heart reposes in greater security on the immensity of Nature's works, expatiates freely there, and finds elbow-room and breathing-space. We are always at home with Nature. There is neither hypocrisy, caprice, nor mental reservation in her favors. Our intercourse with her is not liable to accident or change, suspicion or disappointment: she smiles on us still the same . . . In our love of Nature, there is all the force of individual attachment, combined with the most airy abstraction. It is this circumstance which gives that refinement, expansion and wild interest to feelings of this sort . . . Thus Nature is a sort of universal home, and every object it presents to us is an old acquaintance, with unaltered looks; for there is that constant and mutual harmony among all her works—one undivided spirit pervading them throughout—that to him who has well acquainted himself with them, they speak always the same well-known language, striking on the heart

amidst unquiet thoughts and the tumult of the world, like the music of one's native tongue, heard in some far off country."

1839

For Discussion and Writing

1. Examine the words Kirkland uses to describe her "framed house." What does her tone suggest about her attitude toward her new home?
2. According to Kirkland, what is the difference between men's and women's perceptions of frontier life and their hopes for the future?
3. What is the purpose of the paragraph that Kirkland quotes at the end of her chapter? What is the effect of closing with someone else's words, rather than her own?
4. In an essay, use Frederick Jackson Turner's frontier thesis (elsewhere in this chapter) to interpret Kirkland's experiences. Is Kirkland's first-hand account capable of illustrating or disproving Turner's thesis? In what ways does Turner help readers understand Kirkland, or vice versa?

The New Colossus

EMMA LAZARUS

The child of Portuguese Jewish immigrants, Emma Lazarus studied literature from an early age, and became an accomplished poet and noted translator of Goethe and other European writers. When large numbers of Jewish immigrants began to emigrate from Eastern Europe to America, driven out of their homelands by waves of pogroms, Lazarus became active in teaching the new immigrants. Lazarus is best remembered for her 1883 poem, "The New Colossus," inscribed at the Statue of Liberty in 1903. Its famous words—"Give me your tired, your poor/Your huddled masses yearning to breathe free"—have long represented America's invitation to immigrants, even when anti-immigration sentiment prevails.

Not like the brazen giant of Greek fame,
With conquering limbs astride from land to land;
Here at our sea-washed, sunset gates shall stand
A mighty woman with a torch, whose flame
Is the imprisoned lightning, and her name

Mother of Exiles. From her beacon-hand
Glows world-wide welcome; her mild eyes command
The air-bridged harbor that twin cities frame.
"Keep ancient lands, your storied pomp!" cries she
With silent lips. "Give me your tired, your poor,
Your huddled masses yearning to breathe free,
The wretched refuse of your teeming shore.
Send these, the homeless, tempest-tost to me,
I lift my lamp beside the golden door!"

1883

For Discussion and Writing

1. What implied promises does "The New Colossus" make?
2. What is a colossus? What does Lazarus mean by the "new" colossus?
3. To what extent does America act on the values of Lazarus' poem? Find examples from newspapers or internet news sites that show a variety of ways that Americans greet newcomers.
4. See the readings by Calvin Trillin and Richard Rodriguez elsewhere in this chapter. Would Trillin's father see himself as one of the huddled masses? Would Rodriquez? In an essay, compare the primary image of the poor, tired immigrant in Lazarus' poem with a variety of contemporary immigrant groups.
5. To what extent does the invitation of "The New Colossus" apply to African Americans? To American Indians?

From "The Road to Business Success: A Talk to Young Men"

ANDREW CARNEGIE

After his family emigrated from Scotland to Pennsylvania in 1848, 13 year-old Andrew Carnegie found work as a bobbin boy in a cotton mill. Moving up in the work world, at age 30 Carnegie launched the Pittsburgh steel industry after founding the Carnegie Steel Company. At one time, Carnegie was the richest man in the world, but he was the first prominent industrialist to argue that the rich have a moral obligation to give away their money to charitable causes. He lived by his own words; perhaps his most enduring legacy was funding free public libraries across the country, many of which are still operating.

Andrew Carnegie personified the American Dream, having risen from poverty to great wealth, power, and fame, according to his own account, by working his way up from the very bottom of the business ladder. In the tradition of Benjamin Franklin, Carnegie offered his own life story as an example of how others could achieve the success he enjoyed. The talk excerpted below, widely reprinted, was first delivered to students at Pittsburgh's Curry Commercial College in 1885.

It is well that young men should begin at the beginning and occupy the most subordinate positions. Many of the leading business men of Pittsburgh had a serious responsibility thrust upon them at the very threshold of their career. They were introduced to the broom, and spent the first hours of their business lives sweeping out the office. I notice we have janitors and janitresses now in offices, and our young men unfortunately miss that salutary branch of a business education. But if by chance the professional sweeper is absent any morning the boy who has the genius of the future partner in him will not hesitate to try his hand at the broom. The other day a fond fashionable mother in Michigan asked a young man whether he had ever seen a young lady sweep in a room so grandly as her Priscilla. He said no, he never had, and the mother was gratified beyond measure, but then said he, after a pause, "What I should like to see her do is sweep out a room." It does not hurt the newest comer to sweep out the office if necessary. I was one of those sweepers myself. . . .

Assuming that you have all obtained employment and are fairly started, my advice to you is "aim high." I would not give a fig for the young man who does not already see himself the partner or the head of an important firm. Do not rest content for a moment in your thoughts as head clerk, or foreman, or general manager in any concern, no matter how extensive. Say each to yourself, "My place is at the top." *Be king in your dreams.* Make your vow that you will reach that position, with untarnished reputation, and make no other vow to distract your attention, except the very commendable one that when you are a member of the firm or before that, if you have been promoted two or three times, you will form another partnership with the loveliest of her sex—a partnership to which our new partnership act has no application. The liability there is never limited.

Let me indicate two or three conditions essential to success. Do not be afraid that I am going to moralize, or inflict a homily upon you. I speak upon the subject only from the view of a man of the world, desirous of aiding you to become successful business men. You all know that there is no genuine, praiseworthy success in life if you are not honest, truthful, fair-dealing. I assume you are and will remain all these, and also that you are determined to live pure, respectable lives, free from pernicious or equivocal associations with one sex or the other. There is no creditable future for you else. Otherwise your learning and your advantages not only go for naught, but serve to accentuate your failure and your disgrace. I hope you will not take it amiss if I warn you against three of the gravest dangers which will beset you in your upward path.

The first and most seductive, and the destroyer of most young men, is the drinking of liquor. I am no temperance lecturer in disguise, but a man who knows and tells you what observation has proved to him, and I say to you that you are more likely to fail in your career from acquiring the habit of drinking liquor than from any, or all, the other temptations likely to assail you. You may yield to almost any other temptation and reform—may brace up, and if not recover lost ground, at least remain in the race and secure and maintain a respectable position. But from the insane thirst for liquor escape is almost impossible. I have known but few exceptions to this rule. First, then, you must not drink liquor to excess. Better if you do not touch it at all—much better; but if this be too hard a rule for you then take your stand firmly here. Resolve never to touch it except at meals. A glass at dinner will not hinder your advance in life or lower your tone; but I implore you hold it inconsistent with the dignity and self-respect of gentlemen, with what is due from yourselves to yourselves, being the men you are, and especially the men you are determined to become, to drink a glass of liquor at a bar. Be far too much of the gentleman ever to enter a barroom. You do not pursue your careers in safety unless you stand firmly upon this ground. Adhere to it and you have escaped danger from the deadliest of your foes. . . .

5 Hundreds of young men were tempted in this city not long since to gamble in oil, and many were ruined; all were injured whether they lost or won. You may be, nay, you are certain to be similarly tempted; but when so tempted I hope you will remember this advice. Say to the tempter who asks you to risk your small savings, that if ever you decide to speculate you are determined to go to a regular and well-conducted house where they cheat fair.

You can get fair play and about an equal chance upon the red and black in such a place; upon the Exchange you have neither. You might as well try your luck with the three-card-monte man. There is another point involved in speculation. Nothing is more essential to young business men than untarnished credit, credit begotten of confidence in their prudence, principles and stability of character. Well, believe me, nothing kills credit sooner in any Bank Board than the knowledge that either firms or men engage in speculation. It matters not a whit whether gains or losses be the temporary result of these operations. The moment a man is known to speculate, his credit is impaired, and soon thereafter it is gone. . . . Resolve to be business men, but speculators never.

The third and last danger against which I shall warn you is one which has wrecked many a fair craft which started well and gave promise of a prosperous voyage. It is the perilous habit of indorsing—all the more dangerous, inasmuch as it assails one generally in the garb of friendship. It appeals to your generous instincts, and you say, "How can I refuse to lend my name only, to assist a friend?" It is because there is so much that is true and commendable in that view that the practice is so dangerous. Let me endeavor to put you upon safe honourable grounds in regard to it. I would say to you to make it a rule now, *never indorse*: but this is too much like never taste wine, or never smoke, or any other of the "nevers." They generally result in exceptions. . . . Mark you then, never indorse until you have cash means not required for your own debts, and never indorse beyond those means. Before you indorse at all, consider indorsements as gifts, and ask yourselves whether you wish to make the gift to your friend and whether the money is really yours to give and not a trust for your creditors. . . .

Assuming you are safe in regard to these your gravest dangers, the question now is how to rise from the subordinate position we have imagined you in, through the successive grades to the position for which you are, in my opinion, and, I trust, in your own, evidently intended. I can give you the secret. It lies mainly in this. Instead of the question, "What must I do for my employer?" substitute "What can I do?" Faithful and conscientious discharge of the duties assigned you is all very well, but the verdict in such cases generally is that you perform your present duties so well that you had better continue performing them. Now, young gentlemen, this will not do. It will not do for the coming partners. There must be something beyond this. We make Clerks, Bookkeepers, Treasurers,

Bank Tellers of this class, and there they remain to the end of the chapter. The rising man must do something exceptional, and beyond the range of his special department. HE MUST ATTRACT ATTENTION . . . There is no service so low and simple, neither any so high, in which the young man of ability and willing disposition cannot readily and almost daily prove himself capable of greater trust and usefulness, and, what is equally important, show his invincible determination to rise. . . .

There is one sure mark of the coming partner, the future millionaire; his revenues always exceed his expenditures. He begins to save early, almost as soon as he begins to earn. No matter how little it may be possible to save, save that little. Invest it securely, not necessarily in bonds, but in anything which you have good reason to believe will be profitable, but no gambling with it, remember. A rare chance will soon present itself for investment. The little you have saved will prove the basis for an amount of credit utterly surprising to you. Capitalists trust the saving young man. For every hundred dollars you can produce as the result of hard-won savings, Midas, in search of a partner, will lend or credit a thousand; for every thousand, fifty thousand. It is not capital that your seniors require, it is the man who has proved that he has the business habits which create capital, and to create it in the best of all possible ways, as far as self-discipline is concerned, is, by adjusting his habits to his means. Gentlemen, it is the first hundred dollars saved which tells. Begin at once to lay up something. The bee predominates in the future millionaire.

Of course there are better, higher aims than saving. As an end, the acquisition of wealth is ignoble in the extreme; I assume that you save and long for wealth only as a means of enabling you the better to do some good in your day and generation. Make a note of this essential rule: Expenditure always within income.

You may grow impatient, or become discouraged when year by year you float on in subordinate positions. . . . Still, let me tell you for your encouragement, that there is no country in the world, where able and energetic young men can so readily rise as this. . . .

Young men give all kinds of reasons why in their cases failure was clearly attributable to exceptional circumstances which render success impossible. Some never had a chance, according to their own story. This is simply nonsense. No young man ever lived who had not a chance, and a splendid chance, too, if he ever was employed at all. . . . His ability, honesty, habits, associations, temper, disposition, all these are weighed and analysed. The young man who never had a chance is the same young man who has been canvassed over and over again by his superiors, and found destitute of necessary qualifications, or is deemed unworthy of closer relations with the firm, owing to some objectionable act, habit, or association, of which he thought his employers ignorant.

Another class of young men attribute their failure to employers having relations or favourites whom they advanced unfairly. They also insist that their employers disliked brighter intelligences than their own, and were disposed to discourage aspiring genius, and delighted in keeping young men down. There is nothing in this. . . . There is always a boom in brains, cultivate that crop, for if you grow any amount of that commodity, here is your best market and you cannot overstock it, and the more brains you have to sell, the higher price you can exact. . . .

And here is the prime condition of success, the great secret: concentrate your energy, thought, and capital exclusively upon the business in which you are engaged. Having begun in one line, resolve to fight it out on that line, to lead in it; adopt every improvement, have the best machinery, and know the most about it.

The concerns which fail are those which have scattered their capital, which means that they have scattered their brains also. They have investments in this, or that, or the other, here, there and everywhere. "Don't put all your eggs in one basket" is all wrong. I tell you "put all your eggs in one basket, and then watch that basket." Look round you and take notice; men who do that do not often fail. It is easy to watch and carry the one basket. It is trying to carry too many baskets that breaks most eggs in this country. He who carries three baskets must put one on his head, which is apt to tumble and trip him up. One fault of the American business man is lack of concentration. . . .

I congratulate poor young men upon being born to that 15
ancient and honourable degree which renders it necessary that they should devote themselves to hard work. . . . [T]he vast majority of the sons of rich men are unable to resist the temptations to which wealth subjects them, and sink to unworthy lives. I would almost as soon leave a young man a curse, as burden him with the almighty dollar. It is not from this class you have rivalry to fear. The partner's sons will not trouble you much, but look out that some boys poorer, much poorer than yourselves, whose parents cannot afford to give them the advantages of a course in this institute, advantages which should give you a decided lead in the race—look out that such boys do not challenge you at the post and pass you at the grand stand. Look out for the boy who has to

plunge into work direct from the common school and who begins by sweeping out the office. He is the probable dark horse that you had better watch.

1885

For Discussion and Writing

1. According to Carnegie, what are the conditions for business success? How do these conditions reflect the idea of the American Dream? Do these conditions still apply today?
2. What are the rewards of achieving success using Carnegie's advice?
3. According to Carnegie, what are the moral and ethical requirements for a successful business career? Are these requirements outdated? What incentives exist for business people to adhere to Carnegie's conditions?
4. What are the pitfalls of the behaviors Carnegie warns his audience to avoid?
5. If Carnegie's blueprint for rising in the work world represents dominant ideology, how can we explain the success of people or corporations who ignore Carnegie's moral framework?

From "The Significance of the Frontier in American History"

Frederick Jackson Turner

In 1893, at the Chicago World Columbian Exposition, Frederick Jackson Turner delivered a speech still widely considered the defining explanation of the unique arc of American history. For Turner, the existence of free or inexpensive land and westward expansion was the factor that formed the unique American character. Arguing that America had at last reached the end of the frontier in the late eighteenth century, Turner predicted the dawn of a new age, marked at last by an immovable border: the Pacific Ocean. Turner's "frontier thesis" drew little notice when he delivered his speech, but historians continue to debate the merits of his argument.

The frontier is the line of most rapid and effective Americanization. The wilderness masters the colonist. It finds him a European in dress, industries, tools, modes of travel, and thought. It takes him from the railroad car and puts him in the birch canoe. It strips off the garments of civilization and arrays him in the hunting shirt and the moccasin. It puts him in the log cabin of the Cherokee and Iroquois and runs an Indian palisade around him. Before long he has gone to planting Indian corn and plowing with a sharp stick, he shouts the war cry and takes the scalp in orthodox Indian fashion. In short, at the frontier the environment is at first too strong for the man. He must accept the conditions which it furnishes, or perish, and so he fits himself into the Indian clearings and follows the Indian trails. Little by little he transforms the wilderness, but the outcome is not the old Europe, not simply the development of Germanic germs. . . . The fact is, that here is a new product that is American.

The exploitation of the beasts took hunter and trader to the west, the exploitation of the grasses took the rancher west, and the exploitation of the virgin soil of the river valleys and prairies attracted the farmer. Good soils have been the most continuous attraction to the farmer's frontier. The land hunger of the Virginians drew them down the rivers into Carolina, in early colonial days; the search for soils took the Massachusetts men to Pennsylvania and to New York. As the eastern lands were taken up migration flowed across them to the west. Daniel Boone, the great backwoodsman, who combined the occupations of hunter, trader, cattle-raiser, farmer, and surveyor-learning, probably from the traders, of the fertility of the lands of the upper Yadkin, where the traders were wont to rest as they took their way to the Indians, left his Pennsylvania home with his father, and passed down the Great Valley road to that stream. Learning from a trader of the game and rich pastures of Kentucky, he pioneered the way for the farmers to that region. Thence he passed to the frontier of Missouri, where his settlement was long a landmark on the frontier. Here again he helped to open the way for civilization, finding salt licks, and trails, and land. His son was among the earliest trappers in the passes of the Rocky Mountains, and his party are said to have been the first to camp on the present site of Denver. His grandson, Col. A.J. Boone, of Colorado, was a power among the Indians of the Rocky Mountains, and was appointed an agent by the government. Kit Carson's mother was a Boone. Thus this family epitomizes the backwoodsman's advance across the continent. . . .

Obviously the immigrant was attracted by the cheap lands of the frontier, and even the native farmer felt their influence strongly. Year by year the farmers who lived on soil whose returns were diminished by unrotated crops were offered the virgin soil of the frontier at nominal prices. Their growing families demanded more lands, and these were dear. The competition of the unexhausted, cheap, and easily tilled prairie lands compelled the farmer either to go west and continue the exhaustion of the soil on a new frontier, or to adopt intensive culture. Thus the census of 1890 shows, in the Northwest, many counties in which there is an absolute or a relative decrease of population. These States have been sending farmers to advance the frontier on the plains, and have themselves begun to turn to intensive farming and to manufacture. A decade before this, Ohio had shown the same transition stage. Thus the demand for land and the love of wilderness freedom drew the frontier ever onward. . . . [T]he frontier promoted the formation of a composite nationality for the American people. The coast was preponderantly English, but the later tides of continental immigration flowed across to the free lands. This was the case from the early colonial days. The Scotch-Irish and the Palatine Germans, or "Pennsylvania Dutch," furnished the dominant element in the stock of the colonial frontier. With these peoples were also the freed indented servants, or redemptioners, who at the expiration of their time of service passed to the frontier. Governor Spotswood of Virginia writes in 1717, "The inhabitants of our frontiers are composed generally of such as have been transported hither as servants, and, being out of their time, settle themselves where land is to be taken up and that will produce the necessarys of life with little labour." Very generally these redemptioners were of non-English stock. In the crucible of the frontier the immigrants were Americanized, liberated, and fused into a mixed race, English in neither nationality nor characteristics. The process has gone on from the early days to our own. Burke and other writers in the middle of the eighteenth century believed that Pennsylvania was "threatened with the danger of being wholly foreign in language, manners, and perhaps even inclinations." The German and Scotch-Irish elements in the frontier of the South were only less great. In the middle of the present century the German element in Wisconsin was already so considerable that leading publicists looked to the creation of a German state out of the commonwealth by concentrating their colonization. Such examples teach us to beware of misinterpreting the fact that there is a common English speech in America into a belief that the stock is also English.

5 But the most important effect of the frontier has been in the promotion of democracy here and in Europe. As has been indicated, the frontier is productive of individualism. Complex society is precipitated by the wilderness into a kind of primitive organization based on the family. The tendency is anti-social. It produces

antipathy to control, and particularly to any direct control. The tax-gatherer is viewed as a representative of oppression. Prof. Osgood, in an able article, has pointed out that the frontier conditions prevalent in the colonies are important factors in the explanation of the American Revolution, where individual liberty was sometimes confused with absence of all effective government. The same conditions aid in explaining the difficulty of instituting a strong government in the period of the confederacy. The frontier individualism has from the beginning promoted democracy. The frontier States that came into the Union in the first quarter of a century of its existence came in with democratic suffrage provisions, and had reactive effects of the highest importance upon the older States whose peoples were being attracted there. An extension of the franchise became essential. It was *western* New York that forced an extension of suffrage in the constitutional convention of that State in 1821; and it was *western* Virginia that compelled the tide-water region to put a more liberal suffrage provision in the constitution framed in 1830, and to give to the frontier region a more nearly proportionate representation with the tide-water aristocracy. The rise of democracy as an effective force in the nation came in with western preponderance under Jackson and William Henry Harrison, and it meant the triumph of the frontier—with all of its good and with all of its evil elements. . . .

So long as free land exists, the opportunity for a competency exists, and economic power secures political power. But the democracy born of free land, strong in selfishness and individualism, intolerant of administrative experience and education, and pressing individual liberty beyond its proper bounds, has its dangers as well as its benefits. Individualism in America has allowed a laxity in regard to governmental affairs which has rendered possible the spoils system and all the manifest evils that follow from the lack of a highly developed civic spirit. In this connection may be noted also the influence of frontier conditions in permitting lax business honor, inflated paper currency and wild-cat banking. . . .

From the conditions of frontier life came intellectual traits of profound importance. The works of travelers along each frontier from colonial days onward describe certain common traits, and these traits have, while softening down, still persisted as survivals in the place of their origin, even when a higher social organization succeeded. The result is that to the frontier the American intellect owes its striking characteristics. That coarseness and strength combined with acuteness and inquisitiveness; that practical, inventive turn of mind, quick to find expedients; that masterful grasp of material things, lacking in the artistic but powerful to effect great ends; that restless, nervous energy; that dominant individualism, working for good and for evil, and withal that buoyancy and exuberance which comes with freedom—these are traits of the frontier, or traits called out elsewhere because of the existence of the frontier. Since the days when the fleet of Columbus sailed into the waters of the New World, America has been another name for opportunity, and the people of the United States have taken their tone from the incessant expansion which has not only been open but has even been forced upon them. He would be a rash prophet who should assert that the expansive character of American life has now entirely ceased. Movement has been its dominant fact, and, unless this training has no effect upon a people, the American energy will continually demand a wider field for its exercise. But never again will such gifts of free land offer themselves. For a moment, at the frontier, the bonds of custom are broken and unrestraint is triumphant. There is not *tabula rasa*. The stubborn American environment is there with its imperious summons to accept its conditions; the inherited ways of doing things are also there; and yet, in spite of environment, and in spite of custom, each frontier did indeed furnish a new field of opportunity, a gate of escape from the bondage of the past; and freshness, and confidence, and scorn of older society, impatience of its restraints and its ideas, and indifference to its lessons, have accompanied the frontier. What the Mediterranean Sea was to the Greeks, breaking the bond of custom, offering new experiences, calling out new institutions and activities, that, and more, the ever retreating frontier has been to the United States directly, and to the nations of Europe more remotely. And now, four centuries from the discovery of America, at the end of a hundred years of life under the Constitution, the frontier has gone, and with its going has closed the first period of American history.

1893

For Discussion and Writing

1. According to Turner, how did the frontier forge a uniquely American culture? What elements contributed to this frontier-based culture?
2. What intellectual traits does Turner claim are associated with the conditions of frontier life? Does he use stereotypes in his descriptions?
3. How did the frontier create what Turner calls a "composite nationality for the American people"? Does that composite nationality exist today? How has the paradigm shifted?

4. How does Turner's use of Daniel Boone's story affect the persuasiveness of his argument? Consider Caroline Kirkland's experience, elsewhere in this chapter. How does Turner's historical interpretation provide insight to her life story?
5. Using Turner's thesis, write an essay discussing individualism as a core American trait. Compare Turner's examples of frontier individualism to present-day examples of American individualism.

From *I Came a Stranger: The Story of a Hull-House Girl*

HILDA SATT POLACHECK

The settlement house movement, pioneered in Chicago at Hull House by Jane Addams, became a widely accepted means for immigrant families to assimilate into American life. At Hull House, mostly immigrant women and children might take English classes, join play groups, prepare for U.S. citizenship exams, and receive help in negotiating the confusing aspects of a new culture.

Hilda Satt Polacheck emigrated as a child with her family from Poland to Chicago in 1892. Introduced to Hull House activities soon after her arrival, she remained associated with the settlement house and other progressive causes throughout her life. In the following excerpt from her autobiography, she describes her life as a young immigrant woman at Hull House and as a worker in Chicago.

✦

Being allowed to teach English to immigrants at Hull-House did more for me than anything that I imparted to my students. It gave me a feeling of security that I so sorely needed. What added to my confidence in the future was that my class was always crowded and the people seemed to make good progress. From time to time Jane Addams would visit the class to see what I was doing, and she always left with that rare smile on her face; she seemed to be pleased.

There were no textbooks for adult beginners in English at that time. It soon became evident that it would be a waste of time to talk about cat, rat, mat, fat, sat to people who probably had been to high school in a foreign country.

This situation was emphasized for me one evening when Miss Addams brought a Greek professor to my class. He had come to America for the express purpose of learning English and had come to Chicago because he wanted to see relatives who were living near Hull-House. These relatives had suggested that he find out what Hull-House was doing about teaching English to adults. Miss Addams told me that the professor would stay one or two nights in my class to see what was being done. The crowning glory of my teaching was when he decided to join the class and attended all winter.

But to come back to the subject of textbooks, since there were none, I decided to use the Declaration of Independence as a text. It was a distinct success. The students did not find the words difficult; so in addition to learning English, we all learned the principles of Americanism.

I next introduced the manual on naturalization and the class learned English while studying how to become a citizen. It was all very exciting and stimulating.

My students were now beginning to confide in me. Classes at Hull-House were never just classes where people came to learn a specific subject. There was a human element of friendliness among us. Life was not soft or easy for any of them. They worked hard all day in shops and factories and made this valiant effort to learn the language of their adopted country. At times they needed real help, and they knew that somewhere in this wonderful house on Halsted Street they would get it.

I recall a special case in point. One evening, after the class had been dismissed, one of my students stayed behind. At first he seemed reluctant to tell me his story. But it soon came tumbling out; he had been ill and had gone to a doctor and was told that he would have to have a delicate and rather serious operation. And he had no money.

I looked at the fine young man and the first thought that flashed through my mind was that he must be saved. I told him that I would speak to Miss Addams and that he should see her the next night.

I went in search of Miss Addams. It did not matter that it was late. She was always available when there was a need. I told her about my student.

"Come in and see me before you go to your class tomorrow," she said. "I will write a letter to Dr. McArthur. I think he will take care of the young man."

Dr. McArthur was at that time the outstanding surgeon in Chicago. The young man took Miss Addams's letter to him and he performed the operation. I don't believe that anyone could refuse a request from Miss Addams.

Hull-House had a unique arrangement for getting work done. No teachers or attendants were paid. It was all volunteer work. The residents of Hull-House were occupied with outside work during the day, and each gave a certain number of evenings to teaching and directing clubs. The only people who were paid were those who devoted their full time to the house.

So in the fall, when volunteers returned, I decided to look for a job. I had learned to use a typewriter, so I decided to look for more "genteel" work. I still shuddered when I thought of those cuffs.

I started scanning the want ads, but now I looked under the heading "Office Help."

A large mail-order house, which shall remain unnamed, advertised for bill clerks who could operate billing machines. Since the keyboard of a typewriter was the same as that of a billing machine, I decided to apply. I was pleasantly surprised when I was told to report for work on the following day.

Carrying my lunch, I set out for my new job. I was taken to a large room that was filled with long tables on which the billing machines had been placed. There were about three feet between the machines. I was assigned to a machine and an instructor came to show me how the work was done. She also told me the rules of the office. I was told that no talking was permitted during working hours. I could, however, do what I wanted during the lunch period, which was forty-five minutes, even talk.

In addition to the blank bills, carbon paper, pencil, and eraser, I was given a wire spindle and several cards of different colors. I believe there were seven of these cards. I was told that when I had finished a batch of bills and needed more work, I was to put up a blue card on the spindle. When I needed blank bills, the green card was to be put up, and the supply clerk would bring the needed items. The red card would bring a new pencil. The yellow card meant that I needed an eraser. The purple card was a signal that I needed carbon paper. When my typewriter ribbon was worn out, and I must be sure that it was worn out, the orange card would bring a new ribbon. If I needed cleaning fluid to clean the machine, a pink card would bring it. I was not to leave my machine unless it was absolutely necessary. Then I was told that the toilets were at the end of the hall, and I knew what she meant by "absolutely necessary."

I had no difficulty learning to do the work and at first it was new and exciting. About the third day my mother noticed that my voice was husky, and she wanted to know what was wrong. I suddenly realized that I had not been using my vocal chords for three days and that my voice was beginning to show the lack of exercise. I suddenly realized that "genteel" work can be as deadly monotonous as factory work.

I made a feeble protest. I saw no reason why I could not speak to the girl next to me once in a while. The next day I was told that I was "too smart" for the job, and I was fired.

20 Several years later I went with a group of people on a sightseeing tour that took us to the state penitentiary at Joliet. As I walked through the overall factory, I saw a spindle and several colored cards at each machine. I asked the guide what the cards meant and was told that when a prisoner needed supplies he had to use the cards to indicate what he needed, as no talking was permitted during working hours.

I often wondered whether the mail-order house got the idea from the prison, or the prison from the mail-order house.

I was again looking for a job. Miss Addams suggested that I might try A. C. McClurg & Co., a publishing house and at the time the largest bookstore in Chicago. With a letter of introduction from Jane Addams, I was given a very friendly interview and got the job.

Working among books was almost as good as taking a course in literature. It gave me the opportunity of knowing what books were being published. I was keenly interested in what books people were reading. And I had the great privilege of working at McClurg's when *The Quest of the Silver Fleece* was published. It was the first time that I came across the name of W. E. B. Du Bois. This book aroused a keen interest in the growth of cotton in the South and the part that the Negro played in the industry.

I still spent my evenings at Hull-House, and one evening Miss Addams asked me to help organize a social and literary club for young men and women about my age. We all needed an outlet for recreation. About thirty young people joined the club, which was named the Ariadne Club. I don't know who suggested the name, but like the mythological daughter of Minos, who led Theseus out of the labyrinth by a thread, the club led many of us out of a labyrinth of boredom.

25 I now had the opportunity to come into contact with young men. The club met once a week, and how I looked forward to those meetings. The first order of business, after officers were elected, was to appoint a program committee, whose duty it would be to arrange weekly programs. Since this was a social and

literary club, one week was devoted to dancing and the next to study. For the more serious evening, a member was usually assigned to write a paper and to read it before the club. This was followed by a discussion.

And what subjects we discussed.

Papers were written on the collection of garbage, grand opera, clean streets, single tax, trade unionism, and many others. I think our subjects were influenced by what was going on at Hull-House.

The Ariadne Club soon branched out and launched a series of debates. We would try to find another club that would accept a challenge. If we could not find a club, the members would form opposing teams. The subjects of these debates come back to me: Which is mightier, the sword or the pen? Should women be allowed to vote? Which is stronger, the desire for fame or riches?

The club's next endeavor was book reviewing. A member would be appointed to read a book, write a review, and read it at a meeting. Some of the reviews were of *David Copperfield*, *Ivanhoe*, *The Pickwick Papers*, *The Count of Monte Cristo*, *When Knighthood Was in Flower*, and the various popular books of the day.

It was about this time that I found a copy of *Uncle Tom's* 30
Cabin. I was deeply moved by the misery of the slaves. For the first time I read about slavery. For the first time I found out that people could be bought and sold on the auction block; that children could be taken from parents; that fathers could be sold, never to see their families again.

When it was my turn to write a book review, I chose *Uncle Tom's Cabin*.

A great discussion followed this review. When it was time to adjourn the meeting, we were nowhere near finished with the discussion. It was decided to continue at the next meeting, even though it had previously been decided to devote that evening to dancing.

Most of the club members had no contact with Negroes. We even found that some of the members had never seen a Negro. Dr. James Britton, who was the club leader, told us that most of the Negroes had lived longer in America than any of us present and were fully entitled to anything and everything that the country offered. I thought of all the racial hatreds in Poland, Germany, and Russia, and I was thankful that I was being cured of this disease of intolerance.

In this connection, I recall that shortly after I had arrived in Chicago, one of my playmates told me that I must cross the street when I approached the Chinese laundry on Halsted Street. When I wanted to know why, she told me that if you pass the laundry, the "Chinaman" will come out with a long knife and kill you. I realize now that my playmate must have been told this fantastic tale by someone. Until I found out that the Chinese man who operated this laundry was the soul of kindness, I was afraid to pass the laundry.

35 We also had music in the Ariadne Club. The members who could play an instrument, or sing, would perform; we heard some very good concerts. Many of the members who worked all day would study music at night. I recall when a piano lesson could be had for twenty-five cents. Some of the members attended the Hull-House Music School, and I venture to say that not a few became successful musicians.

The Ariadne Club also produced plays. I recall taking part in *David Garrick*, in which I played a fussy and obnoxious old maid.

My interest in the theater was a direct outgrowth of the dramatics at Hull-House. It was a preparation for life.

1991

For Discussion and Writing

1. How does Polacheck find authority as a teacher of English? What events serve to reassure her that she is a good teacher?
2. Why does Polacheck mention that she used the Declaration of Independence as a text in her class? What point is she making with her readers?
3. What similarities does Polacheck suggest exist between the workplace and prison?

From *The Promised Land*

Mary Antin

Born in 1881 in Polotsk, a town situated in the Pale of Russia, where all Jews were required to live during the tsarist era, Mary Antin emigrated to Boston in 1894 in the midst of a massive influx of immigrants to American cities. Antin caught up to her age group in public school, and later attended Teachers' College at Columbia University in

New York City. She lectured widely on immigrant life in the United States after the publication of her 1912 autobiography, The Promised Land, *which details her transformation into a "real American."*

✦

Our initiation into American ways began with the first step on the new soil. My father found occasion to instruct or correct us even on the way from the pier to Wall Street, which journey we made crowded together in a rickety cab. He told us not to lean out of the windows, not to point, and explained the word "greenhorn." We did not want to be "greenhorns," and gave the strictest attention to my father's instructions. I do not know when my parents found opportunity to review together the history of Polotzk in the three years past, for we children had no patience with the subject; my mother's narrative was constantly interrupted by irrelevant questions, interjections, and explanations.

The first meal was an object lesson of much variety. My father produced several kinds of food, ready to eat, without any cooking, from little tin cans that had printing all over them. He attempted to introduce us to a queer, slippery kind of fruit, which he called "banana," but had to give it up for the time being. After the meal, he had better luck with a curious piece of furniture on runners, which he called "rocking-chair." There were five of us newcomers, and we found five different ways of getting into the American machine of perpetual motion, and as many ways of getting out of it. One born and bred to the use of a rocking-chair cannot imagine how ludicrous people can make themselves when attempting to use it for the first time. We laughed immoderately over our various experiments with the novelty, which was a wholesome way of letting off steam after the unusual excitement of the day.

In our flat we did not think of such a thing as storing the coal in the bathtub. There was no bathtub. So in the evening of the first day my father conducted us to the public baths. As we moved along in a little procession, I was delighted with the illumination of the streets. So many lamps, and they burned until morning, my father said, and so people did not need to carry lanterns. In America, then, everything was free, as we had heard in Russia. Light was free; the streets were as bright as a synagogue on a holy day. Music was free; we had been serenaded, to our gaping delight, by a brass band of many pieces, soon after our installation on Union Place.

Education was free. That subject my father had written about repeatedly, as comprising his chief hope for us children, the essence of American opportunity, the treasure that no thief could touch, not even misfortune or poverty. It was the one thing that he was able to promise us when he sent for us; surer, safer than bread or shelter. On our second day I was thrilled with the realization of what this freedom of education meant. A little girl from across the alley came and offered to conduct us to school. My father was out, but we five between us had a few words of English by this time. We knew the word school. We understood. This child, who had never seen us till yesterday, who could not pronounce our names, who was not much better dressed than we, was able to offer us the freedom of the schools of Boston! No application made, no questions asked, no examinations, rulings, exclusions; no machinations, no fees. The doors stood open for every one of us. The smallest child could show us the way.

5 This incident impressed me more than anything I had heard in advance of the freedom of education in America. It was a concrete proof—almost the thing itself. One had to experience it to understand it.

It was a great disappointment to be told by my father that we were not to enter upon our school career at once. It was too near the end of the term, he said, and we were going to move to Crescent Beach in a week or so. We had to wait until the opening of the schools in September. What a loss of precious time—from May till September!

Not that the time was really lost. Even the interval on Union Place was crowded with lessons and experiences. We had to visit the stores and be dressed from head to foot in American clothing; we had to learn the mysteries of the iron stove, the washboard, and the speaking-tube; we had to learn to trade with the fruit peddler through the window, and not to be afraid of the policeman; and, above all, we had to learn English.

The kind people who assisted us in these important matters form a group by themselves in the gallery of my friends. If I had never seen them from those early days till now, I should still have remembered them with gratitude. When I enumerate the long list of my American teachers, I must begin with those who came to us on Wall Street and taught us our first steps. To my mother, in her perplexity over the cookstove, the woman who showed her how to make the fire was an angel of deliverance. A fairy godmother to us children was she who led us to a wonderful country called "uptown," where, in a dazzlingly beautiful palace called a "department store," we exchanged our hateful homemade European costumes, which pointed us out as "greenhorns" to the children on the street, for real American machine-made garments, and issued forth glorified in each other's eyes.

1912

For Discussion and Writing

1. What is a "greenhorn" and how does such a person behave, dress, eat, and live? Why is Antin so desperate to shed her status as a greenhorn? What are the visual signs of American-ness?
2. What was the "essence of American opportunity" in Antin's father's eyes?
3. What about schooling in America surprises Antin? What is the role of education in attaining the American Dream, in Antin's view? Compare her emphasis on education to that of Richard Rodriguez, Richard Wright, and Helen Polacheck as detailed in the readings found elsewhere in this chapter.
4. Antin points out that much learning took place for her and her siblings outside the formal school setting. What lessons does she describe learning out of school in this excerpt? How central are these lessons to the process of Americanization?
5. How does Antin's attitude toward learning English differ from that described by Richard Rodriquez in the *Hunger of Memory* excerpt?

From *Black Boy*

RICHARD WRIGHT

Not all immigrants came from overseas; as segregation in the United States became more deeply entrenched after Plessy v. Ferguson ruled that "separate but equal" was equal under the law in 1896, many southern blacks moved to northern cities in the early twentieth century in hope of finding better jobs, schools, and homes. Known as the Great Migration, this mass exodus from southern states contributed to a radical shift in the social and economic landscape, arguably leading to the later successes of the civil rights movement. One of these "migrants" was Richard Wright, best remembered as the author of Native Son. *Wright's autobiography, excerpted here, narrates the story of his escape from the repressive South of his youth.*

The accidental visit of Aunt Maggie to Memphis formed a practical basis for my planning to go north. Aunt Maggie's husband, the "uncle" who had fled from Arkansas in the dead of night, had deserted her; and now she was casting about for a living. My mother, Aunt Maggie, my brother, and I held long conferences, speculating on the prospects of jobs and the cost of apartments in Chicago. And every time we conferred, we defeated ourselves. It was impossible for all four of us to go at once; we did not have enough money.

Finally sheer wish and hope prevailed over common sense and facts. We discovered that if we waited until we were prepared to go, we would never leave, we would never amass enough money to see us through. We would have to gamble. We finally decided that Aunt Maggie and I would go first, even though it was winter, and prepare a place for my mother and brother. Why wait until next week or next month? If we were going, why not go at once?

Next loomed the problem of leaving my job cleanly, smoothly, without arguments or scenes. How could I present the fact of leaving to my boss? Yes, I would pose as an innocent boy; I would tell him that my aunt was taking me and my paralyzed mother to Chicago. That would create in his mind the impression that I was not asserting my will; it would block any expression of dislike on his part for my act. I knew that southern whites hated the idea of Negroes leaving to live in places where the racial atmosphere was different.

It worked as I had planned. When I broke the news of my leaving two days before I left—I was afraid to tell it sooner for fear that I would create hostility on the part of the whites with whom I worked—the boss leaned back in his swivel chair and gave me the longest and most considerate look he had ever given me.

"Chicago?" he repeated softly.

"Yes, sir."

"Boy, you won't like it up there," he said.

"Well, I have to go where my family is, sir," I said.

The other white office workers paused in their tasks and listened. I grew self-conscious, tense.

"It's cold up there," he said.

"Yes, sir. They say it is," I said, keeping my voice in a neutral tone.

He became conscious that I was watching him and he looked away, laughing uneasily to cover his concern and dislike.

"Now, boy," he said banteringly, "don't you go up there and fall into that lake."

"Oh, no, sir," I said, smiling as though there existed the possibility of my falling accidentally into Lake Michigan.

He was serious again, staring at me. I looked at the floor.

"You think you'll do any better up there?" he asked.

"I don't know, sir."

"You seem to've been getting along all right down here," he said.

"Oh, yes, sir. If it wasn't for my mother's going, I'd stay right here and work," I lied as earnestly as possible.

"Well, why not stay? You can send her money," he suggested.

He had trapped me. I knew that staying now would never do. I could not have controlled my relations with the whites if I had remained after having told them that I wanted to go north.

"Well, I want to be with my mother," I said.

"You want to be with your mother," he repeated idly. "Well, Richard, we enjoyed having you with us."

"And I enjoyed working here," I lied.

There was silence; I stood awkwardly, then moved to the door. There was still silence; white faces were looking strangely at me. I went upstairs, feeling like a criminal. The word soon spread through the factory and the white men looked at me with new eyes. They came to me.

"So you're going north, hunh?"

"Yes, sir. My family's taking me with 'em."

"The North's no good for your people, boy."

"I'll try to get along, sir."

"Don't believe all the stories you hear about the North."

"No, sir. I don't."

"You'll come back here where your friends are."

"Well, sir. I don't know."

"How're you going to act up there?"

"Just like I act down here, sir."

"Would you speak to a white girl up there?"

"Oh, no, sir. I'll act there just like I act here."

"Aw, no, you won't. You'll change. Niggers change when they go north."

I wanted to tell him that I was going north precisely to change, but I did not.

"I'll be the same," I said, trying to indicate that I had no imagination whatever.

As I talked I felt that I was acting out a dream. I did not want to lie, yet I had to lie to conceal what I felt. A white censor was standing over me and, like dreams forming a curtain for the safety of sleep, so did my lies form a screen of safety for my living moments.

"Boy, I bet you've been reading too many of them damn books."

"Oh, no, sir."

I made my last errand to the post office, put my bag away, washed my hands, and pulled on my cap. I shot a quick glance about the factory; most of the men were working late. One or two looked up. Mr. Falk, to whom I had returned my library card, gave me a quick, secret smile. I walked to the elevator and rode down with Shorty.

"You lucky bastard," he said bitterly.

"Why do you say that?"

"You saved your goddamn money and now you're gone."

"My problems are just starting," I said.

"You'll never have any problems as hard as the ones you had here," he said.

"I hope not," I said. "But life is tricky."

"Sometimes I get so goddamn mad I want to kill everybody," he spat in a rage.

"You can leave," I said.

"I'll never leave this goddamn South," he railed. "I'm always saying I am, but I won't . . . I'm lazy. I like to sleep too goddamn much. I'll die here. Or maybe they'll kill me."

I stepped from the elevator into the street, half expecting someone to call me back and tell me that it was all a dream, that I was not leaving.

This was the culture from which I sprang. This was the terror from which I fled.

1945

For Discussion and Writing

1. Why does Wright feel it is necessary to lie about his reasons for quitting his job? What effect does the "white censor" have on Wright's access to the American Dream?
2. Why would Wright's white co-workers believe that the North is "no good for your people"? What threat might they have perceived to their own access to the American Dream?
3. Examine the differences between Wright's speech to his co-workers as seen in the dialogue portions of the excerpt and the language he uses in the narrative sections. How can these differences be explained?

4. In an essay, explain how Wright might define the American Dream. What is he searching for in order to fulfill the dream? What stands in his way?

From *Death of a Salesman*

ARTHUR MILLER

Perhaps the most famous of American plays, Arthur Miller's Death of a Salesman *won a Pulitzer Prize, a Tony Award, and a New York Drama Critics' Award for best play in 1949. Its central character, Willy Loman, is a traveling salesman who is struggling to make ends meet. Willy claims that he was once a master salesman, but at the end of his career he is deprived of his salary, forced to rely on dwindling commissions. Widely seen as a blistering critique of the American Dream,* Death of a Salesman *asks what happens when an American man does everything he is supposed to do, but still fails to achieve the promised success. In the scene below, Willy pleads with his boss, Howard, a much younger man whose father was once Willy's supervisor, for a reduced work schedule.*

✦

HOWARD: Say, aren't you supposed to be in Boston?

WILLY: That's what I want to talk to you about, Howard. You got a minute? *He draws a chair in from the wing.*

HOWARD: What happened? What're you doing here?

WILLY: Well . . .

HOWARD: You didn't crack up again, did you?

WILLY: Oh, no. No . . .

HOWARD: Geez, you had me worried there for a minute. What's the trouble?

WILLY: Well, tell you the truth, Howard. I've come to the decision that I'd rather not travel any more.

HOWARD: Not travel! Well, what'll you do?

WILLY: Remember, Christmas time, when you had the party here? You said you'd try to think of some spot for me here in town.

HOWARD: With us?

WILLY: Well, sure.

HOWARD: Oh, yeah, yeah. I remember. Well, I couldn't think of anything for you, Willy.

WILLY: I tell ya, Howard. The kids are all grown up, y'know. I don't need much any more. If I could take home—well, sixty-five dollars a week, I could swing it.

HOWARD: Yeah, but Willy, see I—

WILLY: I tell ya why, Howard. Speaking frankly and between the two of us, y'know—I'm just a little tired.

HOWARD: Oh, I could understand that, Willy. But you're a road man, Willy, and we do a road business. We've only got a half-dozen salesmen on the floor here.

WILLY: God knows, Howard, I never asked a favor of any man. But I was with the firm when your father used to carry you in here in his arms.

HOWARD: I know that, Willy, but—

WILLY: Your father came to me the day you were born and asked me what I thought of the name of Howard, may he rest in peace.

HOWARD: I appreciate that, Willy, but there just is no spot here for you. If I had a spot I'd slam you right in, but I just don't have a single solitary spot.

He looks for his lighter. Willy has picked it up and gives it to him. Pause.

WILLY, *with increasing anger*: Howard, all I need to set my table is fifty dollars a week.

HOWARD: But where am I going to put you, kid?

WILLY: Look, it isn't a question of whether I can sell merchandise, is it?

HOWARD: No, but it's a business, kid, and everybody's gotta pull his own weight.

WILLY, *desperately*: Just let me tell you a story, Howard—

HOWARD: 'Cause you gotta admit, business is business.

WILLY, *angrily*: Business is definitely business, but just listen for a minute. You don't understand this. When I was a boy—eighteen, nineteen—I was already on the road. And there was a question in my mind as to whether selling had a future for me. Because in those days I had a yearning to go to Alaska. See, there were three gold strikes in one month in Alaska, and I felt like going out. Just for the ride, you might say.

HOWARD, *barely interested*: Don't say.

WILLY: Oh, yeah, my father lived many years in Alaska. He was an adventurous man. We've got quite a little streak of self-reliance in our family. I thought I'd go out with my older brother and try to locate him, and maybe settle in the North with the old man. And I was almost decided to go, when I met a salesman in the Parker House. His name was Dave Singleman. And he was eighty-four years old, and he'd drummed merchandise in thirty-one states. And old Dave, he'd go up to his room, y'understand, put on his green velvet slippers—I'll never forget—and pick up his phone and call the buyers, and without ever leaving his room, at the age of eighty-four, he made his living. And when I saw that, I realized that selling was the greatest career a man could want. 'Cause what could be more satisfying than to be able to go, at the age of eighty-four, into twenty or thirty different cities, and pick up a phone, and be remembered and loved and helped by so many different people? Do you know? when he died—and by the way he died the death of a salesman, in his green velvet slippers in the smoker of the New York, New Haven and Hartford, going into Boston—when he died, hundreds of salesmen and buyers were at his funeral. Things were sad on a lotta trains for months after that. *He stands up. Howard has not looked at him.* In those days there was personality in it, Howard. There was respect, and comradeship, and gratitude in it. Today, it's all cut and dried, and there's no chance for bringing friendship to bear—or personality. You see what I mean? They don't know me any more.

HOWARD, *moving away, to the right*: That's just the thing, Willy.

WILLY: If I had forty dollars a week—that's all I'd need. Forty dollars, Howard.

HOWARD: Kid, I can't take blood from a stone, I—

WILLY, *desperation is on him now*: Howard, the year Al Smith was nominated, your father came to me and—

HOWARD, *starting to go off*: I've got to see some people, kid.

WILLY, *stopping him*: I'm talking about your father! There were promises made across this desk! You mustn't tell me you've got people to see—I put thirty-four years into this firm, Howard, and now I can't pay my insurance! You can't eat the orange and throw the peel away—a man is not a piece of fruit! *After a pause*: Now pay attention. Your father—in 1928 I had a big year. I averaged a hundred and seventy dollars a week in commissions.

HOWARD, *impatiently*: Now, Willy, you never averaged—

WILLY, *banging his hand on the desk*: I averaged a hundred and seventy dollars a week in the year of 1928! And your father came to me—or rather, I was in the office here—it was right over this desk—and he put his hand on my shoulder—

HOWARD, *getting up*: You'll have to excuse me, Willy, I gotta see some people. Pull yourself together. *Going out*: I'll be back in a little while.

On Howard's exit, the light on his chair grows very bright and strange.

WILLY: Pull myself together! What the hell did I say to him? My God, I was yelling at him! How could I! *Willy breaks off, staring at the light, which occupies the chair, animating it. He approaches this chair, standing across the desk from it.* Frank, Frank, don't you remember what you told me that time? How you put your hand on my shoulder, and Frank . . . *He leans on the desk and as he speaks the dead man's name he accidentally switches on the recorder, and instantly*

HOWARD'S SON: ". . . of New York is Albany. The capital of Ohio is Cincinnati, the capital of Rhode Island is . . ." *The recitation continues.*

WILLY, *leaping away with fright, shouting*: Ha! Howard! Howard! Howard!

HOWARD, *rushing in*: What happened?

WILLY, *pointing at the machine, which continues nasally, childishly, with the capital cities*: Shut it off! Shut it off!

HOWARD, *pulling the plug out*: Look, Willy . . .

WILLY, *pressing his hands to his eyes*: I gotta get myself some coffee. I'll get some coffee . . .

Willy starts to walk out. Howard stops him.

HOWARD, *rolling up the cord*: Willy, look . . .

WILLY: I'll go to Boston.

HOWARD: Willy, you can't go to Boston for us.

WILLY: Why can't I go?

HOWARD: I don't want you to represent us. I've been meaning to tell you for a long time now.

WILLY: Howard, are you firing me?

HOWARD: I think you need a good long rest, Willy.

WILLY: Howard—

HOWARD: And when you feel better, come back, and we'll see if we can work something out.

WILLY: But I gotta earn money, Howard. I'm in no position to—

HOWARD: Where are your sons? Why don't your sons give you a hand?

WILLY: They're working on a very big deal.

HOWARD: This is no time for false pride, Willy. You go to your sons and you tell them that you're tired. You've got two great boys, haven't you?

WILLY: Oh, no question, no question, but in the meantime . . .

HOWARD: Then that's that, heh?

WILLY: All right, I'll go to Boston tomorrow.

HOWARD: No, no.

WILLY: I can't throw myself on my sons. I'm not a cripple!

HOWARD: Look, kid, I'm busy this morning.

WILLY, *grasping Howard's arm*: Howard, you've got to let me go to Boston!

HOWARD, *hard, keeping himself under control*: I've got a line of people to see this morning. Sit down, take five minutes, and pull yourself together, and then go home, will ya? I need the office, Willy. *He starts to go, turns, remembering the recorder, starts to push off the table holding the recorder*. Oh, yeah. Whenever you can this week, stop by and drop of the samples. You'll feel better, Willy, and then come back and we'll talk. Pull yourself together, kid, there's people outside.

1948

For Discussion and Writing

1. What role does respect, camaraderie, and gratitude play in Willy Loman's vision of success?
2. What does Howard give away about his attitude toward Willy by calling him "kid"?
3. What made Willy realize that sales was the "greatest career a man could want"? Does his realization still hold true today? If not, what is today's equivalent?
4. How much responsibility does Willy bear for his own failure?
5. If the American Dream can be seen as a contract between the individual and society, what obligation does a business have to a loyal, hard-working employee? In an essay, consider the iconic story of Willy Loman in light of such events as the collapse of the Enron Corporation. How can a play help us understand a real-life situation?

From *Hunger of Memory: The Education of Richard Rodriguez*

RICHARD RODRIGUEZ

A highly regarded writer and PBS commentator, Rodriguez was born in 1944 to Mexican immigrant parents. He developed a love of reading and literature at a young age, eventually earning a Ph.D. in English literature at the University of California at Berkeley. Though Rodriguez spoke no English until he went to Catholic school, he is a forceful critic of affirmative action and bilingual education, and believes that both stand between the immigrant and his need to become part of his adopted country.

*The memoir excerpted here describes the consciousness of an immigrant family, constantly aware of their difference from the Americans—*los gringos*—that surround them. The language of the immigrant's home and that of the public arena give rise to the child's sense of two separate worlds. Though many emigrate to the U.S. mainly so their children will have the opportunity to get good educations, the result is often that parents and children become estranged from one another.*

Memory teaches me what I know of these matters; the boy reminds the adult. I was a bilingual child, a certain kind—socially disadvantaged—the son of working-class parents, both Mexican immigrants.

In the early years of my boyhood, my parents coped very well in America. My father had steady work. My mother managed at home. They were nobody's victims. Optimism and ambition led them to a house (our home) many blocks from the Mexican south side of town. We lived among *gringos* and only a block from the biggest, whitest houses. It never occurred to my parents that they couldn't live wherever they chose. Nor was the Sacramento of the fifties bent on teaching them a contrary lesson. My mother and father were more annoyed than intimidated by those two or three neighbors who tried initially to make us unwelcome. ("Keep your brats away from my sidewalk!") But despite all they achieved, perhaps because they had so much to achieve, any deep feeling of ease, the confidence of "belonging" in public was withheld from them both. They regarded the people at work, the faces in crowds, as very distant from us. They were the others, *los gringos*. That term was interchangeable in their speech with another, even more telling, *los americanos*.

In public, my father and mother spoke a hesitant, accented, not always grammatical English. And they would have to strain—their bodies tense—to catch the sense of what was rapidly said by *los gringos*. At home they spoke Spanish. The language of their Mexican past sounded in counterpoint to the English of public society. The words would come quickly, with ease. Conveyed through those sounds was the pleasing, soothing, consoling reminder of being at home.

During those years when I was first conscious of hearing, my mother and father addressed me only in Spanish; in Spanish I learned to reply. By contrast, English (*inglés*), rarely heard in the house, was the language I came to associate with *gringos*. I learned my first words of English overhearing my parents speak to strangers. At five years of age, I knew just enough English for my mother to trust me on errands to stores one block away. No more.

I was a listening child, careful to hear the very different sounds 5
of Spanish and English. Wide-eyed with hearing, I'd listen to sounds more than words. First, there were English (*gringo*) sounds. So many words were still unknown that when the butcher or the lady at the drugstore said something to me, exotic polysyllabic sounds would bloom in the midst of their sentences. Often, the speech of people in public seemed to me very loud, booming with confidence. The man behind the counter would literally ask, "What can I do for you?" But by being so firm and so clear, the sound of his voice said that he was a *gringo*; he belonged in public society.

The accent of *los gringos* was never pleasing nor was it hard to hear. Crowds at Safeway or at bus stops would be noisy with sound. And I would be forced to edge away from the chirping chatter above me.

I was unable to hear my own sounds, but I knew very well that I spoke English poorly. My words could not stretch far enough to form complete thoughts. And the words I did speak I didn't know well enough to make into distinct sounds. (Listeners would usually lower their heads, better to hear what I was trying to say.) But it was one thing for *me* to speak English with difficulty. It was more troubling for me to hear my parents speak in public: their high-whining vowels and guttural consonants; their sentences that got stuck with "eh" and "ah" sounds; the confused syntax; the hesitant rhythm of sounds so different from the way *gringos* spoke. I'd notice, moreover, that my parents' voices were softer than those of *gringos* we'd meet.

I am tempted now to say that none of this mattered. In adulthood I am embarrassed by childhood fears. And, in a way, it didn't matter very much that my parents could not speak English with ease. Their linguistic difficulties had no serious consequences. My mother and father made themselves understood at the county hospital clinic and at government offices. And yet, in another way, it mattered very much—it was unsettling to hear my parents struggle with English. Hearing them, I'd grow nervous, my clutching trust in their protection and power weakened.

There were many times like the night at a brightly lit gasoline station (a blaring white memory) when I stood uneasily, hearing my father. He was talking to a teenaged attendant. I do not recall what they were saying, but I cannot forget the sounds my father made as he spoke. At one point his words slid together to form one word—sounds as confused as the threads of blue and green oil in the puddle next to my shoes. His voice rushed through what he had left to say. And, toward the end, reached falsetto notes, appealing to his listener's understanding. I looked away to the lights of passing automobiles. I tried not to hear anymore. But I heard only too well the calm, easy tones in the attendant's reply. Shortly afterward, walking toward home with my father, I shivered when he put his hand on my shoulder. The very first chance that I got, I evaded his grasp and ran on ahead into the dark, skipping with feigned boyish exuberance.

10 But then there was Spanish. *Español*: my family's language. *Español*: the language that seemed to me a private language. I'd hear strangers on the radio and in the Mexican Catholic church across town speaking in Spanish, but I couldn't really believe that Spanish was a public language, like English. Spanish speakers, rather, seemed related to me, for I sensed that we shared—through our language—the experience of feeling apart from *los gringos*. It was thus a ghetto Spanish that I heard and I spoke. Like those whose lives are bound by a barrio, I was reminded by Spanish of my separateness from *los otros, los gringos* in power. But more intensely than for most barrio children—because I did not live in a barrio—Spanish seemed to me the language of home. (Most days it was only at home that I'd hear it.) It became the language of joyful return.

A family member would say something to me and I would feel myself specially recognized. My parents would say something to me and I would feel embraced by the sounds of their words. Those sounds said: *I am speaking with ease in Spanish. I am addressing you in words I never use with* los gringos. *I recognize you as someone special, close, like no one outside. You belong with us. In the family.*

(Ricardo.)

At the age of five, six, well past the time when most other children no longer easily notice the difference between sounds uttered at home and words spoken in public, I had a different experience. I lived in a world magically compounded of sounds. I remained a child longer than most; I lingered too long, poised at the edge of language—often frightened by the sounds of *los gringos*, delighted by the sounds of Spanish at home. I shared with my family a language that was startlingly different from that used in the great city around us.

For me there were none of the gradations between public and private society so normal to a maturing child. Outside the house was public society; inside the house was private. Just opening or closing the screen door behind me was an important experience. I'd rarely leave home all alone or without reluctance. Walking down the sidewalk, under the canopy of tall trees, I'd warily notice the—suddenly—silent neighborhood kids who stood warily watching me. Nervously, I'd arrive at the grocery store to hear there the sounds of the *gringo*—foreign to me—reminding me that in this world so big, I was a foreigner. But then I'd return. Walking back toward our house, climbing the steps from the sidewalk, when the front door was open in summer, I'd hear voices beyond the screen door talking in Spanish. For a second or two, I'd stay, linger there, listening. Smiling, I'd hear my mother call out, saying in Spanish (words): "Is that you, Richard?" All the while her sounds would assure me: *You are home now; come closer; inside. With us.*

"*Si*," I'd reply.

Once more inside the house I would resume (assume) my 15
place in the family. The sounds would dim, grow harder to hear. Once more at home, I would grow less aware of that fact. It required, however, no more than the blurt of the doorbell to alert me to listen to sounds all over again. The house would turn instantly still while my mother went to the door. I'd hear her hard English sounds. I'd wait to hear her voice return to soft-sounding Spanish, which assured me, as surely as did the clicking tongue of the lock on the door, that the stranger was gone.

Plainly, it is not healthy to hear such sounds so often. It is not healthy to distinguish public words from private sounds so easily. I remained cloistered by sounds, timid and shy in public, too dependent on voices at home. And yet it needs to be emphasized: I was an extremely happy child at home. I remember many nights when my father would come back from work, and I'd hear him call out to my mother in Spanish, sounding relieved. In Spanish, he'd sound light and free notes he never could manage in English. Some nights I'd jump up just at hearing his voice. With *mis hermanos* I would come running into the room where he was with my mother. Our laughing (so deep was the pleasure!) became screaming. Like others who know the pain of public alienation, we transformed the knowledge of our public separateness and made it consoling—the reminder of intimacy. Excited, we joined our voices in a celebration of sounds. *We are speaking now the way we never speak out in public. We are alone—together,* voices sounded, surrounded to tell me. Some nights, no one seemed willing to loosen the hold sounds had on us. At dinner, we invented new words. (Ours sounded Spanish, but made sense only to us.) We pieced together new words by taking, say, an English verb and giving it Spanish endings. My mother's instructions at bedtime would be lacquered with mock-urgent tones. Or a word like *sí* would become, in several notes, able to convey added measures of feeling. Tongues explored the edges of words, especially the fat vowels. And we happily sounded that military drum roll, the twirling roar of the Spanish *r*. Family language: my family's sounds. The voices of my parents and sisters and brother. Their voices insisting: *You belong here. We are family members. Related. Special to one another. Listen!* Voices singing and sighing, rising, straining, then surging, teeming with pleasure that burst syllables into fragments of laughter. At times it seemed there was steady quiet only when, from another room, the rustling whispers of my parents faded and I moved closer to sleep.

1981

For Discussion and Writing

1. What difference does language ability make in terms of Rodriguez's parents' ability to move comfortably in their lives? How does he show their comfort level or lack thereof?

2. Why do the English speakers young Richard encounters seem so loud in contrast to his family's voices? How does he interpret this difference?
3. How does Rodriguez respond to his parents' hesitant English?
4. How does Rodriguez indicate his sense of difference from *los gringos*?
5. In an essay, compare the conflict Rodriguez experienced as a child between his parents' world and American culture with that of Pao Her (elsewhere in this chapter). How does each negotiate between the public and private spheres? Would Pao Her agree with Rodriguez that it is unhealthy for a child to "distinguish private words from public sounds"? Why or why not?

From *Messages From My Father*

CALVIN TRILLIN

Calvin Trillin has been a staff writer for The New Yorker *magazine since 1963, writing gently humorous essays marked by detailed and telling descriptions of people and places across the United States. He is also the author of many books on family life, travel, politics, and eating. In this excerpt from his 1996 memoir,* Messages From My Father, *Trillin reflects on how his father taught him to be an American. Unlike the more familiar story of Jewish immigrants flooding New York City, Trillin's family emigrated to Galveston, Texas, and from there to Kansas City.*

✦

We lived on a pleasant street in a city then known as the Heart of America. My father mowed the lawn, just the way Mr. Doty and Mr. Arnold and Mr. Cunningham mowed the lawn. On summer evenings, we caught lightning bugs or we played croquet or kick the can in the Dotys' backyard. We brought our meat loaf to the covered-dish suppers that my Cub Scout pack held regularly at the Broadway Methodist Church—although it is also true that my mother told us to stay away from everyone else's meat loaf, on the theory that you could never tell what "they" put in it. (This warning, I think, did not grow out of her fear that we might find ourselves eating *trayf*—she cheerfully cooked the bacon on family picnics at Shelter House #4 in Swope Park—but out of an unfocused suspicion about how Gentiles lived. She may have suspected that Gentile meat loaf was adulterated not just with pork but with filler or maybe even

Jim Beam.) When the time came, Sukey and I went to a high school that had a strong resemblance to the high schools in the sort of Hollywood movies that featured Andy Hardy—or, as it turned out, the sort of movies that featured Paul Newman and Joanne Woodward, since Southwest was the school attended by the children of Mr. and Mrs. Bridge. After our family had a dog named Buck, we had a dog named Spike. I took it for granted that we were as American as anyone else.

I believe now that my father never took it for granted. It was my father, not his parents or some immigration officer, who changed the family name. I think we lived in that neighborhood precisely because it was where regular middle-class Americans lived. It was a vast section of southwest Kansas City that had been developed largely by a man named J. C. Nichols. He called it the Country Club District. The full name of the shopping district we called the Plaza is the Country Club Plaza, unless it's "the world-famous Country Club Plaza." The baccalaureate service accompanying our high-school graduation was actually in a house of worship called the Country Club Christian Church. Although there were eventually plenty of Jews in the Country Club District, there was a widespread feeling in the late thirties that its developer held the prevailing country club views on how few Jews it took to be too many. Just to be safe, my father had bought the land our house was built on through a Christian acquaintance—a salesman who called on him at the grocery stores.

A writer I know, Victoria Redel, has published a book of connected short stories, *Where the Road Bottoms Out*, about someone growing up in a comfortable suburb of New York in a family of cosmopolitan Jewish refugees, some of whom had made stops along their way in places like Belgium and Constantinople and Mexico. Most of the stops presumably ended badly, and it is assumed by the adults in the book that America, however comfortable and however tolerant, is just another one of these stops. The narrator expresses this in a way that sums up Jews as wanderers in one sentence: "In the easy suburban evenings our parents waited for our American disaster." When the daughters of the family in the book engage in some conventional suburban activity like marching with the school band, their father says to them, "You are not American." He says it, the narrator reports, "the way we heard other fathers tell their children not to run out into the street." When I read that, it occurred to me that my father's message, delivered with such assurance that it did not require articulation, was precisely the opposite: "You are American." It never occurred to him that the Trillins were going anywhere. There weren't any exotic ports of call behind us—just those Kiev suburbs—and there weren't any in our future. We were in America to stay.

I think my father dreamed of my going to Yale partly because that's where he believed the ideal American boy would go. It was all right there in a heroic novel he had read as a boy in St. Joseph—*Stover at Yale*. The longest argument my father and I had during my childhood was over the question of whether I was going to join the Boy Scouts. I didn't want to be a Boy Scout. My father wanted me to be a Boy Scout. American boys were Boy Scouts. I remember the argument as lasting for days, but maybe it just seemed that long. I argued, among other things, that I was being treated unfairly: how come Sukey, who was a year ahead of me in school, hadn't been forced to be a Girl Scout? I considered that a brilliant point, but it was, of course, based on my misreading of the theme that guided our upbringing. I might as well have asked why Sukey wasn't expected to go to Radcliffe or Wellesley. Sukey wasn't the American being fashioned here; I was. I became a Boy Scout—not an enthusiastic Boy Scout, perhaps, but a Boy Scout. I thought I had put up a pretty good argument, but I was, after all, only the second stubbornest person in the house.

5 My father had an American's optimism—the sort of quiet confidence about the future that was not always easy to find among the immigrants or first-generation Americans of that era. The people who came to this country in the great wave of immigration from Southern and Eastern Europe may have looked on America as the land of opportunity, but their experience over generations in the Old Country must have told them that they would be doing well to keep their heads above water. One part of them was waiting for their American disaster. A friend of mine—Joseph Machlis, a musicologist and writer and translator of operas—grew up an immigrant on the Lower East Side at precisely the same time my father was growing up in St. Joseph, Missouri. He says that at the close of the Passover seder, at the moment when it was traditional in Jewish homes to offer in the final prayer the phrase "Next year in Jerusalem," his father would push back from the table and say, in Yiddish, *"Iber a yor nischt erger"*—"Next year no worse."

In the immigrant community of that generation, pessimism and fearfulness were endemic. They were compounded by a conviction common among Jews that no Gentiles could be trusted. When I was in college, a Jewish friend's father—a cultivated man who had left Europe just ahead of the Nazi invasion of his country—often told his son and me that we were naïve to think that we would not be abandoned by our Gentile friends if one of them ever had to choose between us and his own people. My mother came from a background marginally more sophisticated than my father's. She had a regular American name from the start—Edyth. She occasionally mentioned, with some pride, that she was "not from Independence Avenue," where, apparently, the poorest Jewish immigrants in Kansas City had lived. Among the cousins in her generation of the family were college graduates and even doctors. The patriarch who had come to Kansas City from Lithuania in the previous generation was himself referred to as Dr. E.L.—although I suspect his medical credentials would not have borne serious scrutiny. Even so, my mother had more than a trace of the immigrant's fearfulness.

My father seemed to have no trace at all. He feared no pogroms. He saw no limitations. Although my parents' circle of friends was totally Jewish, it would have never occurred to him to question the long-term loyalty of my Gentile friends. He would have considered all of that kvetching. My father did not kvetch—about his health or his childhood or his business.

1996

For Discussion and Writing

1. How did Trillin's father ensure that his children were "as American as anyone else"?
2. Why was it important to Trillin's father that his son go to Yale?
3. Why does Trillin's father see no limitations as an immigrant? How is his view different from the pessimism Trillin describes as widespread among Jews on the Lower East Side of New York?
4. How do the Boy Scouts "train" Americans?
5. In an essay, examine the variety of ways in which Trillin's father, Mary Antin, and Hilda Polacheck define the American Dream and attempt to fulfill it for themselves. Is there any correlation between their definitions and the degree to which they are successful in achieving their goals?

"Stuck in Between"— Interview with Pao Her From *I Begin My Life All Over Again*

LILLIAN FADERMAN

While the U.S. was at war in Vietnam, it was also secretly engaged in fighting Communist forces in nearby Laos, where the CIA recruited ethnic Hmong from the mountainous regions to become soldiers. When at last the U.S. gave up in the mid-1970s and left Southeast Asia, Communist forces targeted the Hmong people for "reeducation" in what were essentially concentration camps. The CIA helped some escape Laos, but most were left to fend for themselves. Since the Laotian war was supposed to be secret, the U.S. government was reluctant for some years to allow significant numbers of Hmong refugees to emigrate. Many Hmong refugees endured a dangerous journey on foot through the Mekong River area to Thailand, where they sometimes waited years in relocation camps before being cleared to emigrate to the U.S., Australia, and France.

Today there are significant numbers of Hmong Americans living in central California, Minnesota, and North Carolina. As with most immigrant groups, adjusting to life in a new country has been difficult for the Hmong; traditionally clan-based farmers, the older generation has had the hardest time. Life in American cities is loud and bewildering compared to the slow pace of the Laotian village, and language barriers create steep hardships. The generation that was young children when they arrived is caught between two worlds; they cannot remember life in Laos, but they feel disloyal "being American." In this oral history, eighteen-year-old Pao Her describes feeling torn about his identity.

✦

I'm eighteen and when I came to America I was about four years old. I didn't speak any English, and my parents still can't speak English that well. But I remember I used to watch television a lot, and I learned that way. I still like programs like *Full House*. It's a comedy about a white family. I think it's fun to watch sometimes because they have some good programs about family problems and stuff. In some ways, they're not that much different from us, but in other ways they are.

I think the big way they're different is the way they show their emotions. They're much more emotional than us—like with hugging. Americans give hugs to each and everybody in the family, but the Hmong—they just don't hug each other or . . . like, kiss you before you got to sleep. They just say, "Go to sleep." Well, sometimes now I kind of question how come we Hmong do it that way. Sometimes I feel like maybe I want to give my family a hug, too. But then I think, "Well, maybe it's not good," because we just don't do that stuff.

Or another difference that I see on American television with families is that they go out, like to restaurants. Sometimes I go with my friends to restaurants. But my parents don't go out that much. They have to stay home and watch the house. I kind of want my family to go to restaurants and eat out once in a while, just see how it's like, but they never do. My mom wants to go out, even just to a fast-food restaurant, but my dad—he goes, "Just stay home and eat." Sometimes he does take my mom and my little baby brother out, but never the whole family. When I get married I think I'll probably be Americanized, so probably the whole family will go out to a restaurant once in a while.

But the truth is, I don't really feel American and I don't feel all Hmong. I don't know that much about the Hmong culture, like my parents say; and I don't know much about the American culture, how their society works or what their laws are. Sometimes I don't feel like I fit in. So I'm just stuck in between, jumping back and forth.

5 My little sister, she was born here and she doesn't even speak that much Hmong. She's like, more Americanized. There's not that many Hmong families living in this neighborhood, except one across the street and they don't have a daughter her age. So she doesn't come in contact with Asian girls that much. She's—like more Americanized by playing with her American friends. She asks for clothes—like bathing suits—that American girls would wear that's different from what Asian girls would wear. She hangs around mostly with the girl next door, and she goes out to their church with them. When she gets home from school, she puts her bag down and goes over there and they just play until it's dark.

When she speaks to my mom it's mostly in Hmong, but when she speaks to us or her friends it's always in English. Sometimes she says the wrong word in Hmong to my mom, and my mom goes, "You don't know that much Hmong anymore!" I imagine this worries my mom, because in our culture, a girl is supposed to be a good daughter, like knowing how to speak her language—so that when she marries she could communicate with her in-laws in a more formal way.

Sometimes I think I'd like to have some American friends too, but—like if they invite me over to their house, I don't feel comfortable going over because I'm afraid they might think I'm different. I might get stereotyped or something by them—like they might think I would steal their stuff. So if they ask me to go, I usually end up making excuses like, "My family's going out and I gotta be there."

I don't invite them over to my house either because there's a lot of people in my family, and I know they're not used to that. And my parents are not like American families where you go over, and they really invite you in, they say "take a seat" and they give you refreshments, stuff like that. I've been over to American families, like for a party and stuff. Even though they may not know you, they kind of make you feel like it's okay. But Hmong families . . . well, they're the same way too, but they don't have that much to offer, like food or anything. So I don't want to invite kids over and then just sit around. We don't have games like in American families, where they all play board games together like Monopoly, or they have all these other games, or they say "Let's play on the backyard swings." We don't have stuff like that.

And then they might not like . . . uh, all of us speaking Hmong. They might think we're talking about them, and then that might make them feel uncomfortable—because my parents don't know that much English. I just feel like it's kind of embarrassing to invite them over to my house. But then I go, "Why should I feel embarrassed?" But sometimes I just feel that way.

When I invite my Hmong friends over, it just feels like they're 10
my brothers and sisters. It's like they're just there. They don't expect to have games or things to have fun with. We can just talk or listen to music, watch TV, maybe do homework or something. And they don't even notice my mom and them. It's like we're all the same.

But usually I don't feel like I'm a real Hmong either because . . . for example, I don't know that much about the Hmong language. I kind of feel angry at myself because I should know what my parents or grandparents are saying to me. Sometimes I find it really hard to understand what they mean. There are a lot of words they use that I don't know. Like sometimes they tell me, "Go and get something in the backyard," like parsley. They say it and I go, but then I ask myself, "Wait, what did they mean? Is it this, or is it this?" . . . I didn't know what the word meant, but I didn't want to be embarrassed in front of them, so I just take my chances at guessing which. Half the time I would get the right one. But the other times I would get it wrong, and they would just think I was absentminded, like they'd say, "How can you be so forgetful? It was the same one you picked last time."

I'm not keeping my own culture, that's how I'm feeling. And I'm keeping the culture that is not even mine. It's confusing—even with Hmong kids I know, they're becoming more Americanized, and they speak more English to you than Hmong. You want to speak Hmong to them, but then you might not feel comfortable—because they may not want to speak Hmong, or they may not know as much Hmong as you and then they would feel uncomfortable.

It's so easy to forget your language and the culture because you don't come in contact with it as much as you would if you were back in Laos. Like, my parents want me to learn the bamboo pipes. Sometimes I feel that I want to, but usually I don't because I don't see much use for them everyday. If I was back in Laos, I would be learning to play the bamboo pipes, but since I'm here, I'm more into American stuff, like playing volleyball and basketball and football and going out with my friends.

Here you're in so much contact with American things, like on TV: you don't see anything about your own culture, but you see everything about American culture, so that's what you learn.

1998

For Discussion and Writing

1. What concrete objects and behaviors does Pao Her associate with American-ness? How does he contrast those things with Hmong-ness?
2. Examine Her's discussion of his feelings. Where does he express contradictory ideas? What effect do these contradictory feelings have on his sense of identity?
3. Compare Pao Her's ways of being American with Mary Antin's. Do they express similar conflicts? Explain.
4. Write a letter to Pao Her in which you suggest ways in which he might be able to be both Hmong and American. How can he resolve his conflict about being neither?

From "The *Pineros*"

Tom Knudson

Sweatshops might conjure up images of the early 1900s, but they thrive in twenty-first century America as well. As in earlier eras, they are dangerous, exploitive workplaces, filled with foreign-born workers who fear they will lose their jobs if they complain or ask for changes. Many live with the constant fear of deportation. Similar conditions are the norm in agricultural and forest work, where most of the laborers are from Mexico and South American countries. While the U.S. has at times actively encouraged and invited these experienced workers in order to cope with labor shortages, whenever there is a perceived threat to American jobs, "guest workers" are often deported. Despite more than a century of labor reforms, foreign-born workers remain as vulnerable as their early twentieth century counterparts.

✦

In the impoverished Guatemala border town of La Mesilla, 15-year old Santa Pablo Bautista failed to heed her father's pleas to stay home on their tiny hillside farm.

Juan Carlos Rios, 22, was equally dismissive when his mother begged him not to leave Jerez, Mexico.

Born into poverty, both felt the tug of money to be made in *El Norte.*

Two months after arriving to harvest brush in Washington state, Santa Pablo lay in a hospital with a fractured arm, broken jaw and cuts across her face. Days after taking a job as a tree planter in Oregon, Juan Carlos Rios returned home in a casket.

Forest work has always been dangerous. But Juan Carlos was 5
not killed, nor Santa Pablo injured, in the woods. Instead, disaster struck on the highway—on long-distance, pre-dawn commutes in unsafe, unstable vans that tumbled and veered out-of-control on windy mountain roads.

The number one cause of death among *pineros*—Latino forest workers—is not the slip of a chain saw or the falling trees known as widow-makers. It is van accidents. And unlike most highway tragedies, the crashes that claim migrant lives are not born of chance alone.

They are the by-products of fatigue, poorly maintained vehicles, ineffective state and federal laws, inexperienced drivers and poverty-stricken workers hungry for jobs.

"When you add everything up, it's a formula for disaster," said Robert Perez, a Fresno lawyer who has represented scores of Latino laborers hurt and killed in van accidents.

All told, 21 pineros are known to have died in van accidents over just the last three years: 14 in Maine, five in Washington and two in Oregon. But those numbers don't begin to measure the pain: across Guatemala and Honduras, at least 15 women have lost their partners and 69 children no longer have their fathers.

10 Six years ago, the deaths of 13 San Joaquin Valley farmworkers in a van crash prompted California legislators to pass the nation's toughest migrant vehicle safety law. The law made seat belts compulsory for everyone riding in vans carrying nine or more passengers and required that bench seats be bolted to the floor. It mandated that vans be inspected and certified safe yearly and that drivers pass a driver-training course for multipassenger vans.

Other states have not been so vigilant. In Oregon and Washington, for example, migrant labor law does not require annual vehicle inspections or a special test for drivers who transport migrant workers in vans.

"California has done it," said Matthew Geyman, a Seattle attorney representing the families of four forest workers from Guatemala who died in the 2004 van crash in Washington. "We could use California as a model. It would save lives."

But even California's tough law goes only so far. Last year, 1,300 migrant worker vans were pulled over by the California Highway Patrol and 2,882 citations were issued, up 150 percent from 2002. And many violations go undetected.

"I don't want to put the finger on nobody because I'm in this business. But I see a lot of contractors with vans with no certification, nothing," said Raul Acevedo, a supervisor for Central Valley Forestry, a reforestation contractor based in Exeter.

15 "Why do I have to spend so much money myself fixing my vans . . . and why don't (other) guys?" Acevedo asked. "It's not fair. I wish somebody could do something."

At the federal level, the Migrant and Seasonal Agricultural Worker Protection Act requires that vans pass a safety test for such things as brakes, wipers and mirrors. But unlike California's law, it does not mandate that every passenger have a seat belt. And inspections are rare.

"This is a national problem and one which calls for a national solution," said Sen. Dianne Feinstein, D-Calif., who plans to reintroduce legislation, modeled on California's law, requiring seat belts for all migrant workers riding in vans.

"Migrant workers should not have to put their lives at risk just to travel to their job site," she said.

Feinstein first tried to pass such a law in 2000, following the San Joaquin Valley tragedy, but her effort failed after farm interests objected to the cost of retrofitting older vans with seat belts.

Unlike California's law, the existing federal migrant worker 20
statute does not require drivers to take and pass a special safe-driving course for multi-passenger vans. Instead, it requires only that they pass a physical exam.

"A physical is fine and well and dandy. But it doesn't have anything to do with safety," said Martin Desmond, former executive director of the Northwest Reforestation Contractors Association. "It is just sort of a meaningless exercise."

The road has long been a risky place for farmworkers. But over the past two decades, as Latinos have moved rapidly into the forest work force, timber country highways have turned deadly, too.

"Most of the liability in our industry is on the transportation side," said Robert "Wade" Zaharie, an Idaho reforestation contractor who employs Latino crews and requires all workers—not just drivers—to attend a defensive driving class.

"We're telling (employees) if they ever observe that a foreman is not driving safely, let the office know immediately," Zaharie said. "You just can't afford that liability."

Zaharie blamed the problem on bad habits learned south of 25
the border. "Unfortunately, we're dying for people that have more common sense in our industry," he said "If you follow this back into Mexico, or any of your Latin countries, there are tons of accidents down there. They don't have as dear a respect for life, in general."

The life of Alberto Martín Calmo is remembered every day in his parents' adobe home in the hardscrabble hills outside the village of Todos Santos in northern Guatemala. His grave is a mile or so away—on a scenic knoll in a neighborhood of pines. A picture of his body in a casket hangs near the front door.

"I look at that picture and I cry," said his mother, 60-year-old Luisa Calmo Ramírez. "All I do is cry."

Her 31-year-old son died in the van accident in Washington in March 2004. Today, Luisa and her 70-year-old husband, Macario Martín Ordóñez, are raising three of their son's children—ages 8,

10 and 12. In the months after their father's death, the children seemed not to comprehend the loss.

"They would ask me, 'When is papa coming home?'" said Luisa. As she spoke, she hovered over a wood fire on the dirt floor of her living room, cooking tortillas for the family.

30 "I would tell them: 'Please be quiet. He'll come back someday.' But of course he won't," she said, speaking in her native Mam language and struggling to hold back tears.

Her dead son's wife stayed in the United States with two younger children—leaving the rest to her and Macario.

"I am old and it is hard to work," Macario said one windy afternoon this spring. "My son used to send home money. He was taking care of us. Now there is nothing."

All highway travel is dangerous. But for the pineros, it is a roller-coaster ride. Mountain roads twist, dip, climb and corkscrew. Often the weather is hostile.

Fatigue compounds the risk. Crews routinely work six days a week, sometimes seven. Just getting to work is an ordeal. Commutes of 100 miles are not unusual, beginning before dawn and dragging on for hours. The three fatal forest labor crashes all happened in the early morning: at 6:08 A.M. in Oregon, 6:45 A.M. in Washington and 7:55 A.M. in Maine.

35 Forest Service work notes reflect that peril, too: "Contractor arrived at 7 A.M. They still haven't found a place to stay. . . . It takes them four hours driving time each way," wrote Karen Bell, a contract inspector on the Sierra National Forest in 2003.

"Reforestation workers don't get paid for travel time," said Dan Robertson, president of the Northwest Reforestation Contractors Association. "So in order to get in an eight-hour day, they get up at four in the morning." . . . .

Around 3 A.M. on Monday, Jan. 3, 2005, a van pulled up at an apartment complex in Salem, Ore. Inside, Francisco Sánchez Rios and his cousin Juan Carlos were waiting—eager to begin new jobs as tree planters. They stepped out into the darkness and hopped in the vehicle: a silver 2002 Ford E350 with a bald left rear tire.

Three hours and 150 miles later, on an icy stretch of road near the coast, Francisco felt the van veer to the right. "We were skidding," he said. As the van plunged off the road, the driver screamed.

Pinned beneath the overturned vehicle, Francisco remembers crying out: "Juan! Where are you?" In the darkness, Francisco said he heard a reply from his cousin: "Please help me." Then, on the wet ground along the right side of the vehicle, Rios died of massive chest and abdominal injuries, just three days shy of his 23rd birthday.

An Oregon State Police investigator later found that three factors had contributed to the crash: poor driving, icy conditions and the bald tire that failed to grip the road.

The tire "was worn down to the cords in areas throughout the circumference. . . . The spare tire was located and found to be inflated, having more than adequate tread depth," the inspector wrote in his report.

"The night before we had dinner together," said Juan Carlos' sister, Lorena Rodarte Rios, of Salem, choked by grief a week after the accident. "He was very happy because the job was going to pay well, around $10 an hour. It was his dream to provide for his mother in Mexico. He was his mother's right hand."

In a dry, dusty neighborhood in Jerez, Mexico—southwest of Zacatecas—Rios' mother, Nicolasa, took the news hard. For days, she cried. When her son's body arrived on Saturday, Jan. 15, Nicolasa was stricken with anguish—too stunned to even attend a wake in the carport outside her home.

Finally, as mourners wailed and a hearse arrived Sunday to take Juan Carlos' body to church for a funeral Mass, Nicolasa stepped outside to say goodbye. She leaned over the coffin and rubbed her son's face, gently at first, then more forcefully.

"Please let me go with him," she sobbed, inconsolably.

"I am going crazy!" she screamed. "Let me go with him!"

As her older son, Javier, struggled to pull her away, Nicolasa tugged desperately at the coffin, then let go, wobbled a few steps and fainted.

Juan Carlos Rios was hired to plant trees on property owned by Menasha Forest Products Corp., a major U.S. timber firm. But Menasha maintains it bears no responsibility for the death because it, in turn, hired a labor contractor to plant the trees and transport the workers.

"It was not our vehicle. They were not our employees. They were contract employees," said Barbara Bauder, director of human resources and community relations for Menasha in the Oregon coastal community of North Bend.

"It was a tragedy," Bauder added. "But since it wasn't people we knew and they really weren't from our area, it didn't hit quite so close to home."

In August, the U.S. Department of Labor agreed with Menasha's assessment of blame. It fined the timber company's contractor—BP Reforestation—$3,000, saying it failed to provide safe transportation. The contracting company has appealed the fine. . . .

2006

For Discussion and Writing

1. A reforestation contractor quoted on p. 177 claims that the reason there are so many vehicle accidents among forest workers is that "there are tons of accidents down there [in Mexico and South America]. They don't have as dear a respect for life, in general." What is the effect of this statement in the context of the individual stories?
2. How does this article try to create outrage and sympathy for the workers? What effect do the individual stories have on the larger story of the status of forest workers in America?
3. How can we explain the contradictions between the situation described in "The *Pineros*" and the American Dream? Is it possible to believe in the American Dream, and also to believe that there is nothing wrong with the way Latino forest workers are treated?
4. In an essay, consider Carnegie's advice to young men to start with menial jobs and work their way up in the context of the *pineros*. Can a *pinero* realistically expect to move on to bigger and better jobs by following Carnegie's advice? Does some or all of Carnegie's advice still hold up? What evidence could be given to a *pinero* that menial labor will some day pay off?

"The Day an Immigrant Refugee Can Say, 'I'm an American'"

HELENE COOPER

Helene Cooper has been a member of the New York Times *editorial board since 2004. She has extensive experience reporting on foreign affairs and economics, and in 2002, she edited* At Home in the World, *a collection of writings by Daniel Pearl, the* Wall Street Journal *writer who was kidnapped and murdered by extremists in Pakistan. A native of Liberia, Cooper became an American citizen in 1997.*

My mom sounded both rushed and chirpy when she called Wednesday morning: "I'm driving myself to the beauty parlor to get my hair done."

"What are you, crazy?" I said. She got out of the hospital a week and a half ago after orthopedic surgery, and can't really walk yet, let alone drive.

"Tomorrow I become an American citizen, and I am not taking the oath of citizenship with dirty hair."

As the debate over immigration reform swirls in Washington and around the country, the emotional significance behind the phrase "path to citizenship" can be lost. I've been reading articles about border patrols and National Guardsmen; I've seen TV reports conjuring up the fearsome specter of classrooms filled with children speaking Spanish, as if that would somehow threaten the very American-ness of our existence.

What I hadn't seen, and had somehow managed to forget, was 5
why the path to citizenship is so important. Why isn't the green card or the work permit enough?

My family moved here in bits and pieces from Liberia, fleeing coups, revolutions and civil wars. My mom came in 1990, after Charles Taylor invaded Liberia and started a war that would kill 500,000 people in Liberia, Ivory Coast and Sierra Leone.

She came on a one-month tourist visa, and initially got a job as a home health aide. It was a far cry from our well-off existence in Liberia. But who wouldn't rather be poor in America than rich in a country where soldiers could enter your home, rape your children and murder your parents? Eventually she got a green card, and has since retired. I became a citizen in 1997, but for 16 years, my mother could not call herself an American.

Yesterday, my younger sister and I drove her to the Homeland Security Department's office in suburban Virginia, where 63 immigrants were to become citizens. We were late, and everyone looked tense, as if they were afraid that something they wanted so badly could be yanked away at the last minute.

Standing at the front of the room was Robert Schofield, the supervisory adjudications officer. At first, he rubbed me the wrong way. He kept repeating that people should come up as their names were called, but not to come up if they hadn't filled out citizenship forms. My mom became flustered—of course she hadn't filled out her form. As soon as I handed her a pen, Mr. Schofield called out her name. My mom reached for her walker, grabbed her bag, dropped the pen, dropped the form. "It's O.K., Mommy," my sister said.

10 Eventually all 63 people were seated in front of the dais. Mr. Schofield smiled at them. "All right, folks," he said. "Today you are going to become U.S. citizens."

Suddenly he didn't seem so officious anymore, and the tension in the room started to ease. The 63—from El Salvador, the Philippines, China, South Korea, Afghanistan, Bolivia and Liberia—all stood. The woman from Afghanistan was wearing a gorgeous cream abaya, her eyes lined with kohl. She looked at my mom and smiled.

A woman named Phyllis Howard, the immigration agency's district director, administered the oath of allegiance. My mom teared up while singing "The Star-Spangled Banner," but not when they played a patriotic video with Lee Greenwood singing "God Bless the USA."

I've always thought that was a sappy song, too, but I felt the tears start to well as I watched my mom staring at images meant to arouse patriotism: that great statue of the marines at Iwo Jima, the Washington Monument at sunset, a bald eagle, cherry blossoms around the Jefferson Memorial.

Whenever Lee Greenwood sang the chorus—"And I gladly stand up next to you, and defend her still today"—the video showed a graduating Coast Guard class, standing up. When he sang, "'Cause there ain't no doubt I love this land," it showed newly minted immigrants gazing reverently at the American flag and reciting the Pledge of Allegiance.

15 This, I suddenly thought, is why a green card isn't enough. There is something about being able to say you're American that can get you in your gut. Maybe it's because being American pretty much means you, or your parents or grandparents, came from somewhere else. For all the national debate about immigration, this remains a country defined by the diversity of its people. Once you take that oath, all you have to do is say you're American, and you are.

After the song, Mr. Schofield called out names and handed each person a naturalization certificate. Everyone posed with him in front of the flag to have pictures taken.

My mom was the last called. "Calista Cooper." She was standing up, trying to get her walker. "Wait, I'll bring it to you," he said.

My mom shook her head. "No," she said, pushing her walker up to the dais. "I want to be next to the flag."

2006

For Discussion and Writing

1. What does Cooper's mother's experience say about the path to American citizenship?
2. Cooper asks, "Why isn't the green card or the work permit enough?" Why might immigrants want more than legal permission to work in the U.S.?
3. Why are the immigrants nervous about their impending American citizenship?
4. What is there about being an American "that can get you in the gut"?
5. In an essay, discuss how does Cooper's definition of Americans compares with Frederick Jackson Turner's, found elsewhere in this chapter. In what ways has the definition shifted for Cooper?

Chapter 3: For Further Research and Writing

1. What does it mean to assimilate in American society? What is expected of an assimilated immigrant? How should s/he look, behave, think?
2. In what ways have diverse immigrant groups helped to shape American identity? Choose three specific groups and trace their influence on American culture.
3. In his 1782 book, *Letters from an American Farmer,* Hector St. John de Crèvecoeur wrote that in America, "individuals of all nations are melted into a new race of men, whose labours and posterity will one day cause great changes in the world." In your view, to what extent was Crèvecoeur's description accurate? To what extent was it *not* accurate?
4. Crèvecoeur anticipated the still-influential "melting pot" image, which stipulates that immigrants will "melt" into the culture of their adopted nation and become indistinguishable from native-born citizens. While this process is generally presented as positive, what is lost when individuals shed some or all of their identity? To what extent is it possible for all individuals to melt and disappear into the general population? To what extent is it *not* possible?
5. The motto of the United States, *E Pluribus Unum,* translates as "From the many, one." Explain how this ideal might be seen both as a unifying ideology and as a means of exclusion.
6. One of the central ideologies of the American Dream is that work is rewarded in equal measure to effort, regardless of an individual's background. Citing readings in this chapter, write an essay explaining how this and other ideologies can hinder or help in attaining the American Dream.

CHAPTER 4

Sustaining the Dream

The United States has always been a diverse nation that has met its challenges fully; however, technology has altered twenty-first century life in ways the colonists could never have imagined. For example, the oceans that flank our country are no longer the isolating elements that they once were. We've experienced wars and scandals, natural crises, and crises of the soul.

The American Dream has been manipulated throughout the last 200 years to promote various agendas. Its reputation has been tarnished. Some believe it's meant for others, but not for them. Yet the Dream has endured. The prominence of some elements has increased, and that of others has diminished.

As you read the selections in Chapter 4, consider the variety of ways that the American Dream has been sustained, altered, or abandoned. The readings move chronologically from the lives of pre-Depression Americans to the concerns of what the media likes to call Generation Next. As you read these selections, focus on how we have changed, and look for ways in which the visions of people like Thomas Jefferson, Horatio Alger, and Martin Luther King, Jr., have attempted to sustain the American Dream.

Little Boxes

MALVINA REYNOLDS

In 1947, Levitt & Sons construction company began building the first of 2000 mass-produced homes outside New York City. By 1951, Levittown, New York, was a community of 17,447 homes—arguably the first suburb in the United States. Today more Americans live in suburbs than in either cities or rural areas.

Malvina Reynolds (1900–1978), a political activist and singer/songwriter, wrote "Little Boxes." Recorded by Pete Seeger in 1962,

"Little Boxes" became an anthem for suburbia's greatest critics—those who decry its perceived conformity and emphasis on materialism.

Little boxes on the hillside,
Little boxes made of ticky tacky
Little boxes on the hillside,
Little boxes all the same,
There's a green one and a pink one
And a blue one and a yellow one
And they're all made out of ticky tacky
And they all look just the same.

And the people in the houses
All went to the university
Where they were put in boxes
And they came out all the same
And there's doctors and lawyers
And business executives
And they're all made out of ticky tacky
And they all look just the same.

And they all play on the golf course
And drink their martinis dry
And they all have pretty children
And the children go to school,
And the children go to summer camp
And then to the university
Where they are put in boxes
And they come out all the same.

And the boys go into business
And marry and raise a family
In boxes made of ticky tacky
And they all look just the same,
There's a green one and a pink one
And a blue one and a yellow one
And they're all made out of ticky tacky
And they all look just the same.

1962

For Discussion and Writing

1. Can you name other "boxes" besides those Reynolds names in her lyrics?
2. We hear a lot about "comfort zones" and "thinking outside the box." To what extent has your education boxed you in? To what extent has it taught you to think outside the box?
3. You won't find "ticky tacky" in the dictionary, but people generally see a negative connotation in the term. What does "ticky tacky" suggest to you? What, in the term, fosters that suggestion?
4. Write a critique of suburban life as you see it, including both its advantages and its disadvantages. As you think about this assignment, be sure you understand the relevance of your perspective as either having grown up in a suburb or not, and to allow for that perspective in your critique.

Address at Rice University on the Space Effort: The New Frontier

John F. Kennedy

John F. Kennedy (1917–1963) served as our nation's thirty-fifth president (from 1961–1963) at a time when the American Dream was being challenged from within and from without the United States. Kennedy's term saw the emergence of the national Civil Rights movement and the beginning of the Vietnam War. In addition, Kennedy served at a time when the Cold War was at its height; events such as the building of the Berlin Wall, the Bay of Pigs invasion, and The Cuban Missile Crisis defined America's global status. The Space Race, which this speech addresses, was partly the result of ongoing conflict between the United States and the Soviet Union.

Kennedy's assassination on November 22, 1963, changed life and the perception of the American Dream for many Americans.

✦

We meet at a college noted for knowledge, in a city noted for progress, in a State noted for strength, and we stand in need of all three, for we meet in an hour of change and challenge, in a decade of hope and fear, in an age of both knowledge and ignorance. The greater our knowledge increases, the greater our ignorance unfolds.

Despite the striking fact that most of the scientists that the world has ever known are alive and working today, despite the fact that this Nation's own scientific manpower is doubling every 12 years in a rate of growth more than three times that of our population as a whole, despite that, the vast stretches of the unknown and the unanswered and the unfinished still far out-strip our collective comprehension.

No man can fully grasp how far and how fast we have come, but condense, if you will, the 50,000 years of man's recorded history in a time span of but a half century. Stated in these terms, we know very little about the first 40 years, except at the end of them advanced man had learned to use the skins of animals to cover them. Then about 10 years ago, under this standard, man emerged from his caves to construct other kinds of shelter. Only 5 years ago man learned to write and use a cart with wheels. Christianity began less than 2 years ago. The printing press came this year, and then less than 2 months ago, during this whole 50-year span of human history, the steam engine provided a new source of power.

Newton explored the meaning of gravity. Last month electric lights and telephones and automobiles and airplanes became available. Only last week did we develop penicillin and television and nuclear power, and now if America's new spacecraft succeeds in reaching Venus, we will have literally reached the stars before midnight tonight.

5 This is a breathtaking pace, and such a pace cannot help but create new ills as it dispels old, new ignorance, new problems, new dangers. Surely the opening vistas of space promise high costs and hardships, as well as high reward.

So it is not surprising that some would have us stay where we are a little longer to rest, to wait. But this city of Houston, this State of Texas, this country of the United States was not built by those who waited and rested and wished to look behind them. This country was conquered by those who moved forward—and so will space.

William Bradford, speaking in 1630 of the founding of the Plymouth Bay Colony, said that all great and honorable actions are accompanied with great difficulties, and both must be enterprised and overcome with answerable courage.

If this capsule history of our progress teaches us anything, it is that man, in his quest for knowledge and progress, is determined and cannot be deterred. The exploration of space will go ahead, whether we join in it or not, and it is one of the great adventures of all time, and no nation which expects to be the leader of other nations can expect to stay behind in this race for space.

Those who came before us made certain that this country rode the first waves of the industrial revolutions, the first waves of modern invention, and the first wave of nuclear power, and this generation does not intend to founder in the backwash of the coming age of space. We mean to be a part of it—we mean to lead it. For the eyes of the world now look into space, to the moon and to the planets beyond, and we have vowed that we shall not see it governed by a hostile flag of conquest, but by a banner of freedom and peace. We have vowed that we shall not see space filled with weapons of mass destruction, but with instruments of knowledge and understanding.

Yet the vows of this Nation can only be fulfilled if we in this 10
Nation are first, and, therefore, we intend to be first. In short, our leadership in science and in industry, our hopes for peace and security, our obligations to ourselves as well as others, all require us to make this effort, to solve these mysteries, to solve them for the good of all men, and to become the world's leading space-faring nation.

We set sail on this new sea because there is new knowledge to be gained, and new rights to be won, and they must be won and used for the progress of all people. For space science, like nuclear science and all technology, has no conscience of its own. Whether it will become a force for good or ill depends on man, and only if the United States occupies a position of pre-eminence can we help decide whether this new ocean will be a sea of peace or a new terrifying theater of war. I do not say that we should or will go unprotected against the hostile misuse of space any more than we go unprotected against the hostile use of land or sea, but I do say that space can be explored and mastered without feeding the fires of war, without repeating the mistakes that man has made in extending his writ around this globe of ours.

There is no strife, no prejudice, no national conflict in outer space as yet. Its hazards are hostile to us all. Its conquest deserves the best of all mankind, and its opportunity for peaceful cooperation may never come again. But why, some say, the moon? Why choose this as our goal? And they may well ask why climb the highest mountain. Why, 35 years ago, fly the Atlantic? Why does Rice play Texas?

We choose to go to the moon. We choose to go to the moon in this decade and do the other things, not because they are easy, but because they are hard, because that goal will serve to organize and measure the best of our energies and skills, because that challenge is one that we are willing to accept, one we are unwilling to postpone, and one which we intend to win, and the others, too.

It is for these reasons that I regard the decision last year to shift our efforts in space from low to high gear as among the most important decisions that will be made during my incumbency in the Office of the Presidency.

15 In the last 24 hours we have seen facilities now being created for the greatest and most complex exploration in man's history. We have felt the ground shake and the air shattered by the testing of a Saturn C-1 booster rocket, many times as powerful as the Atlas which launched John Glenn, generating power equivalent to 10,000 automobiles with their accelerators on the floor. We have seen the site where five F-1 rocket engines, each one as powerful as all eight engines of the Saturn combined, will be clustered together to make the advanced Saturn missile, assembled in a new building to be built at Cape Canaveral as tall as a 48-story structure, as wide as a city block, and as long as two lengths of this field.

Within these last 19 months at least 45 satellites have circled the earth. Some 40 of them were "made in the United States of America" and they were far more sophisticated and supplied far more knowledge to the people of the world than those of the Soviet Union.

The Mariner spacecraft now on its way to Venus is the most intricate instrument in the history of space science. The accuracy of that shot is comparable to firing a missile from Cape Canaveral and dropping it in this stadium between the 40-yard lines.

Transit satellites are helping our ships at sea to steer a safer course. Tiros satellites have given us unprecedented warnings of hurricanes and storms, and will do the same for forest fires and icebergs.

We have had our failures, but so have others, even if they do not admit them. And they may be less public.

20 To be sure, we are behind, and will be behind for some time in manned flight. But we do not intend to stay behind, and in this decade we shall make up and move ahead.

The growth of our science and education will be enriched by new knowledge of our universe and environment, by new techniques of learning and mapping and observation, by new tools and computers for industry, medicine, the home as well as the school. Technical institutions, such as Rice, will reap the harvest of these gains.

And finally, the space effort itself, while still in its infancy, has already created a great number of new companies, and tens of thousands of new jobs. Space and related industries are generating new demands in investment and skilled personnel, and this city and this State, and this region, will share greatly in this growth.

What was once the furthest outpost on the old frontier of the West will be the furthest outpost on the new frontier of science and space. Houston, your City of Houston, with its Manned Spacecraft Center, will become the heart of a large scientific and engineering community. During the next 5 years the National Aeronautics and Space Administration expects to double the number of scientists and engineers in this area, to increase its outlays for salaries and expenses to $60 million a year; to invest some $200 million in plant and laboratory facilities; and to direct or contract for new space efforts over $1 billion from this Center in this City.

To be sure, all this costs us all a good deal of money. This year's space budget is three times what it was in January 1961, and it is greater than the space budget of the previous 8 years combined. That budget now stands at $5,400 million a year—a staggering sum, though somewhat less than we pay for cigarettes and cigars every year. Space expenditures will soon rise some more from 40 cents per person per week to more than 50 cents a week for every man, woman, and child in the United States, for we have given this program a high national priority even though I realize that this is in some measure an act of faith and vision, for we do not now know what benefits await us. But if I were to say, my fellow citizens, that we shall send to the moon, 240,000 miles away from the control station in Houston, a giant rocket more than 300 feet tall, the length of this football field, made of new metal alloys, some of which have not yet been invented, capable of standing heat and stresses several times more than have ever been experienced, fitted together with a precision better than the finest watch, carrying all the equipment needed for propulsion, guidance, control, communications, food and survival, on an untried mission, to an unknown celestial body, and then return it safely to earth, reentering the atmosphere at speeds of over 25,000 miles per hour, causing heat about half that of the temperature of the sun—almost as hot as it is here today—and do all this, and do it right, and do it first before this decade is out, then we must be bold.

However, I think we're going to do it, and I think that we must pay what needs to be paid. I don't think we ought to waste any money, but I think we ought to do the job. And this will be done in the decade of the sixties. It may be done while some of you are still here at school at this college and university. It will be done during the terms of office of some of the people who sit here on this platform. But it will be done. And it will be done before the end of this decade.

Many years ago the great British explorer George Mallory, 25
who was to die on Mount Everest, was asked why did he want to climb it. He said, "Because it is there."

Well, space is there, and we're going to climb it, and the moon and the planets are there, and new hopes for knowledge and peace are there. And, therefore, as we set sail we ask God's blessing on the most hazardous and dangerous and greatest adventure on which man has ever embarked.

1962

For Discussion and Writing

1. As Chapter 3 has illustrated, expansion played a large part in the American Dream, and the move westward was a defining element of nineteenth century America. Eventually, of course, restless Americans found an insurmountable object in their path: the Pacific Ocean. How does Kennedy's quest for space revive expansion as an element of the American Dream?
2. John F. Kennedy was a compelling speaker. Note particularly paragraphs three and eight, which illustrate two speech patterns of his style: parallel statements ("The greater our knowledge increases, the greater our ignorance unfolds") and series of (usually three) items ("at a college noted for knowledge, in a city noted for progress, in a State noted for strength"). What other examples of parallel structure do you see in the *Address at Rice University*? How do parallel structures unify and simplify a speech for an audience? What other patterns define Kennedy's style?
3. Kennedy stresses the value of exploration of space to scientific and educational growth, technological advancement, and economic gain, but the space race with the Soviet Union is an underlying reason for space exploration. Why does Kennedy feel that space exploration is necessary for American security?
4. Kennedy compares George Mallory's famous reason for climbing Mount Everest, "Because it is there," with his own reason: "Well, space is there, and we're going to climb it, and the moon and the planets are there, and new hopes for knowledge and peace are there." What effect does this final statement of the speech have on audience emotions?

Great Society Speech

Lyndon B. Johnson

Lyndon Baines Johnson (1908–1978), 36th president of the United States, assumed the presidency upon the assassination of President John F. Kennedy in 1963 and served until 1969. As president he pushed through an extensive program of legislation dealing with domestic issues. On the national front, he was responsible for the escalation of the Vietnam War. Although he was re-elected by a landslide in 1964, his popularity declined, leading to his decision not to run for the presidency in 1968.

Johnson's Great Society speech *was delivered to the graduating class of 1964 at the University of Michigan in Ann Arbor.*

I have come today from the turmoil of your Capital to the tranquility of your campus to speak about the future of your country.

The purpose of protecting the life of our Nation and preserving the liberty of our citizens is to pursue the happiness of our people. Our success in that pursuit is the test of our success as a Nation.

For a century we labored to settle and to subdue a continent. For half a century we called upon unbounded invention and untiring industry to create an order of plenty for all of our people.

The challenge of the next half century is whether we have the wisdom to use that wealth to enrich and elevate our national life, and to advance the quality of our American civilization.

Your imagination, your initiative, and your indignation will 5
determine whether we build a society where progress is the servant of our needs, or a society where old values and new visions are buried under unbridled growth. For in your time we have the opportunity to move not only toward the rich society and the powerful society, but upward to the Great Society.

The Great Society rests on abundance and liberty for all. It demands an end to poverty and racial injustice, to which we are totally committed in our time. But that is just the beginning.

The Great Society is a place where every child can find knowledge to enrich his mind and to enlarge his talents. It is a place where leisure is a welcome chance to build and reflect, not a feared cause of boredom and restlessness. It is a place where the city of man serves not only the needs of the body and the demands of commerce but the desire for beauty and the hunger for community.

It is a place where man can renew contact with nature. It is a place which honors creation for its own sake and for what is adds to the understanding of the race. It is a place where men are more concerned with the quality of their goals than the quantity of their goods.

But most of all, the Great Society is not a safe harbor, a resting place, a final objective, a finished work. It is a challenge constantly renewed, beckoning us toward a destiny where the meaning of our lives matches the marvelous products of our labor.

10 So I want to talk to you today about three places where we begin to build the Great Society—in our cities, in our countryside, and in our classrooms.

Many of you will live to see the day, perhaps 50 years from now, when there will be 400 million Americans—four-fifths of them in urban areas. In the remainder of this century urban population will double, city land will double, and we will have to build homes, highways, and facilities equal to all those built since this country was first settled. So in the next 40 years we must rebuild the entire urban United States.

Aristotle said: "Men come together in cities in order to live, but they remain together in order to live the good life." It is harder and harder to live the good life in American cities today.

The catalog of ills is long: there is the decay of the centers and the despoiling of the suburbs. There is not enough housing for our people or transportation for our traffic. Open land is vanishing and old landmarks are violated.

Worst of all expansion is eroding the precious and time honored values of community with neighbors and communion with nature. The loss of these values breeds loneliness and boredom and indifference.

15 Our society will never be great until our cities are great. Today the frontier of imagination and innovation is inside those cities and not beyond their borders.

New experiments are already going on. It will be the task of your generation to make the American city a place where future generations will come, not only to live but to live the good life.

I understand that if I stayed here tonight I would see that Michigan students are really doing their best to live the good life.

This is the place where the Peace Corps was started. It is inspiring to see how all of you, while you are in this country, are trying so hard to live at the level of the people.

A second place where we begin to build the Great Society is in our countryside. We have always prided ourselves on being not only America the strong and America the free, but America the beautiful. Today that beauty is in danger. The water we drink, the food we eat, the very air that we breathe, are threatened with pollution. Our parks are overcrowded, our seashores overburdened. Green fields and dense forests are disappearing.

20 A few years ago we were greatly concerned about the "Ugly American." Today we must act to prevent an ugly America.

For once the battle is lost, once our natural splendor is destroyed, it can never be recaptured. And once man can no longer walk with beauty or wonder at nature his spirit will wither and his sustenance be wasted.

A third place to build the Great Society is in the classrooms of America. There your children's lives will be shaped. Our society will not be great until every young mind is set free to scan the farthest reaches of thought and imagination. We are still far from that goal.

Today, 8 million adult Americans, more than the entire population of Michigan, have not finished 5 years of school. Nearly 20 million have not finished 8 years of school. Nearly 54 million—more than one quarter of all America—have not even finished high school.

Each year more than 100,000 high school graduates, with proved ability, do not enter college because they cannot afford it. And if we cannot educate today's youth, what will we do in 1970 when elementary school enrollment will be 5 million greater than 1960? And high school enrollment will rise by 5 million. College enrollment will increase by more than 3 million.

25 In many places, classrooms are overcrowded and curricula are outdated. Most of our qualified teachers are underpaid, and many of our paid teachers are unqualified. So we must give every child a place to sit and a teacher to learn from. Poverty must not be a bar to learning, and learning must offer an escape from poverty.

But more classrooms and more teachers are not enough. We must seek an educational system which grows in excellence as it grows in size. This means better training for our teachers. It means preparing youth to enjoy their hours of leisure as well as their hours of labor. It means exploring new techniques of teaching, to find new ways to stimulate the love of learning and the capacity for creation.

These are three of the central issues of the Great Society. While our Government has many programs directed at those issues, I do not pretend that we have the full answer to those problems.

But I do promise this: We are going to assemble the best thought and the broadest knowledge from all over the world to find those answers for America. I intend to establish working groups to prepare a series of White House conferences and meetings—on the cities, on natural beauty, on the quality of education, and on other emerging challenges. And from these meetings and from this inspiration and from these studies we will begin to set our course toward the Great Society.

The solution to these problems does not rest on a massive program in Washington, nor can it rely solely on the strained resources of local authority. They require us to create new concepts of cooperation, a creative federalism, between the National Capital and the leaders of local communities.

Woodrow Wilson once wrote: "Every man sent out from his university should be a man of his Nation as well as a man of his time."

Within your lifetime powerful forces, already loosed, will take us toward a way of life beyond the realm of our experience, almost beyond the bounds of our imagination.

For better or for worse, your generation has been appointed by history to deal with those problems and to lead America toward a new age. You have the chance never before afforded to any people in any age. You can help build a society where the demands of morality, and the needs of the spirit, can be realized in the life of the Nation.

So, will you join in the battle to give every citizen the full equality which God enjoins and the law requires, whatever his belief, or race, or the color of his skin?

Will you join in the battle to give every citizen an escape from the crushing weight of poverty?

Will you join in the battle to make it possible for all nations to live in enduring peace—as neighbors and not as mortal enemies?

Will you join in the battle to build the Great Society, to prove that our material progress is only the foundation on which we will build a richer life of mind and spirit?

There are those timid souls who say this battle cannot be won; that we are condemned to a soulless wealth. I do not agree. We have the power to shape the civilization that we want. But we need your will, your labor, your hearts, if we are to build that kind of society.

Those who came to this land sought to build more than just a new country. They sought a new world. So I have come here today to your campus to say that you can make their vision our reality. So let us from this moment begin our work so that in the future men will look back and say: It was then, after a long and weary way, that man turned the exploits of his genius to the full enrichment of his life.

1964

For Discussion and Writing

1. Johnson echoes Jefferson's *Declaration of Independence* in his focus on the pursuit of happiness as part of the American Dream. To do this, he proposes a Great Society, using that term ten times in his speech. What, to Johnson, were the major components of the Great Society?
2. Johnson proposed programs to improve cities by controlling urban expansion and enhancing housing and transportation, to improve the countryside

through conservation, and to improve education through better classrooms, curricula, and teacher preparation. To what extent has the United States succeeded in resolving these problems? To what extent are the concerns expressed in the Great Society speech still concerns today?

3. Johnson pledged to end poverty and racial injustice, asserting that without meeting these goals, America would have "a soulless wealth." What does he mean by this? What is the moral call he makes?

"On Being Asian American"

Lawson Fusao Inada

During World War II, Lawson Inada was one of thousands of Japanese Americans torn from their homes and interned in camps in the western United States. Viewed as potential if not probable enemies of state after Japan's attack on Pearl Harbor, Japanese Americans lost personal property, rights, and freedoms. In 1998, the United States made a formal public apology and paid reparations to the survivors and the descendants of those interned at the camps. Inada's story is typical of his generation; born in Fresno, he is a Sansei, *or a second generation Japanese American. His book,* Before the War: Poems as They Happened, *was the first collection of poetry by an Asian American released by a major publisher. His poetry reflects the experience of Japanese Americans in the camps, and also the diversity of sounds and voices of his native California.*

On Being Asian American

For Our Children

Of course, not everyone
can be an Asian American.
Distinctions are earned
and deserve dedication.

Thus, from time of birth,
the journey awaits you
ventures through time,
the turns of the earth.

When you seem to arrive,
the journey continues;
when you seem to arrive,
the journey continues.

Take me as I am, you cry.
I, I, am an individual.
Which certainly is true.
Which generates an echo.

Who are all your people
assembled in celebration,
with wisdom and strength,
to which you are entitled.

For you are at the head
of succeeding generations,
as the rest of the world
comes forward to greet you.

1972

For Discussion and Writing

1. Why does the poem begin with the words, "Of course"?
2. What could the poet mean by "the journey"? Why does he refer to it so often?
3. How does Inada indicate the benefits and drawbacks of being Asian American?
4. What differences in tone do you detect between Inada's poem and Pao Her's feelings, as described in his oral history in Chapter 3?

"My American Dream"— Interview with Rafael Rosa

From *American Dreams: Lost and Found*

Studs Terkel

Studs Terkel has been the leading oral historian in America for the past half century, having collected and edited firsthand accounts and viewpoints from a vast number of "regular people" on such subjects as race, the Great Depression, World War II, death, and work. His interview subjects come from all over the United States and represent all social groups, from the nearly invisible to the wealthy and famous. In the oral history excerpted here, a young man born of Puerto Rican parents describes, in rich terms, his particular version of the American Dream.

✦

My American Dream is to be famous. Like a big boss at a big firm, sit back, relax, and just collect. Oh, I treat my employees nice, pay 'em real good, don't overwork 'em too much, not like most bosses, they fire you right away.

I really would like to have a chauffeur-driven limousine, have a bar one side, color TV on the other. The chicks, the girls, oh yeah. Instead of coming in at eight in the morning and leavin' at eight in the afternoon. Maybe I'll invent something one of these days and wind up a millionaire. As for now, I'd really like to be chief pilot at the air force.

As I ride my bike here in New York, I see all these elegant-looking people, fancy-dressed, riding around in a limousine, just looking all normal. I figured if they can do, why can't I? Why can't I just go out there and get myself driven around for a while? I haven't hit it big yet, but I'm still working on it.

As I started growing older, I figured it's a jungle out there, you better grab a vine. So I grabbed a vine, and here I landed. (Laughs.) It's really hard out there in the city; you can't get a job any more. I would just like to be on TV, a newsman or something.

My friends are always talkin' about havin' a nice sheen. That's a 5
nice car or van, something set up real nice on the inside with fold-away beds and wall-to-wall carpeting and paneling, fat tires, mufflers sticking out on the side, and speeding. Usually, they get together on this highway and they would race each other at the flat. It's really incredible. I don't see how these guys can do that. Drag racing.

I wanted to be a taxi driver. I figured it would be an exciting job, just riding around all day. Plus I had that driving fever. Most of the time, I dream I can fly, be all the way up there on the top. But I don't see how, unless I invent something, eh? Anti-gravity belt or something like that. It would cost a lot of loot just to make one of those. I'm a bicycle mechanic now. I ride 'em on one wheel also, but I don't think that's gonna get me far. I'd really like to be a motorcycle driver and explore the world.

Most of the time, I'm usually out in the streets, lookin' around. Scope on the nice women who pass by. I like their wardrobes and the way they walk, the way they talk. I should really be a gift to all women. I don't know how I'm gonna do it, but it's gotta be done somehow. (Laughs.)

My brother works in the post office, makin' some all-right money. My other brother works in a factory, getting some good money as long as he can put in overtime. We're all in the same business, tryin' to move up, tryin' to see if we can get this "flat fixed" place or a grocery store. With the right location, we'll move up.

I would really like to invest in something *real big*, like in baby food. You can never run out of baby food. And cars. We'll never run out of cars as long as we don't run out of people. I could invest in tires. Where there's tires, there's automobiles. I guess I'm gonna have to hit it big.

10 People today are more like keepin' it to themselves. They don't let their emotions show. They're afraid to lose respect, cool. I'm open most of the time, I kinda like to turn off and on. I'm the kind of guy that gets along with everybody. I'm Puerto Rican and I got the complexion of a Negro, so I can fall to either side. I've been chased by whites a couple of times, but nothing special happens.

What's goin' on these days with all the violence, a person's gotta think twice of walking down the street. One time I got mugged in the South Bronx. Three guys jumped me as I was walking down this dark street. One guy stops me for a cigarette, and as I go to give him one, two guys grab me from behind. They just started beatin' on me and took all my money and left me on the floor and fled. I recovered, and now I think twice about it. Before I was mugged, I walked down any street. I'd rather walk around a dark street than go through it, no matter how much time it's gonna take me to get there. If people call ya, I just keep on walking if I don't know the person. I look back and just keep walking.

I suggest: Don't walk alone at night. Walk with a stick to protect yourself. Don't get too high because it slows down your reflexes. You gotta keep your head clear. They say: Never look back. In real life, you gotta look back.

1980

For Discussion and Writing

1. What progression of ideas do you see taking place here as Rafael Rosa moves from fame to safety as his opening and closing topics?
2. Citing specific lines or sections of Rosa's account as support, how would you classify his attitude toward being able to achieve success in America? How

does that attitude help to sustain popular notions of what "success" means in American society?

3. If Rosa were to draw a map showing the path toward attaining the American Dream, what steps would be on that path?
4. In an essay, compare and contrast the viewpoints expressed by Rafael Rosa and Kanye West (elsewhere in this chapter) on the subject of material wealth and its role in becoming a successful American.

"Take The Power Back" (Text through Internet Search)

RAGE AGAINST THE MACHINE

Led by vocalist Zach de la Rocha and guitarist Tom Morello, the band Rage Against the Machine debuted in late 1992 and unleashed a steady torrent of hard-edged music and angry, confrontational lyrics to listeners throughout the 1990s. Taking on a wide range of issues from the imprisonment of Indian activist Leonard Peltier ("Freedom") to the corporate greed represented by the stock market ("Bulls on Parade"), de la Rocha and Morello carried on in the traditions of their fathers—a pro-Chicano street artist and a Kenyan guerilla fighter, respectively. With such intensity at its core, the band did not sustain itself for long, and in late 2000 de la Rocha left for a solo career that never materialized. The song "Take the Power Back," in typical Rage fashion, addresses in blunt terms a problem with the American education system and the materials it chooses to sanction. To find the lyrics to this song, simply type its title, plus the word "lyrics," into an Internet search engine, such as Google.

✦

For Discussion and Writing

1. Based on the specific complaints raised in the song, what do you suppose the "right light" mentioned in line one would be by the band's definition?
2. What other readings, elsewhere in this book, would support the band's claim that a Eurocentric viewpoint is harmful to Americans who represent other cultural backgrounds?

3. Toward the end of the song, the band says that the Weathermen should serve as an example for changing current models of education in the United States. After conducting research into the 1960s militant group by that name, would you agree with that sentiment?
4. In an essay, describe the role that education plays in a citizen's ability to achieve the American Dream—or to be locked out of it. Cite lyrics from this song and historical examples as your support in arguing in support for, or against, the central argument that the band presents here.

From "Kids in the Mall: Growing Up Controlled"

William Severini Kowinski

William Severini Kowinski (1946–), a freelance writer who has published in such periodicals as Esquire, Rolling Stone, The New York Times *and the* Los Angeles Times, *has studied mall life for over twenty years. The latest revision of his work appears in* The Malling of America: Travels in the United States of Shopping, *published in 2002.*

> Butch heaved himself up and loomed over the group. "Like it was different for me," he piped. "My folks used to drop me off at the shopping mall every morning and leave me all day. It was like a big free babysitter, you know? One night they never came back for me. Maybe they moved away. Maybe there's some kind of a Bureau of Missing Parents I could check with."
>
> — Richard Peck
> *Secrets of the Shopping Mall,*
> a novel for teenagers

From his sister at Swarthmore, I'd heard about a kid in Florida whose mother picked him up after school every day, drove him straight to the mall, and left him there until it closed—all at his insistence. I'd heard about a boy in Washington who, when his family moved from one suburb to another, pedaled his bicycle five miles every day to get back to his old mall, where he once belonged.

These stories aren't unusual. The mall is a common experience for the majority of American youth; they have probably been going there all their lives. Some ran within their first large open space, saw their first fountain, bought their first toy, and read their first book in a mall. They may have smoked their first cigarette or first joint, or turned them down, had their first kiss or lost their virginity in the mall parking lot. Teenagers in America now spend more time in the mall than anywhere else but home and school. Mostly it is their choice, but some of that mall time is put in as the result of two-paycheck and single-parent households, and the lack of other viable alternatives. But are these kids being harmed by the mall?

I wondered first of all what difference it makes for adolescents to experience so many important moments in the mall. They are, after all, at play in the fields of its little world and they learn its ways; they adapt to it and make it adapt to them. It's here that these kids get their street sense, only it's mall sense. They are learning the ways of a large-scale, artificial environment; its subtleties and flexibilities, its particular pleasures and resonances, and the attitudes it fosters.

The presence of so many teenagers for so much time was not something mall developers planned on. In fact, it came as a big surprise. But kids became a fact of mall life very easily, and the International Council of Shopping Centers found it necessary to commission a study, which they published along with a guide to mall managers on how to handle the teenage incursion.

The study found that "teenagers in suburban centers are 5
bored and come to the shopping centers mainly as a place to go. Teenagers in suburban centers spent more time fighting, drinking, littering and walking than did their urban counterparts, but presented fewer overall problems." The report observed that "adolescents congregated in groups of two to four and predominantly at locations selected by them rather than management." This probably had something to do with the decision to install game arcades, which allow management to channel these restless adolescents into naturally contained areas away from major traffic points of adult shoppers.

The guide concluded that mall management should tolerate and even encourage the teenage presence because, in the words of the report, "The vast majority support the same set of values as does shopping center management." *The same set of values* means simply that mall kids are already preprogrammed to be consumers and that the mall can put the finishing touches to them as hard-core, lifelong shoppers just like everybody else. That, after all, is what the mall is about. So it shouldn't be surprising that in spending a lot of time there, adolescents find little that challenges the assumption that the goal of life is to make money and buy products, or that just about everything else in life is to be used to serve those ends.

Growing up in a high-consumption society already adds inestimable pressure to kids' lives. Clothes consciousness has invaded the grade schools, and popularity is linked with having the best, newest clothes in the currently acceptable styles. Even what they read has been affected. "Miss [Nancy] Drew wasn't obsessed with her wardrobe," noted the *Wall Street Journal*. "But today the mystery in teen fiction for girls is what outfit the heroine will wear next." Shopping has become a survival skill and there is certainly no better place to learn it than the mall, where its importance is powerfully reinforced and certainly never questioned.

The mall as a university of suburban materialism, where Valley Girls and Boys from coast to coast are educated in consumption, has its other lessons in this era of change in family life and sexual mores and their economic and social ramifications. The plethora of products in the mall, plus the pressure on teens to buy them, may contribute to the phenomenon that psychologist David Elkind calls "the hurried child": kids who are exposed to too much of the adult world too quickly and must respond with a sophistication that belies their still-tender emotional development. Certainly the adult products marketed for children—form-fitting designer jeans, sexy tops for preteen girls—add to the social pressure to look like an adult, along with the home-grown need to understand adult finances (why mothers must work) and adult emotions (when parents divorce).

Kids spend so much time at the mall partly because their parents allow it and even encourage it. The mall is safe, doesn't seem to harbor any unsavory activities, and there is adult supervision; it is, after all, a controlled environment. So the temptation, especially for working parents, is to let the mall be their baby-sitter. At least the kids aren't watching TV. But the mall's role as a surrogate mother may be more extensive and more profound.

10 Karen Lansky, a writer living in Los Angeles, has looked into the subject, and she told me some of her conclusions about the effects on its teenaged denizens of the mall's controlled and controlling environment. "Structure is the dominant idea, since true 'mall rats' lack just that in their home lives," she said, "and adolescents about to make the big leap into growing up crave more structure than our modern society cares to acknowledge." Karen pointed out some of the elements malls supply that kids used to

get from their families, like warmth (Strawberry Shortcake dolls and similar cute and cuddly merchandise), old-fashioned mothering ("We do it all for you," the fast-food slogan), and even home cooking (the "homemade" treats at the food court).

The problem in all this, as Karen Lansky sees it, is that while families nurture children by encouraging growth through the assumption of responsibility and then by letting them rest in the bosom of the family from the rigors of growing up, the mall as a structural mother encourages passivity and consumption, as long as the kid doesn't make trouble. Therefore all they learn about becoming adults is how to act and how to consume.

Kids are in the mall not only in the passive role of shoppers—they also work there, especially as fast-food outlets infiltrate the mall's enclosure. There they learn how to hold a job and take responsibility, but still within the same value context. When *CBS Reports* went to Oak Park Mall in suburban Kansas City, Kansas, to tape part of their hour-long consideration of malls, "After the Dream Comes True," they interviewed a teenaged girl who worked in a fast-food outlet there. In a sequence that didn't make the final program, she described the major goal of her present life, which was to perfect the curl on top of the ice-cream cones that were her store's specialty. If she could do that, she would be moved from the lowly soft-drink dispenser to the more prestigious ice-cream division, the curl on top of the status ladder at her restaurant. These are the achievements that are important at the mall.

Other benefits of such jobs may also be overrated, according to Laurence D. Steinberg of the University of California at Irvine's social ecology department, who did a study on teenage employment. Their jobs, he found, are generally simple, mindlessly repetitive and boring. They don't really learn anything, and the jobs don't lead anywhere. Teenagers also work primarily with other teenagers; even their supervisors are often just a little older than they are. "Kids need to spend time with adults," Steinberg told me. "Although they get benefits from peer relationships, without parents and other adults it's one-side socialization. They hang out with each other, have age-segregated jobs, and watch TV."

Perhaps much of this is not so terrible or even so terribly different. Now that they have so much more to contend with in their lives, adolescents probably need more time to spend with other adolescents without adult impositions, just to sort things out. Though it is more concentrated in the mall (and therefore perhaps a clearer target), the value system there is really the dominant one of the whole society. Attitudes about curiosity, initiative, self-expression, empathy, and disinterested learning aren't necessarily made in the mall; they are mirrored there, perhaps a bit more intensely—as through a glass brightly.

15 Besides, the mall is not without its educational opportunities. There are bookstores, where there is at least a short shelf of classics at great prices, and other books from which it is possible to learn more than how to do sit-ups. There are tools, from hammers to VCRs, and products, from clothes to records, that can help the young find and express themselves. There are older people with stories, and places to be alone or to talk one-on-one with a kindred spirit. And there is always the passing show.

The mall itself may very well be an education about the future. I was struck with the realization, as early as my first forays into Greengate, that the mall is only one of a number of enclosed and controlled environments that are part of the lives of today's young. The mall is just an extension, say, of those large suburban schools—only there's Karmelkorn instead of chem lab, the ice rink instead of the gym: It's high school without the impertinence of classes.

Growing up, moving from home to school to the mall—from enclosure to enclosure, transported in cars—is a curiously continuous process, without much in the way of contrast or contact with unenclosed reality. Places must tend to blur into one another. But whatever differences and dangers there are in this, the skills these adolescents are learning may turn out to be useful in their later lives. For we seem to be moving inexorably into an age of preplanned and regulated environments, and this is the world they will inherit.

Still, it might be better if they had more of a choice. One teenaged girl confessed to *CBS Reports* that she sometimes felt she was missing something by hanging out at the mall so much. "But I'm here," she said, "and this is what I have."

1985

For Discussion and Writing

1. How does Kowinski explain the attraction of malls? Is his explanation plausible? Why or why not?
2. Kowinski argues that mall owners and kids in the mall share the same values, and that the mall is a "university of suburban materialism." The word "values"

is commonly used today by political and religious leaders. How do you define "values?" Is materialism a "value?"

3. According to Kowinski, the structure of the mall, which leads to passivity and consumption, prepares young people for the planned, regulated environments they will enter in adulthood. How do planning and regulation mesh with the earliest conceptions of the American Dream? With contemporary conceptions?
4. Kowinski lists elements which he finds absent from the mall experience: curiosity, initiative, self-expression, empathy, and engaged learning. Write an essay defining and evaluating the benefits and disadvantages of any one of these elements.
5. Kowinski published this article 20 years ago. Are his observations about malls still true, or has social networking replaced malls as the gathering place of choice for adolescent Americans? How do Facebook and MySpace function like a mall, according to Kowinski's description?

Argument in Favor of Proposition 227

In 1998, voters in California overwhelmingly passed into law a proposal to eliminate bilingual education and to restrict the language spoken in the state's schools to English. The campaign to convince voters included a great deal of information and discussion, appealing to parents, teachers, politicians, and especially ethnic groups for their consent and agreement. Groups advocating for Proposition 227 were careful to present their case in reasoned terms, hoping to appeal to voters who valued cultural diversity and those who valued assimilation, focusing on both the "melting pot" ideology and unique cultural identity. More than anything else, advocates for the law emphasized the benefits to the state's children and students of a single-language education.

WHY DO WE NEED TO CHANGE CALIFORNIA'S BILINGUAL EDUCATION SYSTEM?

Begun with the best of intentions in the 1970s, bilingual education has failed in actual practice, but the politicians and administrators have refused to admit this failure. For most of California's non-English speaking students, bilingual education actually means monolingual, SPANISH-ONLY education for the first 4 to 7 years of school. The current system fails to teach children to read and write English. Last year, only 6.7 percent of limited-English students in California learned enough English to be moved into mainstream classes.

Latino immigrant children are the principal victims of bilingual education. They have the lowest test scores and the highest dropout rates of any immigrant group. There are 140 languages spoken by California's schoolchildren. To teach each group of children in their own native language before teaching them English is educationally and fiscally impossible. Yet this impossibility is the goal of bilingual education.

COMMON SENSE ABOUT LEARNING ENGLISH

Learning a new language is easier the younger the age of the child. Learning a language is much easier if the child is immersed in that language. Immigrant children already know their native language; they need the public schools to teach them English. Children who leave school without knowing how to speak, read, and write English are injured for life economically and socially.

WHAT "ENGLISH FOR THE CHILDREN" WILL DO:

- Require children to be taught English as soon as they start school.
- Provide "sheltered English immersion" classes to help non-English speaking students learn English; research shows this is the most effective method.
- Allow parents to request a special waiver for children with individual educational needs who would benefit from another method.

WHAT "ENGLISH FOR THE CHILDREN" WON'T DO:

It will NOT throw children who can't speak English into regular classes where they would have to "sink or swim." It will NOT cut special funding for children learning English. It will NOT violate any federal laws or court decisions.

WHO SUPPORTS THE INITIATIVE?

- Teachers worried by the undeniable failure of bilingual education and who have long wanted to implement a successful alternative—sheltered English immersion.
- Most Latino parents, according to public polls. They know that Spanish-only bilingual education is preventing their children from learning English by segregating them into an educational dead-end.
- Most Californians. They know that bilingual education has created an educational ghetto by isolating non-English speaking students and preventing them from becoming successful members of society.

WHO OPPOSES THE INITIATIVE?

- Individuals who profit from bilingual education. Bilingual teachers are paid up to $5,000 extra annually and the program provides jobs to thousands of bilingual coordinators and administrators.
- Schools and school districts which receive HUNDREDS OF MILLIONS of extra dollars for schoolchildren classified as not knowing English and who, therefore, have a financial incentive to avoid teaching English to children.
- Activist groups with special agendas and the politicians who support them.

1998

For Discussion and Writing

1. How would you describe the overall tone of this writing? What specific aspects of the language give it that quality?
2. What are the authors' attitudes toward opponents of the Proposition? What seems to be the authors' primary complaint about those opponents?
3. What information in the writing requires more specific evidence or fuller explanation? Why?
4. If bilingual education was "begun with the best of intentions," as the authors point out, what are the alternatives to abolishing the practice completely?
5. The authors state that "bilingual education has created an educational ghetto by isolating non-English speaking students and preventing them

from becoming successful members of society." Conduct research to fill in some of the informational gaps you identified in question #3 above, then explain in an essay whether you agree or disagree with the authors' statement, supporting your response with evidence from your research.

From *Nickel and Dimed*

BARBARA EHRENREICH

Trained as a scientist, Barbara Ehrenreich opted instead to pursue writing and social activism. Her essays have appeared in publications such as Time, The New Republic, *and* The New York Times. *She is the author of thirteen books.*

Nickel and Dimed, *subtitled* On (Not) Getting By in America, *recounts Ehrenreich's undercover experiment in working low-wage jobs. Spending one month each as a waitress, maid-service employee, and Wal-Mart associate, Ehrenreich attempted to pay rent, utilities, transportation, and food costs on the pay she received from each of these jobs. She learned what millions of Americans already know—that it is not possible to make ends meet working low-wage jobs.*

In this excerpt, Ehrenreich discusses why it is so difficult for many Americans to improve their economic status.

At The Maids, the boss—who, as the only male in our midst, exerted a creepy, paternalistic kind of power—had managed to convince some of my coworkers that he was struggling against difficult odds and deserving of their unstinting forbearance. Wal-Mart has a number of more impersonal and probably more effective ways of getting its workers to feel like "associates." There was the profit-sharing plan, with Wal-Mart's stock price posted daily in a prominent spot near the break room. There was the company's much-heralded patriotism, evidenced in the banners over the shopping floor urging workers and customers to contribute to the construction of a World War II veterans' memorial (Sam Walton having been one of them). There were "associate" meetings that served as pep rallies, complete with the Wal-Mart cheer: "Gimme a 'W,'" etc.

The chance to identify with a powerful and wealthy entity—the company or the boss—is only the carrot. There is also a stick. What surprised and offended me most about the low-wage workplace (and yes, here all my middle-class privilege is on full display) was the extent to which one is required to surrender one's basic civil rights and—what boils down to the same thing—self-respect. I learned this at the very beginning of my stint as a waitress, when I was warned that my purse could be searched by management at any time. I wasn't carrying stolen salt shakers or anything else of a compromising nature, but still, there's something about the prospect of a purse search that makes a woman feel a few buttons short of fully dressed. After work, I called around and found that this practice is entirely legal: if the purse is on the boss's property—which of course it was—the boss has the right to examine its contents.

Drug testing is another routine indignity. Civil libertarians see it as a violation of our Fourth Amendment freedom from "unreasonable search"; most jobholders and applicants find it simply embarrassing. In some testing protocols, the employee has to strip to her underwear and pee into a cup in the presence of an aide or technician. Mercifully, I got to keep my clothes on and shut the toilet stall door behind me, but even so, urination is a private act and it is degrading to have to perform it at the command of some powerful other. I would add pre-employment personality tests to the list of demeaning intrusions, or at least much of their usual content. Maybe the hypothetical types of questions can be justified—whether you would steal if an opportunity arose or turn in a thieving coworker and so on—but not questions about your "moods of self-pity," whether you are a loner or believe you are usually misunderstood. It is unsettling, at the very least, to give a stranger access to things, like your self-doubts and your urine, that are otherwise shared only in medical or therapeutic situations.

There are other, more direct ways of keeping low-wage employees in their place. Rules against "gossip," or even "talking," make it hard to air your grievances to peers or—should you be so daring—to enlist other workers in a group effort to bring about change, through a union organizing drive, for example. Those who do step out of line often face little unexplained punishments, such as having their schedules or their work assignments unilaterally changed. Or you may be fired; those low-wage workers who work without union contracts, which is the great majority of them, work "at will," meaning at the will of the employer, and are subject to dismissal without explanation. The AFL-CIO estimates that ten thousand workers a year are fired for participating in union organizing drives, and since it is illegal to fire people for union activity, I suspect that these firings are usually justified in terms of unrelated minor infractions. Wal-Mart employees who have bucked the company—by getting involved in a unionization drive or by suing the company for failing to pay overtime—have been fired for breaking the company rule against using profanity.[1]

5 So if low-wage workers do not always behave in an economically rational way, that is, as free agents within a capitalist democracy, it is because they dwell in a place that is neither free nor in any way democratic. When you enter the low-wage workplace—and many of the medium-wage workplaces as well—you check your civil liberties at the door, leave America and all it supposedly stands for behind, and learn to zip your lips for the duration of the shift. The consequences of this routine surrender go beyond the issues of wages and poverty. We can hardly pride ourselves on being the world's preeminent democracy, after all, if large numbers of citizens spend half their waking hours in what amounts, in plain terms, to a dictatorship.

Any dictatorship takes a psychological toll on its subjects. If you are treated as an untrustworthy person—a potential slacker, drug addict, or thief—you may begin to feel less trust-worthy yourself. If you are constantly reminded of your lowly position in the social hierarchy, whether by individual managers or by a plethora of impersonal rules, you begin to accept that unfortunate status. To draw for a moment from an entirely different corner of my life, that part of me still attached to the biological sciences, there is ample evidence that animals—rats and monkeys, for example—that are forced into a subordinate status within their social systems adapt their brain chemistry accordingly, becoming "depressed" in humanlike ways. Their behavior is anxious and withdrawn; the level of serotonin (the neurotransmitter boosted by some antidepressants) declines in their brains. And—what is especially relevant here—they avoid fighting even in self-defense.[2]

---

[1]Bob Ortega, *In Sam We Trust*, p. 356; "Former Wal-Mart Workers File Overtime Suit in Harrison County," *Charleston Gazette*, January 24, 1999.

[2]See, for example, C. A. Shively, K. Laber-Laird, and R. F. Anton, "Behavior and Physiology of Social Stress and Depression in Female Cynomolgous Monkeys," *Biological Psychiatry* 41:8 (1997), pp. 871–82, and D. C. Blanchard et al., "Visible Burrow System as a Model of Chronic Social Stress: Behavioral and Neuroendocrine Correlates," *Psychoneuroendocrinology* 20:2 (1995), pp. 117–34.

Humans are, of course, vastly more complicated; even in situations of extreme subordination, we can pump up our self-esteem with thoughts of our families, our religion, our hopes for the future. But as much as any other social animal, and more so than many, we depend for our self-image on the humans immediately around us—to the point of altering our perceptions of the world so as to fit in with theirs.[3] My guess is that the indignities imposed on so many low-wage workers—the drug tests, the constant surveillance, being "reamed out" by managers—are part of what keeps wages low. If you're made to feel unworthy enough, you may come to think that what you're paid is what you are actually worth.

It is hard to imagine any other function for workplace authoritarianism. Managers may truly believe that, without their unremitting efforts, all work would quickly grind to a halt. That is not my impression. While I encountered some cynics and plenty of people who had learned to budget their energy, I never met an actual slacker or, for that matter, a drug addict or thief. On the contrary, I was amazed and sometimes saddened by the pride people took in jobs that rewarded them so meagerly, either in wages or in recognition. Often, in fact, these people experienced management as an obstacle to getting the job done as it should be done. Waitresses chafed at managers' stinginess toward the customers; housecleaners resented the time constraints that sometimes made them cut corners; retail workers wanted the floor to be beautiful, not cluttered with excess stock as management required. Left to themselves, they devised systems of cooperation and work sharing; when there was a crisis, they rose to it. In fact, it was often hard to see what the function of management was, other than to exact obeisance.

There seems to be a vicious cycle at work here, making ours not just an economy but a culture of extreme inequality. Corporate decision makers, and even some two-bit entrepreneurs like my boss at The Maids, occupy an economic position miles above that of the underpaid people whose labor they depend on. For reasons that have more to do with class—and often racial—prejudice than with actual experience, they tend to fear and distrust the category of people from which they recruit their workers. Hence the perceived need for repressive management and

[3]See, for example, chapter 7, "Conformity," in David G. Myers, *Social Psychology* (McGraw-Hill, 1987).

intrusive measures like drug and personality testing. But these things cost money—$20,000 or more a year for a manager, $100 a pop for a drug test, and so on—and the high cost of repression results in ever more pressure to hold wages down. The larger society seems to be caught up in a similar cycle: cutting public services for the poor, which are sometimes referred to collectively as the "social wage," while investing ever more heavily in prisons and cops. And in the larger society, too, the cost of repression becomes another factor weighing against the expansion or restoration of needed services. It is a tragic cycle, condemning us to ever deeper inequality, and in the long run, almost no one benefits but the agents of repression themselves.

10 But whatever keeps wages low—and I'm sure my comments have barely scratched the surface—the result is that many people earn far less than they need to live on. How much is that? The Economic Policy Institute recently reviewed dozens of studies of what constitutes a "living wage" and came up with an average figure of $30,000 a year for a family of one adult and two children, which amounts to a wage of $14 an hour. This is not the very minimum such a family could live on; the budget includes health insurance, a telephone, and child care at a licensed center, for example, which are well beyond the reach of millions. But it does not include restaurant meals, video rentals, Internet access, wine and liquor, cigarettes and lottery tickets, or even very much meat. The shocking thing is that the majority of American workers, about 60 percent, earn less than $14 an hour. Many of them get by by teaming up with another wage earner, a spouse or grown child. Some draw on government help in the form of food stamps, housing vouchers, the earned income tax credit, or—for those coming off welfare in relatively generous states—subsidized child care. But others—single mothers for example—have nothing but their own wages to live on, no matter how many mouths there are to feed.

Employers will look at that $30,000 figure, which is over twice what they currently pay entry-level workers, and see nothing but bankruptcy ahead. Indeed, it is probably impossible for the private sector to provide everyone with an adequate standard of living through wages, or even wages plus benefits, alone: too much of what we need, such as reliable child care, is just too expensive, even for middle-class families. Most civilized nations compensate for the inadequacy of wages by providing relatively generous public services such as health insurance, free or subsidized child care, subsidized housing, and effective public transportation. But the United States, for all its wealth, leaves its citizens to fend for themselves—facing market-based rents, for example, on their wages alone. For millions of Americans, that $10—or even $8 or $6—hourly wage is all there is.

It is common, among the nonpoor, to think of poverty as a sustainable condition—austere, perhaps, but they get by somehow, don't they? They are "always with us." What is harder for the nonpoor to see is poverty as acute distress: The lunch that consists of Doritos or hot dog rolls, leading to faintness before the end of the shift. The "home" that is also a car or a van. The illness or injury that must be "worked through," with gritted teeth, because there's no sick pay or health insurance and the loss of one day's pay will mean no groceries for the next. These experiences are not part of a sustainable lifestyle, even a lifestyle of chronic deprivation and relentless low-level punishment. They are, by almost any standard of subsistence, emergency situations. And that is how we should see the poverty of so many millions of low-wage Americans—as a state of emergency.

In the summer of 2000 I returned—permanently, I have every reason to hope—to my customary place in the socioeconomic spectrum. I go to restaurants, often far finer ones than the places where I worked, and sit down at a table. I sleep in hotel rooms that someone else has cleaned and shop in stores that others will tidy when I leave. To go from the bottom 20 percent to the top 20 percent is to enter a magical world where needs are met, problems are solved, almost without any intermediate effort. If you want to get somewhere fast, you hail a cab. If your aged parents have grown tiresome or incontinent, you put them away where others will deal with their dirty diapers and dementia. If you are part of the upper-middle-class majority that employs a maid or maid service, you return from work to find the house miraculously restored to order—the toilet bowls shit-free and gleaming, the socks that you left on the floor levitated back to their normal dwelling place. Here, sweat is a metaphor for hard work, but seldom its consequence. Hundreds of little things get done, reliably and routinely every day, without anyone's seeming to do them.

The top 20 percent routinely exercises other, far more consequential forms of power in the world. This stratum, which contains what I have termed in an earlier book the "professional-managerial class," is the home of our decision makers, opinion shapers, culture creators—our professors, lawyers, executives, entertainers, politicians, judges, writers, producers, and editors.[4] When they speak, they are listened to. When they complain, someone usually scurries to correct the problem and apologize for it. If they complain often enough, someone far below them in wealth and influence may be chastised or even fired. Political power, too, is concentrated within the top 20 percent, since its members are far more likely than the poor—or even the middle class—to discern the all-too-tiny distinctions between candidates that can make it seem worthwhile to contribute, participate, and vote. In all these ways, the affluent exert inordinate power over the lives of the less affluent, and especially over the lives of the poor, determining what public services will be available, if any, what minimum wage, what laws governing the treatment of labor.

So it is alarming, upon returning to the upper middle class from a sojourn, however artificial and temporary, among the poor, to find the rabbit hole close so suddenly and completely behind me. You were *where*, doing *what*? Some odd optical property of our highly polarized and unequal society makes the poor almost invisible to their economic superiors. The poor can see the affluent easily enough—on television, for example, or on the covers of magazines. But the affluent rarely see the poor or, if they do catch sight of them in some public space, rarely know what they're seeing, since—thanks to consignment stores and, yes, Wal-Mart—the poor are usually able to disguise themselves as members of the more comfortable classes. Forty years ago the hot journalistic topic was the "discovery of the poor" in their inner-city and Appalachian "pockets of poverty." Today you are more likely to find commentary on their "disappearance," either as a supposed demographic reality or as a shortcoming of the middle-class imagination.

In a 2000 article on the "disappearing poor," journalist James Fallows reports that, from the vantage point of the Internet's nouveaux riches, it is "hard to understand people for whom a million dollars would be a fortune . . . not to mention those for whom $246 is a full week's earnings."[5] Among the reasons he and others

[4] *Fear of Falling: The Inner Life of the Middle Class* (Pantheon, 1989).
[5] "The Invisible Poor," *New York Times Magazine*, March 19, 2000.

have cited for the blindness of the affluent is the fact that they are less and less likely to share spaces and services with the poor. As public schools and other public services deteriorate, those who can afford to do so send their children to private schools and spend their off-hours in private spaces—health clubs, for example, instead of the local park. They don't ride on public buses and subways. They withdraw from mixed neighborhoods into distant suburbs, gated communities, or guarded apartment towers; they shop in stores that, in line with the prevailing "market segmentation," are designed to appeal to the affluent alone. Even the affluent young are increasingly unlikely to spend their summers learning how the "other half" lives, as lifeguards, waitresses, or housekeepers at resort hotels. *The New York Times* reports that they now prefer career-relevant activities like summer school or interning in an appropriate professional setting to the "sweaty, low-paid and mind-numbing slots that have long been their lot."[6]

Then, too, the particular political moment favors what almost looks like a "conspiracy of silence" on the subject of poverty and the poor. The Democrats are not eager to find flaws in the period of "unprecedented prosperity" they take credit for; the Republicans have lost interest in the poor now that "welfare-as-we-know-it" has ended. Welfare reform itself is a factor weighing against any close investigation of the conditions of the poor. Both parties heartily endorsed it, and to acknowledge that low-wage work doesn't lift people out of poverty would be to admit that it may have been, in human terms, a catastrophic mistake. In fact, very little is known about the fate of former welfare recipients because the 1996 welfare reform legislation blithely failed to include any provision for monitoring their postwelfare economic condition. Media accounts persistently bright-side the situation, highlighting the occasional success stories and downplaying the acknowledged increase in hunger.[7] And sometimes there seems to be almost deliberate deception. In June 2000, the press rushed to hail a study

---

[6]"Summer Work Is Out of Favor with the Young," *New York Times*, June 18, 2000.

[7]The *National Journal* reports that the "good news" is that almost six million people have left the welfare rolls since 1996, while the "rest of the story" includes the problem that "these people sometimes don't have enough to eat" ("Welfare Reform, Act 2," June 24, 2000, pp. 1, 978–93).

supposedly showing that Minnesota's welfare-to-work program had sharply reduced poverty and was, as *Time* magazine put it, a "winner."[8] Overlooked in these reports was the fact that the program in question was a pilot project that offered far more generous child care and other subsidies than Minnesota's actual welfare reform program. Perhaps the error can be forgiven—the pilot project, which ended in 1997, had the same name, Minnesota Family Investment Program, as Minnesota's much larger, ongoing welfare reform program.[9]

You would have to read a great many newspapers very carefully, cover to cover, to see the signs of distress. You would find, for example, that in 1999 Massachusetts food pantries reported a 72 percent increase in the demand for their services over the previous year, that Texas food banks were "scrounging" for food, despite donations at or above 1998 levels, as were those in Atlanta.[10] You might learn that in San Diego the Catholic Church could no longer, as of January 2000, accept homeless families at its shelter, which happens to be the city's largest, because it was already operating at twice its normal capacity.[11] You would come across news of a study showing that the percentage of Wisconsin food-stamp families in "extreme poverty"—defined as less than 50 percent of the federal poverty line—has tripled in the last decade to more than 30 percent.[12] You might discover that, nationwide, America's food banks are experiencing "a torrent of need which [they] cannot meet" and that, according to a survey conducted by the U.S. Conference of Mayors, 67 percent of the adults requesting emergency food aid are people with jobs.[13]

One reason nobody bothers to pull all these stories together and announce a widespread state of emergency may be that

---

[8]"Minnesota's Welfare Reform Proves a Winner," *Time*, June 12, 2000.

[9]Center for Law and Social Policy, "Update," Washington, D.C., June 2000.

[10]"Study: More Go Hungry since Welfare Reform," *Boston Herald*, January 21, 2000; "Charity Can't Feed All while Welfare Reforms Implemented," *Houston Chronicle*, January 10, 2000; "Hunger Grows as Food Banks Try to Keep Pace," *Atlanta Journal and Constitution*, November 26, 1999.

[11]"Rise in Homeless Families Strains San Diego Aid," *Los Angeles Times*, January 24, 2000.

[12]"Hunger Problems Said to Be Getting Worse," *Milwaukee Journal Sentinel*, December 15, 1999.

[13]Deborah Leff, the president and CEO of the hunger-relief organization America's Second Harvest, quoted in the *National Journal*, op. cit.; "Hunger Persists in U.S. despite the Good Times," *Detroit News*, June 15, 2000.

Americans of the newspaper-reading professional middle class are used to thinking of poverty as a consequence of unemployment. During the heyday of downsizing in the Reagan years, it very often was, and it still is for many inner-city residents who have no way of getting to the proliferating entry-level jobs on urban peripheries. When unemployment causes poverty, we know how to state the problem—typically, "the economy isn't growing fast enough"—and we know what the traditional liberal solution is—"full employment." But when we have full or nearly full employment, when jobs are available to any job seeker who can get to them, then the problem goes deeper and begins to cut into that web of expectations that make up the "social contract." According to a recent poll conducted by Jobs for the Future, a Boston-based employment research firm, 94 percent of Americans agree that "people who work full-time should be able to earn enough to keep their families out of poverty."[14] I grew up hearing over and over, to the point of tedium, that "hard work" was the secret of success: "Work hard and you'll get ahead" or "It's hard work that got us where we are." No one ever said that you could work hard—harder even than you ever thought possible—and still find yourself sinking ever deeper into poverty and debt.

20 When poor single mothers had the option of remaining out of the labor force on welfare, the middle and upper middle class tended to view them with a certain impatience, if not disgust. The welfare poor were excoriated for their laziness, their persistence in reproducing in unfavorable circumstances, their presumed addictions, and above all for their "dependency." Here they were, content to live off "government handouts" instead of seeking "self-sufficiency," like everyone else, through a job. They needed to get their act together, learn how to wind an alarm clock, get out there and get to work. But now that government has largely withdrawn its "handouts," now that the overwhelming majority of the poor are out there toiling in Wal-Mart or Wendy's—well, what are we to think of them? Disapproval and condescension no longer apply, so what outlook makes sense?

Guilt, you may be thinking warily. Isn't that what we're supposed to feel? But guilt doesn't go anywhere near far enough; the appropriate emotion is shame—shame at our *own* dependency, in this case, on the underpaid labor of others. When someone

---

[14]"A National Survey of American Attitudes toward Low-Wage Workers and Welfare Reform," Jobs for the Future, Boston, May 24, 2000.

works for less pay than she can live on—when, for example, she goes hungry so that you can eat more cheaply and conveniently—then she has made a great sacrifice for you, she has made you a gift of some part of her abilities, her health, and her life. The "working poor," as they are approvingly termed, are in fact the major philanthropists of our society. They neglect their own children so that the children of others will be cared for; they live in substandard housing so that other homes will be shiny and perfect; they endure privation so that inflation will be low and stock prices high. To be a member of the working poor is to be an anonymous donor, a nameless benefactor, to everyone else. As Gail, one of my restaurant coworkers put it, "you give and you give."

Someday, of course—and I will make no predictions as to exactly when—they are bound to tire of getting so little in return and to demand to be paid what they're worth. There'll be a lot of anger when that day comes, and strikes and disruption. But the sky will not fall, and we will all be better off for it in the end.

2001

For Discussion and Writing

1. A major tenet of the American Dream is that people who work hard will succeed. What arguments does Ehrenreich use to dispute this belief in the case of America's working poor?
2. What demeaning practices cause Ehrenreich to see employers of the working poor as dictators? Do you agree with her assessment of employers?
3. On page 213, Ehrenreich states that "If you're made to feel unworthy enough, you may come to think that what you're paid is what you are actually worth." To what extent do you believe that self-image can determine actual achievement?
4. Ehrenreich compares the behavior of rats and monkeys that have been forced into subservient positions to the behavior of Americans who live in poverty. Does her comparison work? Why or why not?
5. What were some of the differences Ehrenreich noticed once she returned to her previous state of affluence? In what ways does affluence blind people to the living conditions of the poor?

What Sacagawea Means to Me

SHERMAN ALEXIE

Born in 1966, acclaimed writer, filmmaker, and teacher Sherman Alexie was raised on the Spokane Indian Reservation by a Spokane father and a C'oeur d'Alene mother. Alexie planned to study medicine, but realizing he lacked the stomach, he looked elsewhere for a vocation. With the encouragement of a poetry teacher, Alexie began a prolific career as a writer. The author of Reservation Blues, The Lone Ranger and Tonto Fistfight in Heaven, *and* Indian Killer, *Alexie writes of the America that is a third world country; his characters reverberate with the history of American Indians. In the following essay, as in much of his fiction and poetry, Alexie imagines the life of a woman whose name many Americans know but whose life is shrouded in mystery. Sacagawea was kidnapped as a child and sold as a slave to a French-Canadian fur trader who eventually made her one of his wives. Sacagawea carried her infant son, Jean-Baptiste, on her back as she traveled the continent, serving as an unpaid translator and horse trader for Lewis and Clark on their—and her—epic journey.*

In the future, every U.S. citizen will get to be Sacagawea for 15 minutes. For the low price of admission, every American, regardless of race, religion, gender and age, will climb through the portal into Sacagawea's Shoshone Indian brain. In the multicultural theme park called Sacagawea Land, you will be kidnapped as a child by the Hidatsa tribe and sold to Toussaint Charbonneau, the French-Canadian trader who will take you as one of his wives and father two of your children. Your first child, Jean-Baptiste, will be only a few months old as you carry him during your long journey with Lewis and Clark. The two captains will lead the adventure, fighting rivers, animals, weather and diseases for thousands of miles, and you will march right beside them. But you, the aboriginal multitasker, will also breast-feed. And at the end of your Sacagawea journey, you will be shown the exit and given a souvenir T shirt that reads, IF THE U.S. IS EDEN, THEN SACAGAWEA IS EVE.

Sacagawea is our mother. She is the first gene pair of the American DNA. In the beginning, she was the word, and the word was possibility. I revel in the wondrous possibilities of Sacagawea. It is good to be joyous in the presence of her spirit, because I hope she had moments of joy in what must have been a grueling life. This much is true: Sacagawea died of some mysterious illness when she was only in her 20s. Most illnesses were mysterious in the 19th century, but I suspect that Sacagawea's indigenous immune system was defenseless against an immigrant virus. Perhaps Lewis and Clark infected Sacagawea. If true, then certain postcolonial historians would argue that she was murdered not by germs but by colonists who carried those germs. I don't know much about the science of disease and immunities, but I know enough poetry to recognize that individual human beings are invaded and colonized by foreign bodies, just as individual civilizations are invaded and colonized by foreign bodies. In that sense, colonization might be a natural process, tragic and violent to be sure, but predictable and ordinary as well, and possibly necessary for the advance, however constructive and destructive, of all civilizations.

After all, Lewis and Clark's story has never been just the triumphant tale of two white men, no matter what the white historians might need to believe. Sacagawea was not the primary hero of this story either, no matter what the Native American historians and I might want to believe. The story of Lewis and Clark is also the story of the approximately 45 nameless and faceless first- and second-generation European Americans who joined the journey, then left or completed it, often without monetary or historical compensation. Considering the time and place, I imagine those 45 were illiterate, low-skilled laborers subject to managerial whims and 19th century downsizing. And it is most certainly the story of the black slave York, who also cast votes during this allegedly democratic adventure. It's even the story of Seaman, the domesticated Newfoundland dog who must have been a welcome and friendly presence and who survived the risk of becoming supper during one lean time or another. The Lewis and Clark Expedition was exactly the kind of multicultural, trigenerational, bigendered, animal-friendly, government-supported, partly French-Canadian project that should rightly be celebrated by liberals and castigated by conservatives.

In the end, I wonder if colonization might somehow be magical. After all, Miles Davis is the direct descendant of slaves and slave owners. Hank Williams is the direct descendant of poor whites and poorer Indians. In 1876 Emily Dickinson was writing her poems in an Amherst attic while Crazy Horse was killing Custer on the banks of the Little Big Horn. I remain stunned by these contradictions, by the successive generations of social, political and artistic mutations that can be so beautiful and painful. How did we get from there to here? This country somehow gave life to Maria Tallchief and Ted Bundy, to Geronimo and Joe McCarthy, to Nathan Bedford Forrest and Toni Morrison, to the Declaration of Independence and Executive Order No. 9066, to Cesar Chavez and Richard Nixon, to theme parks and national parks, to smallpox and the vaccine for smallpox.

As a Native American, I want to hate this country and its con- 5
tradictions. I want to believe that Sacagawea hated this country and its contradictions. But this country exists, in whole and in part, because Sacagawea helped Lewis and Clark. In the land that came to be called Idaho, she acted as diplomat between her long-lost brother and the Lewis and Clark party. Why wouldn't she ask her brother and her tribe to take revenge against the men who had enslaved her? Sacagawea is a contradiction. Here in Seattle, I exist, in whole and in part, because a half-white man named James Cox fell in love with a Spokane Indian woman named Etta Adams and gave birth to my mother. I am a contradiction; I am Sacagawea.

2002

For Discussion and Writing

1. How does Alexie's version of the Lewis and Clark expedition differ from that told in American history textbooks?
2. What contradictions does Alexie find in American culture and history? What is significant about these contradictions?
3. How can colonization be explained as magical, according to Alexie?
4. Why does Alexie want to hate America? Why is he unable to do so?
5. Write an essay in which you consider American history's treatment of such figures as Sacagawea and the thousands of Chinese laborers who built the railroads. What does this pattern suggest about the possibility of attaining the American Dream?

The Death of Horatio Alger

PAUL KRUGMAN

In the nineteenth century, Horatio Alger Jr.'s highly popular pulp fiction stories chronicled the rise from poverty of street boys who worked hard to earn their way to middle class financial security. Because of this familiar plot pattern, the name "Horatio Alger" became shorthand for the uniquely American idea of pulling oneself "up by one's bootstraps" and the work ethic that accompanies it. In this excerpt, economist and editorial writer Paul Krugman argues that the time for true class mobility has passed, and that the "bootstraps" ideology no longer holds.

We were a relatively middle-class nation [in 1974.] It had not always been thus: Gilded Age America was a highly unequal society, and it stayed that way through the 1920s. During the 1930s and '40s, however, America experienced what the economic historians Claudia Goldin and Robert Margo have dubbed the Great Compression: a drastic narrowing of income gaps, probably as a result of New Deal policies. And the new economic order persisted for more than a generation: Strong unions; taxes on inherited wealth, corporate profits and high incomes; close public scrutiny of corporate management—all helped to keep income gaps relatively small. The economy was hardly egalitarian, but a generation ago the gross inequalities of the 1920s seemed very distant.

Now they're back. According to estimates by the economists Thomas Piketty and Emmanuel Saez confirmed by data from the Congressional Budget Office—between 1973 and 2000 the average real income of the bottom 90 percent of American taxpayers actually fell by 7 percent. Meanwhile, the income of the top 1 percent rose by 148 percent, the income of the top 0.1 percent rose by 343 percent and the income of the top 0.01 percent rose 599 percent. (Those numbers exclude capital gains, so they're not an artifact of the stock-market bubble.) The distribution of income in the United States has gone right back to Gilded Age levels of inequality.

Never mind, say the apologists, who churn out papers with titles like that of a 2001 Heritage Foundation piece, "Income Mobility and the Fallacy of Class-Warfare Arguments." America, they say, isn't a caste society—people with high incomes this year may have low incomes next year and vice versa, and the route to wealth is open to all. . . .

The myth of income mobility has always exceeded the reality: As a general rule, once they've reached their 30s, people don't move up and down the income ladder very much. Conservatives often cite studies like a 1992 report by Glenn Hubbard, a Treasury official under the elder Bush who later became chief economic adviser to the younger Bush, that purport to show large numbers of Americans moving from low-wage to high-wage jobs during their working lives. But what these studies measure, as the economist Kevin Murphy put it, is mainly "the guy who works in the college bookstore and has a real job by his early 30s." Serious studies that exclude this sort of pseudo-mobility show that inequality in average incomes over long periods isn't much smaller than inequality in annual incomes.

It is true, however, that America was once a place of substan- 5
tial intergenerational mobility: Sons often did much better than their fathers. A classic 1978 survey found that among adult men whose fathers were in the bottom 25 percent of the population as ranked by social and economic status, 23 percent had made it into the top 25 percent. In other words, during the first thirty years or so after World War II, the American Dream of upward mobility was a real experience for many people.

[A] new survey of today's adult men . . . finds that this number has dropped to only 10 percent. That is, over the past generation upward mobility has fallen drastically. Very few children of the lower class are making their way to even moderate affluence. This goes along with other studies indicating that rags-to-riches stories have become vanishingly rare, and that the correlation between fathers' and sons' incomes has risen in recent decades. In modern America, it seems, you're quite likely to stay in the social and economic class into which you were born.

Business Week attributes this to the "Wal-Martization" of the economy, the proliferation of dead-end, low-wage jobs and the disappearance of jobs that provide entry to the middle class. That's surely part of the explanation. But public policy plays a role—and will, if present trends continue, play an even bigger role in the future.

Put it this way: Suppose that you actually liked a caste society, and you were seeking ways to use your control of the government to further entrench the advantages of the haves against the have-nots. What would you do?

One thing you would definitely do is get rid of the estate tax, so that large fortunes can be passed on to the next generation. More broadly, you would seek to reduce tax rates both on corporate profits and on unearned income such as dividends and capital gains, so that those with large accumulated or inherited wealth could more easily accumulate even more. You'd also try to create tax shelters mainly useful for the rich. And more broadly still, you'd try to reduce tax rates on people with high incomes, shifting the burden to the payroll tax and other revenue sources that bear most heavily on people with lower incomes.

10 Meanwhile, on the spending side, you'd cut back on healthcare for the poor, on the quality of public education and on state aid for higher education. This would make it more difficult for people with low incomes to climb out of their difficulties and acquire the education essential to upward mobility in the modern economy.

And just to close off as many routes to upward mobility as possible, you'd do everything possible to break the power of unions, and you'd privatize government functions so that well-paid civil servants could be replaced with poorly paid private employees.

It all sounds sort of familiar, doesn't it?

Where is this taking us? Thomas Piketty, whose work with Saez has transformed our understanding of income distribution, warns that current policies will eventually create "a class of rentiers in the U.S., whereby a small group of wealthy but untalented children controls vast segments of the US economy and penniless, talented children simply can't compete." If he's right—and I fear that he is—we will end up suffering not only from injustice, but from a vast waste of human potential.

Goodbye, Horatio Alger. And goodbye, American Dream.

2004

For Discussion and Writing

1. According to Krugman, what historical factors have accounted for a narrowing of income gaps in the United States?
2. In the author's view, what is the main flaw with arguments that claim it is still easy to move from one income class to another?
3. Based on your own experience as a job seeker and as an employee hoping for advancement and promotion, has class mobility stalled in recent years? Why or why not?
4. Interview members of your family to discover your family's work and economic past. Write an essay in which you tell the story of your family's American journey.

"All Falls Down" (Text through Internet Search)

Kanye West

Known within the rap community for years as a producer for fellow music acts such as Jay-Z and Janet Jackson, Chicago's Kanye West, the son of an English professor, was a radical departure from the stereotypical and corporate-promoted "thug" image of a rapper when he arrived on the scene as a performer in his own right. Neatly dressed in "preppy" clothing and with no "gangsta" content in his lyrics, West nonetheless soared to near-instant popularity with listeners and critics, proving wrong those in the music industry who had warned that his look and lyrical content were unmarketable. In one of his first hits, "All Falls Down," West manages to look both outward and inward at the roles and effects of materialism and consumerism, two deeply-ingrained components of the American Dream. To find the lyrics of this song, simply type its title, and the word "lyrics," into an Internet search engine, such as Google.

✦

For Discussion and Writing

1. How many different products does Kanye West "name drop" in this song? What is the overall effect of those specific mentions?
2. While many listeners have cited this song as being anti-materialistic, how does that interpretation clash with West's mention of Jacob & Co. (a.k.a. "Jacob the Jeweler") in the last verse?
3. Immediately after West mentions "living the American Dream," what aspects of that dream does he call into question, especially in regards to America's black citizens?
4. In an essay, craft an argument around the line, "The things we buy to cover up what's inside," focusing not on the individual, but on the larger society.

Superman Is An Illegal

Jorge Lerma

Corridos *have been sung by Mexicans and Mexican-Americans for at least two hundred years. Passed down through the generations as part of an oral tradition,* corrido *themes were originally tales of legendary folk heroes. In recent years, this musical form has expanded to include themes of political protest and the exploits of druglords. In the following corrido, the situation of the illegal Mexican immigrant is playfully compared to Superman's uncertain citizenship.*

✦

Supermán es ilegal

(Hablado) ¡Es un pájaro!
¡Es un avión!
No, hombre, ¡es un mojado!
(Cantado) Llegó del cielo y no es un avión.
Venía en su nave, desde Criptón,
y por lo visto, ne es un Americano
sino otro igual como yo, indocumentado.
Así es que Migra, él no debe de trabajar
porque aunque duela, Superman es ilegal.
Es periodista, también yo soy
y no fue el Army, a que camión.
Y aquel es güero, ojos azules, bien formado
y yo prietito, gordiflón y muy chaparro.
Pero yo al menos en mi patria ya marché
con el coyote que pagué cuando cruzé
No cumplió con el servicio militar,
no paga impuestos y le hace al judicial.
No tiene mica ni permiso pa' volar.
Y les apuesto que ni seguro social.
Hay que hechar a Superman se esta región
y si se puede, regresarlo pa' Cripton.
¿Dónde está esa autoridad de emigración?
¿Qué hay de nuevo, Don Racismo, en la nación?
De que yo sepa no lo multan por volar
sino al contrario, lo declaran Superman.
No cumplió con el servicio militar,
no paga impuestos y le hace al judicial.
No tiene mica ni permiso pa' volar.
Y les apuesto que ni seguro social.
Hay que hechar a Superman se esta región
y si se puede, regresarlo pa' Criptón.
¿Dónde está esa autoridad de emigración?
¿Qué hay de nuevo, Don Racismo, en la nación?

1979

Superman Is an Illegal

Jorge Lerma
English Translation by Alex and Nina Hidalgo

(Spoken) It's a bird!
It's a plane!
No man, it's a wetback!
(Sung) He came from the sky, but he is not a plane.
He came in his spaceship from Krypton,
And by the looks of him, he's not American.
He's someone like me—undocumented.
So the migrant should not work
Because even though it hurts, Superman is an illegal.
He's a journalist, and I am too;
He didn't serve in the army (what a bum!)
He is white, has blue eyes and is well-formed;
I'm dark-skinned, chubby, and short.
But in my homeland I already marched
With the coyote I paid when I crossed.

He didn't serve in the military
He doesn't pay taxes and he wants to pass judgment
He doesn't have diamonds or a license to fly.
I'll bet he doesn't even have a social security card.

We need to kick Superman out of here
And if it's possible, send him back to Krypton.
Where is the emigration authority?
What's the news, Mr. Racism, in the nation?
For all I know they don't fine him for flying
But on the contrary, they declare he's Superman.

He didn't serve in the military
He doesn't pay taxes and he wants to pass judgment
He doesn't have diamonds or a license to fly.
I'll bet he doesn't even have a social security card.
We need to kick Superman out of here
And if it's possible, send him back to Krypton.
Where is the emigration authority?
What's new, Mr. Racism, in the nation?

(translation) 2007

For Discussion and Writing

1. The term "wetback" is usually considered offensive. What is the effect of attaching the term to Superman?
2. How is Superman like an illegal immigrant? What argument is being made by comparing the two?
3. The *corrido* implies that Superman has physical characteristics that make him a more desirable illegal alien than a Mexican. What are these characteristics? What do these characteristics reveal about who is and is not considered a desirable citizen?
4. In both contemporary and past controversies about immigration, one prominent issue continually arises: some claim that illegal immigrants take jobs that rightfully belong to American citizens, while others argue that illegal immigrants work at jobs that citizens refuse to take. In a country that was founded by immigrants, when and how should immigration be regulated?

The Power of Our Pastime

MARC GELLMAN

The game of baseball has long been America's "national pastime." Before the introduction of television to American living rooms, most Americans followed news of their favorites teams in the newspapers and on the radio. As a major part of the common culture through most of the twentieth century, baseball is a cultural touchstone, and in the following MSNBC column, Rabbi Marc Gellman uses baseball as an extended analogy to argue for the assimilation of new immigrants.

The arrival of the World Series this year convinced me that God is dead (proof: the Mets are gone) and that God is not dead (proof: the Yankees are also gone). Trying to stretch beyond my own parochial rooting interests, I want to make a serious case for the proposition that baseball is the most powerful path to assimilation into American culture. Without assimilation America dies and immigrant cultures are radicalized. America is not just another country, not just another culture, not just another experiment in democracy. America stands for a single great truth, *e pluribus unum*, "out of many, one." Our self-understanding demands that we welcome and assimilate all those storm-tossed travelers who pass beneath the golden torch.

The ways this assimilation has proceeded are well known to us all. We speak English. We have no monarchy. We have no inherited ruling class. We believe in public education. We gather in public parks. We live in integrated neighborhoods. We respect all religions and establish no religion. Our humor does not insult. Most of us buy our clothes from the same stores and most all of us own blue jeans. We don't all like the same music, but we know the same music. We can all sing "God Bless America" and we can all say the Pledge of Allegiance. Mostly, nobody cares when your ancestors came to America or if they were here all along. We celebrate very few holidays together, but the ones we do celebrate, like July Fourth and Thanksgiving, are celebrated by all Americans. We all eat pizza and the same junk food.

Not all these paths of assimilation are working now as well as they once worked. Many immigrants don't learn English; this hurts them and it hurts America. Many people are so rich that their children are beginning to behave like royalty; this hurts them and it hurts America. Our parks are not all as safe as they should be, and some neighborhoods remain frosty to "others." The status of public schools and public-school teachers is too low. The music my kids like is violent noise. But on balance, America is still able to gently seduce, not coerce, millions of immigrants into a passionate love for this place.

Of all the ways we have tried to make one out of many, the most powerful cultural force has been baseball. Basketball is too small and too new, soccer is too European, hockey is too white. The football season is too short and the squads too few. Baseball provides America with emotionally compelling teams, and these teams allow anyone to be a fanatic—a culturally constructive fanatic. At 162 games, the baseball season is long enough to get deeply involved in your team's fate and gives you a chance to attend a game (there are 81 home games, compared with eight in football). The teams have enough players so that, no matter what your ethnic background is, there is bound to be a professional baseball player whose grandma served him the same greasy, artery-clogging ethnic food you were forced to eat as a child. Baseball is just as good on the radio (I think it's better), so you don't need a television to watch it. It is filled with stupid and important statistics that kids can memorize. It also has neat packs of player cards.

5 I do not believe that beginning every baseball game with the national anthem is an instance of excessive patriotic zeal. I believe it to be a joyous and unifying secular hymn whose last words are always overwhelmed by fans cheering their team and their country and their freedom and their joy at being blessed to live here: "O say, does that star-spangled banner yet wave/O'er the land of the free and the home of the brave?"

In participating in these secular rituals of baseball, you make a team *your* team—and you make America *your* America. Your team divides you from the fans of other teams, but that's strangely unifying. All the fans of all the teams love the game. Your team is different from your religion, which can be divisive and is usually grimly serious. Your team is different than being an American, which is so big a characterization that it is almost meaningless. Your team is the way you break up America into bite-sized pieces. And when you are at a game, and when your team scores, you slap hands with people you do not know. This, and not your passport, is what really makes you into an American.

2006

For Discussion and Writing

1. Why does Gellman believe that assimilation is so important? How does it hurt immigrants if they don't learn to speak English?
2. According to the author, how is baseball an effective path to assimilation?
3. What examples does Gellman provide of American assimilation? What other examples can you think of?
4. Gellman uses a baseball analogy to explain what "really makes you into an American." Do you agree with his definition? What other aspects of U.S. culture help make immigrants into Americans?

Special Comment of October 18, 2006

Keith Olbermann

Since 2003, former ESPN sportscaster Keith Olbermann has hosted "Countdown" on the MSNBC cable news network, where he offers viewers a mix of light humor offset by frequent "special comments" to end the hour-long show. In these closing comments, Olbermann often addresses political issues, as in this scathing opinion about President George W. Bush's signing of the Military Commissions Act, which legally suspended the right of habeus corpus *that served as the backbone of the American legal system for over 200 years.*

We have lived as if in a trance.

We have lived as people in fear.

And now—our rights and our freedoms in peril—we slowly awaken to learn that we have been afraid of the wrong thing.

Therefore, tonight have we truly become the inheritors of our American legacy.

5 For, on this first full day that the Military Commissions Act is in force, we now face what our ancestors faced, at other times of exaggerated crisis and melodramatic fear-mongering:

A government more dangerous to our liberty, than is the enemy it claims to protect us from.

We have been here before—and we have been here before, led here by men better and wiser and nobler than George W. Bush.

We have been here when President John Adams insisted that the Alien and Sedition Acts were necessary to save American lives, only to watch him use those acts to jail newspaper editors.

American newspaper editors, in American jails, for things they wrote about America.

10 We have been here when President Woodrow Wilson insisted that the Espionage Act was necessary to save American lives, only to watch him use that Act to prosecute 2,000 Americans, especially those he disparaged as "Hyphenated Americans," most of whom were guilty only of advocating peace in a time of war.

American public speakers, in American jails, for things they said about America.

And we have been here when President Franklin D. Roosevelt insisted that Executive Order 9066 was necessary to save American lives, only to watch him use that order to imprison and pauperize 110,000 Americans while his man in charge, General DeWitt, told Congress: "It makes no difference whether he is an American citizen—he is still a Japanese."

American citizens, in American camps, for something they neither wrote nor said nor did, but for the choices they or their ancestors had made about coming to America.

Each of these actions was undertaken for the most vital, the most urgent, the most inescapable of reasons.

And each was a betrayal of that for which the president who advocated them claimed to be fighting.

Adams and his party were swept from office, and the Alien and Sedition Acts erased.

Many of the very people Wilson silenced survived him, and one of them even ran to succeed him, and got 900,000 votes, though his presidential campaign was conducted entirely from his jail cell.

And Roosevelt's internment of the Japanese was not merely the worst blight on his record, but it would necessitate a formal apology from the government of the United States to the citizens of the United States whose lives it ruined.

The most vital, the most urgent, the most inescapable of reasons.

In times of fright, we have been only human.

We have let Roosevelt's "fear of fear itself" overtake us.

We have listened to the little voice inside that has said, "the wolf is at the door; this will be temporary; this will be precise; this too shall pass."

We have accepted that the only way to stop the terrorists is to let the government become just a little bit like the terrorists.

Just the way we once accepted that the only way to stop the Soviets was to let the government become just a little bit like the Soviets.

Or substitute the Japanese.

Or the Germans.

Or the Socialists.

Or the Anarchists.

Or the Immigrants.

Or the British.

Or the Aliens.

The most vital, the most urgent, the most inescapable of reasons.

And, always, always wrong.

"With the distance of history, the questions will be narrowed and few: Did this generation of Americans take the threat seriously, and did we do what it takes to defeat that threat?"

Wise words.

And ironic ones, Mr. Bush.

Your own, of course, yesterday, in signing the Military Commissions Act.

You spoke so much more than you know, Sir.

Sadly—of course—the distance of history will recognize that the threat this generation of Americans needed to take seriously was you.

We have a long and painful history of ignoring the prophecy 40
attributed to Benjamin Franklin that "those who would give up essential liberty to purchase a little temporary safety, deserve neither liberty nor safety."

But even within this history we have not before codified the poisoning of habeas corpus, that wellspring of protection from which all essential liberties flow.

You, sir, have now befouled that spring.

You, sir, have now given us chaos and called it order.

You, sir, have now imposed subjugation and called it freedom.

For the most vital, the most urgent, the most inescapable of 45
reasons.

And—again, Mr. Bush—all of them, wrong.

We have handed a blank check drawn against our freedom to a man who has said it is unacceptable to compare anything this country has ever done to anything the terrorists have ever done.

We have handed a blank check drawn against our freedom to a man who has insisted again that "the United States does not torture. It's against our laws and it's against our values" and who has said it with a straight face while the pictures from Abu Ghraib Prison and the stories of waterboarding figuratively fade in and out, around him.

We have handed a blank check drawn against our freedom to a man who may now, if he so decides, declare not merely any non-American citizens "unlawful enemy combatants" and ship them somewhere—anywhere—but may now, if he so decides, declare you an "unlawful enemy combatant" and ship you somewhere—anywhere.

And if you think this hyperbole or hysteria, ask the newspaper 50
editors when John Adams was president or the pacifists when Woodrow Wilson was president or the Japanese at Manzanar when Franklin Roosevelt was president.

And if you somehow think habeas corpus has not been suspended for American citizens but only for everybody else, ask yourself this: If you are pulled off the street tomorrow, and they call you an alien or an undocumented immigrant or an "unlawful enemy combatant"—exactly how are you going to convince them to give you a court hearing to prove you are not? Do you think this attorney general is going to help you?

This President now has his blank check.

He lied to get it.

He lied as he received it.

Is there any reason to even hope he has not lied about how he intends to use it nor who he intends to use it against?

"These military commissions will provide a fair trial," you told us yesterday, Mr. Bush, "in which the accused are presumed innocent, have access to an attorney and can hear all the evidence against them."

"Presumed innocent," Mr. Bush?

The very piece of paper you signed as you said that, allows for the detainees to be abused up to the point just before they sustain "serious mental and physical trauma" in the hope of getting them to incriminate themselves, and may no longer even invoke The Geneva Conventions in their own defense.

"Access to an attorney," Mr. Bush?

Lieutenant Commander Charles Swift said on this program, Sir, and to the Supreme Court, that he was only granted access to his detainee defendant on the promise that the detainee would plead guilty.

"Hearing all the evidence," Mr. Bush?

The Military Commissions Act specifically permits the introduction of classified evidence not made available to the defense.

Your words are lies, Sir.

They are lies that imperil us all.

"One of the terrorists believed to have planned the 9/11 attacks," you told us yesterday, "said he hoped the attacks would be the beginning of the end of America."

That terrorist, sir, could only hope.

Not his actions, nor the actions of a ceaseless line of terrorists (real or imagined), could measure up to what you have wrought.

Habeas corpus? Gone.

The Geneva Conventions? Optional.

The moral force we shined outwards to the world as an eternal beacon, and inwards at ourselves as an eternal protection? Snuffed out.

These things you have done, Mr. Bush, they would be "the beginning of the end of America."

And did it even occur to you once, sir—somewhere in amidst those eight separate, gruesome, intentional, terroristic invocations of the horrors of 9/11—that with only a little further shift in this world we now know—just a touch more repudiation of all of that for which our patriots died—did it ever occur to you once that in just 27 months and two days from now when you leave office, some irresponsible future president and a "competent tribunal" of lackeys would be entitled, by the actions of your own hand, to declare the status of "unlawful enemy combatant" for—and convene a Military Commission to try—not John Walker Lindh, but George Walker Bush?

For the most vital, the most urgent, the most inescapable of reasons.

And doubtless, Sir, all of them—as always—wrong.

2006

For Discussion and Writing

1. Olbermann's tone in this essay can be described as indignant—but what elements of the writing make it so? Do you think his commentary is fair to the President?
2. In how many ways does the author use comparison or contrast to illustrate his points?
3. Olbermann repeats a key line from the President's speech: "For the most vital, the most urgent, the most inescapable of reasons." What is the impact of this repetition? How can the audience apply those words to the right of *habeus corpus* which has been altered?
4. If the American legal system has been an integral part of the American Dream for millions of citizens over the centuries, what would you say is the single most important aspect of Olbermann's address for future generations?
5. Write an essay in which you take the role of someone who has been arrested for speaking out against the government, as Olbermann has spoken out. What can you depend upon as assurance of a fair and speedy trial?

"I Have a Dream" (Text through Internet Search)

Common (Lonnie Rashid Lynn, Jr.)

Rapper, actor, and animal-rights activist Common broke into mainstream hip-hop popularity with his CD, Like Water for Chocolate. *The Chicago rapper earned praise from fans and critics for the lyrical content of his songs, but what helped the disc to stand out on music store shelves was its cover—a photo of a black woman, wearing a Sunday dress, bending to drink from a fountain marked "Colored Only" while her daughter, also wearing a fine dress, stands nearby while looking into a restaurant that bars "colored" customers from entering. With songs that celebrated, promoted, but also criticized Black culture, Common has preserved a reputation as a "conscious" or "alternative" rapper while managing the rare feat of preserving his mainstream popularity. His song, "I Have a Dream," which samples Dr. Martin Luther King delivering his famous speech by the same name, appeared on the soundtrack for the film,* Freedom Writers. *To find the lyrics of this song, simply type its title, and the word "lyrics," into an Internet search engine, such as Google.*

For Discussion and Writing

1. Common claims that he is fighting "the same fight that made Martin Luther the king." What was that fight, and what lyrical content do you see that would support the claim the author makes about it?
2. How many specific aspects to sustaining a belief in the American Dream do you see being referenced in the song? What would the American Dream be, by Common's implied definition?
3. Research the story of Erin Gruwell and the origins of the Freedom Writers Foundation. What connections do you see between the original students in Gruwell's class and the message of Common's song?
4. In an essay, explain whether a popular performer like Common could some day take the place of a charismatic figure like Dr. Martin Luther King in shaping American society and continuing the struggle to make the American Dream more accessible to all of the nation's citizens.

Chapter 4: For Further Research and Writing

1. This chapter has included examples of lyrics written and performed by artists whose work has, for many audience members, helped to shape conceptions of the American Dream. What additional examples can you think of that would also fit the chapter well? Consider the many television, film, and music performers with which you are familiar. How do they influence ongoing discussions of the American Dream and its definitions?
2. What is the role that government, whether at the local, state, or national level, can play in helping citizens to achieve—or prevent citizens from attaining—the American Dream? What role should those levels of government play?

3. Compare John F. Kennedy's definition of patriotism with the rebellious patriotism of David Walker and Frederick Douglass. How does patriotism differ when it is expressed by rebels and dissidents? Can a critic of the United States also be considered a patriot?
4. The "War on Poverty" was one of the most influential movements of the late twentieth century. Given Barbara Ehrenreich's and Paul Krugman's analyses on low-wage work and the loss of class mobility, how would you evaluate the success of Johnson's Great Society program?
5. This book has traced the evolution of the American Dream from its early foundations, to efforts made to expand its scope, to its realization for generations of immigrants, through its development in the twentieth century and beyond. Based on specific evidence from preceding chapters, what predictions can you make for how the American Dream may change in the future? What effects might evolving technology, continuing climate change, and increased economic globalization have on the Dream for your generation and the next? Citing sources from this book and elsewhere, support a 5–7 page picture of the American Dream as you see it being defined in the future.

CREDITS

Alexie, Sherman. "What Sacagawea Means to Me (and Perhaps to You)." Copyright © 2002, Time Inc. All rights reserved. Reprinted by permission.

"Argument in Favor of Proposition 227." California Secretary of State.

Black Panther Manifesto. "The Ten-Point Program." Reprinted by permission of The Dr. Huey Newton Foundation.

Cooper, Helene. "The Day an Immigrant Refugee Can Say, 'I'm an American.'" Copyright © 2006, by The New York Times Co. Reprinted by permission.

Ehrenreich, Barbara. Excerpt from "Evaluation" from NICKEL AND DIMED: On (Not) Getting By in America. © 2001 by Barbara Ehrenreich. Reprinted by permission of Henry Holt and Company, LLC.

Faderman, Lillian (Pao Her). "Stuck in Between," From *I Begin My Life All Over*. Copyright © 1998 by Lillian Faderman. Reprinted by permission of Beacon Press, Boston.

Gellman, Marc. "The Power of Our Pastime." From *Newsweek*, October 25, 2006 © 2006 Newsweek, Inc. All rights reserved. Used by permission and protected by the Copyright Laws of the United States. The printing, copying, redistribution, or retransmission of the Material without express written permission is prohibited.

Guthrie, Woody. "This Land is Your Land." Words and music by Woody Guthrie. TRO-© Copyright 1956 (Renewed), 1958 (Renewed), Ludlow Music, Inc., New York, New York. Used by Permission.

Inada, Lawson. "On Being Asian-American." From *Legends from Camp: Poems* by Lawson Fusao Inada. Copyright © 1993 by Lawson Fusao Inada. Reprinted by permission of the author.

King, Martin Luther, Jr. "The American Dream" speech. Copyright 1961, Martin Luther King, Jr.: copyright renewed 1989, Coretta Scott King.

Knudson, Tom. "The Pineros" (excerpt). © The Sacramento Bee, 2005.

Kowinski, William Severini. "Kids in the Mall: Growing Up Controlled." Copyright © 1985 by William Severini Kowinski. By permission of the author.

Krugman, Paul. "The Death of Horatio Alger." Reprinted with permission from the January 5, 2004 issue of *The Nation*. Portions of each week's Nation magazine can be accessed at http://www.thenation.com.

Lerma, Jorge. "Superman El Ilegal." © 1979 by Peer International Corporation. Used by Permission. All Rights Reserved.

Miller, Arthur. From DEATH OF A SALESMAN. Copyright 1949, renewed ©1977 by Arthur Miller. Used by permission of Viking Penguin, a division of Penguin Group (USA) Inc.

NOW Statement of Purpose. Reprinted by permission of the National Organization of Women. This is a historical document (1966) and may not reflect the current language or priorities of the organization.

Olberman, Keith. "Special Comment of October 18, 2006." © 2007 MSNBC Interactive.

Polacheck, Hilda Satt. From *I Came a Stranger: The Story of a Hull-House Girl.* Copyright 1989 by the Board of Trustees of the University of Illinois. Used with permission of the University of Illinois Press.

Reynolds, Malvina. From the song: "Little Boxes." Words and music by Malvina Reynolds © 1962 Schroder Music Co. (ASCAP) Renewed 1990. Used by permission. All rights reserved.

Rodriguez, Richard. From *Hunger of Memory* by Richard Rodriguez. Reprinted by permission of David R. Godine, Publisher, Inc. Copyright ©1982 by Richard Rodriguez.

Rosa, Rafael. "My American Dream." © 1980 by Studs Terkel. This piece originally appears in *American Dreams: Lost and Found* by Studs Terkel. Reprinted with the permission of The New Press. www.thenewpress.com

Small, Tolbert. "America." Poems by Dr. Tolbert Small, reprinted by permission of the author.

Trillin, Calvin. Excerpt from *Messages from My Father.* Copyright © 1996 by Calvin Trillin. Reprinted by permission of Farrar, Straus & Giroux, Inc.

Wright, Richard. Chapter XIV from BLACK BOY by Richard Wright. Copyright, 1937, 1942, 1944, 1945 by Richard Wright; renewed © 1973 by Ellen Wright. Reprinted by permission of HarperCollins Publishers.